Assessing Rational
Expectations

Assessing Rational Expectations

Sunspot Multiplicity and Economic Fluctuations

Roger Guesnerie

The MIT Press
Cambridge, Massachusetts
London, England

This book was set in Palatino by Best-set Typesetter Ltd., Hong Kong

Printed and bound in the United States of America.

Library of Congress Cataloging-in-Publication Data

Guesnerie, R.
  Assessing rational expectations : sunspot multiplicity and economic
  fluctuations / Roger Guesnerie.
      p.   cm.
  Includes bibliographical references and index.
  ISBN 0-262-07207-6 (hc. : alk. paper)
  1. Business cycles. 2. Rational expectations (Economic theory).
3. Monetary policy. 4. Economic policy. I. Title.

HB3711 .G82   2001
339'.01'5195—dc21   00-055448

Contents

Contents

Preface

1 Introduction

The need for an assessment of Rational Expectations is amply justified by the dominant position they have now in economic modeling. This state of business will be briefly discussed (1.1). The general intellectual perspective of the book, as well as the specific options that have determined the selection of its contents, will then be presented (1.2).

1.1 The Hegemonic Position of the Rational Expectations Hypothesis

The Rational Expectations Hypothesis, REH for short, the development of which in modern economic theory starts from the pioneering proposition of John Muth (1961), has taken over the economic modeling of expectations in almost all fields. The snapshots of different subjects that follow provide eloquent testimonies of the hegemony of the hypothesis in present formalized economic theory.

Macroeconomic theory and monetary theory were the first to bring rationality of expectations to the forefront of the intellectual debate, a debate that was marked in particular by R. Lucas's contribution (1972). Even if applied macroeconomics has resisted the innovation for a time, the main protagonists of modern macroeconomic theory, who may be antagonistic, seem nowadays to accept the idea that macroeconomic phenomena have to be explained within the rational expectations paradigm. A similar trend toward the broad acceptance of the hypothesis is observed in the domain of general equilibrium; switching from the Arrow-Debreu complete markets to settings of incomplete markets, most present studies put little emphasis on the concept "Temporary Equilibrium," a construct that avoids explaining expectations, and instead accept the concept of "Equilibrium of Plans, Prices, and Price Expectations" (Radner [1972]), the precise name given here to an equilibrium with self-fulfilling expectations.

A brief look at different specialized fields shows a unified picture in the treatment of expectations. To name a few active sectors, growth theory, international trade, and finance routinely adopt the Rational Expectations Hypothesis.

Last but not least, the reconsideration in the eighties of the theory of industrial organization, within the conceptual framework of Game Theory, reflects, so far as expectations are concerned, the same situation, a counterpart to the conceptual proximity of the concepts of Nash Equilibrium and Rational Expectations Equilibria.

This overwhelming presence of the Rational Expectations Hypothesis in formalized economic theory justifies a particularly careful evaluation of its pertinence. Indeed, the papers gathered in this book attempt to contribute, within a particular but well-specificied perspective, a critical assessment of the hypothesis.

1.2   The Assessment of the "Rationality" of Expectations: Forms and Background

Such a critical assessment has a priori many possible dimensions. For example, post-Marxist terminology, which was popular in

Europe in the sixties, stresses two broad categories of the assessment, labeled, respectively, "external criticism," here a critical assessment of the hypothesis itself through the discussion of its foundations, and "internal criticism," a critical assessment of the consequences of the hypothesis. In this terminology, the texts gathered in the present book relate to the "internal criticism" viewpoint: They do not question the foundations of the hypothesis but aim at developing a better understanding of the Rational Expectations Hypothesis through a better appraisal of its consequences. As stressed in the title *Assessing Rational Expectations: Sunspot Multiplicity and Economic Fluctuations*, the connecting thread of the investigation is the multiplicity question that arises in (infinite horizon) Rational Expectations models and its implications for a theory of "endogenous" fluctuations.

A companion book, whose provisional title is *Assessing Rational Expectations: Common Knowledge, Rationality, and Learning* will take the "external" criticism viewpoint, focusing attention, not on the possibly counterintuitive implications of the Rational Expectations Equilibria, but on its "rationality" foundations.

Let us make it clear that the assessment of rational expectations is not a gratuitous enterprise. For example, it should have implications for the general theory of markets, a subject at the heart of the economist's reflection. Indeed, historically, the Rational Expectations Hypothesis has often been associated with an optimistic view of the working of markets, which might possibly be challenged by any critical assessment of the hypothesis itself. Three examples, chosen among others, will serve as a brief historical reminder of the implications of the Rational Expectations Hypothesis for the general theory of markets.

Although in Lucas's model (1972) the market does not deliver first-best efficient outputs, it is still the case that the invariance proposition of Friedman holds: Inflation cannot be used to (durably) lower unemployment or raise economic activity.

Commenting on the "flexible price models of the Rational Expectations school," Shefrin (1983) argues that "the (alternative) vision is close to (Tobin's characterization of) prekeynesian economists."

At a, perhaps, more basic level, as suggested by Arrow (1953), there is a one-to-one correspondence between the Arrow-Debreu contingent allocations of a finite horizon model and the intertemporal contingent allocations of a Radner Equilibrium of Plans, Prices, and Price Expectations, as soon as the structure of spot asset markets is "rich" enough (Guesnerie and Jaffray 1974). Hence, the Rational Expectations Hypothesis may appear as the missing link between the Arrow-Debreu's abstract world and the anterior "extensive" forms of the Walrasian tradition: "rational" or self-fufilling expectations are necessary conditions for the first-best Pareto optimality of intertemporal allocations of a truly sequential economy, sufficient when, besides standard conditions, the market structure is "essentially" complete.

Last, most of the comments that arouse from the study of transmission of information through prices[1] undertaken at the end of the seventies (Grossmann 1976) overstressed, from a dubious interpretation of correct statements, the quality of the performance of markets in transmitting information.

There, the perceived connection between the Rational Expectations Equilibria and an optimistic vision of the working of the markets is well founded. However, such an optimistic view of the virtues of rational expectations like coordination becomes problematic when the Rational Expectations Equilibria can deliver an embarassing number of solutions that are not equally satisfactory on efficiency grounds, as will occur in the infinite horizon models we are going to study. The analysis might then challenge the efficiency conclusions stressed from models of the Walrasian tradition and meet instead more skeptical a priori views of the virtues of the market that have a "Keynesian" flavor.

This background is essential. It is, however, somewhat too general; before presenting the content of the book in section 2, the next section will attempt to present a more precise intellectual perspective.

2 Intellectual Perspective

The discussion of the intellectual perspective will introduce the multiplicity problem as it was envisaged in an earlier literature of the seventies (2.1); the intellectual debate will then be better appraised (2.2), and the presentation of the switch of research toward nonlinear general equilibrium models (2.3) will precede a brief review of the main questions under scrutiny (2.4).

2.1 Bubble Solutions in Linear Rational Expectations Models

The Rational Expectations Hypothesis, when incorporated into formal models, leads to the consideration of equilibria, called Rational Expectations Equilibria. It is not surprising that the Rational Expectations Hypothesis may generate multiple equilibria or, in other words, that several Rational Expectations Equilibria emerge from a given model.[2] However, the type of multiplicity that is emphasized here, a continuum of equilibria that are not even "isolated" or "determinate," is more perplexing. Indeed, the phenomenon has first been pointed out and scrutinized, not by the literature on "endogenous (sunspot) fluctuations" developed in the eighties, and to which many texts of this book do belong, but by an earlier literature on linear rational expectations models, which is indeed the ancestor of the first one.

In order to provide an insight into the concern and message of this early reflection, and to introduce at the same time the multiplicity concern that lies at the heart of this book, we will, first, focus attention on a reduced form of a simple dynamical linear model:

$$x_t = aE(x_{t+1}^e) \tag{1}$$

Here, x_t is a number and $E(x_{t+1}^e)$ is the mean taken at t of the random variable x_{t+1}^e, expected value of x at the period $t + 1$. Up to an additional constant term that we do not consider here, Equation (1) describes for example, the price of a stock or the (log) of the price level in a Cagan like model.[3] A priori, the anticipations determining the value of the right hand side of the equation may be arbitrary. If they are rational, they may be associated either with a *perfect foresight equilibrium*: a sequence of numbers x_t, $t = 0, 1, \ldots +\infty$, such that $x_t = ax_{t+1}$; or with *a stochastic equilibrium*, a sequence of random variables $\tilde{x}_t$, $t = 0, 1, \ldots +\infty$, such that $x_t(w_t) = aE_{w_t}(\widetilde{x_{t+1}})$, where w_t denotes the subset of states of nature associated with the history of the stochastic process up to time t. Defining $X_t = a^t x_t$, the preceding equation can be read $X_t = E(X_{t+1})$ and accordingly defines a "martingale." Hence, every solution x_t of the preceding equation is such that $a^t x_t$ is a (possibly degenerate) martingale. When this solution is actually stochastic, it can be reinterpreted in the terminology of note 2 as a *bubble equilibrium*, or viewed as what the succeding sunspot literature will call a *sunspot equilibrium*. The solution may be tied to the realization of a random process in some sense exogenous to the system and foreign to its (here somewhat hidden!) fundamentals, something that we shall later call *extrinsic uncertainty*.

A similar point can be made in more complex models (see Gourieroux, Laffont, and Monfort 1982, and Broze and Szafars 1985, among many others). The message delivered, however, has limits and weaknesses that can be assessed from the simple protoype model just under scrutiny. Indeed, the analysis faces two obvious objections.

The first obvious objection is the *linearity* objection: The model is linear and it goes without saying that the extension of the analysis to nonlinear settings is, and was (even at the end of the seventies), overdue.

The second objection is the *general equilibrium* objection: The theory considers reduced forms of models when the analysis of equilibria, with or without rational expectations, calls for the complete specification of agents, markets, . . . etc., that is required by general equilibrium theory. This second objection is at the heart of an intellectual debate that we are going now to present: Is (bubble-like) multiplicity an artifact of partial equilibrium analysis?

2.2 An Intellectual Debate: Multiplicity as an Artifact of Partial Equilibrium Analysis?

The "general equilibrium" objection to the multiplicity results of subsection 2.1, which has just been evoked, has several aspects. We shall come back to others, but let me now stress the subtlest one, let us call it the "insurance objection": In general equilibrium models of the Arrow-Debreu tradition, undesirable noise will be eliminated by insurance markets. This is called the "ineffectivity theorem" (Cass and Shell 1983). Its conclusions[4] are clearly pertinent to general equilibrium theory: The predictions of an Arrow-Debreu model, when agents are risk averse and when (contingent) markets are complete, are robust to changes in delicate modeling options that concern the a priori choice of the uncertainty to be incorporated into the model.[5] The so-called insurance objection then relies on the powerful effects of completeness stressed by the ineffectivity theorem: In the presence of "extrinsic" noise, possibly generated by arbitrary beliefs, full insurance restores the efficiency of market equilibria à la Arrow-Debreu, and hence of the corresponding sequential Rational Expectations Equilibria. In particular, the undesirable noise that appears in solutions to linear rational expectations models and that is likely to be inefficient in a world of risk-averse agents might disappear in well-specified general equilibrium models in which enough insurance is provided.

I believe that this objection has been considerably overstated, for at least two reasons: First, insurance markets on "extrinsic" noise should be numerous in order to counteract all possible "extrinsic" coordination devices; second, and more important, any of them is quite unlikely. As suggested by contract theory, contractible variables should be "observable" and "verifiable." "States of mind," associated with bubbles or sunspot equilibria, doubtfully fit the first requirement and clearly do not fit the second one. This point seems now, after the development and diffusion of the concepts and analysis of the theory of contracts, well recognized. Most of the present literature on endogenous cycles dismisses the so-called "insurance" objection and, if one follows the above argument, rightly so, although sometimes with too little discussion.[6]

However, the insurance question should be kept in mind, first for keeping the appropriate theoretical light on the subject, and second for understanding the intellectual context in which the switch from the "bubble" viewpoint of the linear rational expectations models to the "sunspot" viewpoint of the nonlinear OLG models has taken place at the beginning of the eighties.

2.3 Nonlinear Models and Sunspot Fluctuations

A great merit of Azariadis 1981b, which is the starting point of the literature on endogenous fluctuations to which the papers of the first part do belong, was to propose a stochastic equilibrium in an infinite horizon model that was immune to all the above-mentioned objections. The model under consideration was an Overlapping Generations (OLG) model, indeed both a nonlinear model and a general equilibrium model. Also, the insurance objection could simply be dismissed, since in the standard interpretation of the model, the required insurance markets should have involved transactions between agents that were not simultaneously alive.[7]

Azariadis exhibited stochastic sunspot equilibria, and in particular Markovian Stationary Sunspot Equilibria, for short Markovian SSE, in an OLG model where the representative agent has a separable utility function. The nature of these equilibria can simply be understood by returning to the linear equation (1). Indeed, in a small enough neighborhood of the steady state of the OLG model, where the model is only "slightly" nonlinear, there exist stochastic equilibria (SSE) having their support in this neighborhood that are close to the stochastic equilibria of the linear model, that is, that can be approximately described from the linear Equation (1). Indeed, let us consider two numbers, positive and negative, $\bar{x}$ et $-\bar{x}'$; let us suppose $|a| > 1$ so that $\bar{x}/a$ as well as $-\bar{x}'/a$ are between $\bar{x}$ and $-\bar{x}'$. One can then find two positive numbers between 0 and 1, π et π', such that:

$$\bar{x}/a = \pi\bar{x} + (1-\pi)(-\bar{x}')$$

$$-\bar{x}'/a = \pi'(-\bar{x}') + (1-\pi')(\bar{x})$$

The stochastic process, the support of which at each period consists of the points $\bar{x}$ and $-\bar{x}'$ and which switches from $\bar{x}$ to $\bar{x}$ with probability π and from $-\bar{x}'$ to $-\bar{x}'$ with probability π', is a solution of Equation (1). It is also the linear approximation, when the number $\bar{x}$ is small, of a "local" Markovian SunSpot Equilibrium, a concept that is central to the articles in this book. Let us note that the solution is reminiscent of a cycle: The system oscillates indefinitely between $\bar{x}$ and $-\bar{x}'$; but the oscillation, contrary to what happens in a deterministic cycle where $\bar{x}$ is surely the successor of $-\bar{x}'$, has a random nature; it is a kind of *quasi-cycle*.

Azariadis's message is then: In a simple OLG model without intrinsic uncertainty, extrinsic uncertainty, "states of mind," trigger endogenous fluctuations that are perfectly correlated with, and hence can be viewed as triggered by, an exogenous phenomenon, a *sunspot* if you like. The phenomenon can either be local and generate small fluctuations homeomorphic to those that would occur in the linear system that approximates the nonlinear system, or global and then generate large fluctuations. Finally, local fluctuations occur, as in the linear case, when the steady state is indeterminate ($|a| \geq 1$ implies that all perfect foresight trajectories starting close to the steady state converge to it, that is, that the steady state is not isolated, with respect to some well chosen topology, that is, not determinate).[8]

2.4   Questions

The above review provides a brief reminder of the reflection on the subject of the present book, which was anterior at the year 81. In some sense, this is the beginning of the a story that is continued here. The questions that are at the heart of the papers reproduced in this book are those suggested by the provisional conclusions raised by the examination of earlier literature.

• Arbitrary beliefs, that is, based on "extrinsic" rather than "intri sic" uncertainty, reflecting "animal spirits" rather than "fundamentals," can sustain rational expectations equilibria of a (nonlinear, infinite horizon) general equilibrium model. What are the characteristics of such self-fulfilling beliefs? How do they relate to the fundamentals of the economy, to the characteristics of its equilibria?

• The relationships between stochastic equilibria in linear models and stochastic equilibria in nonlinear models, which have been briefly sketched, seem to have a general scope. Can we ascertain, by using appropriate tools, the generality of the connection and clarify, at the same time, the specific role played by nonlinearities?

• The above story suggests that, in the simple model à la Azariadis, the value of money, and also the level of activity, may be determined according to different self-fulfilling beliefs. What are the consequences for monetary theory, for macroeconomic theory? Can several "true" theories coexist?

• Fluctuations triggered by stochastic beliefs are "endogenous fluctuations." Do they have relationships with endogenous deterministic fluctuations (like deterministic cycles)? Is there a connection between endogenous fluctuations and fluctuations that are triggered by some exogenous shocks to fundamentals, or are they entirely unconnected? If there are connections, can we build, at least in some given class of models, a comprehensive enough "theory of endogenous fluctuations" that incorporates both cases?

3   Content of the Book

The questions raised above are examined here in models that are rather special, in particular that mostly adopt the simple assumption that agents need only to be *one-step forward looking*.

The underlying choice is depth rather than breadth. The bet implicit to this choice is that a deep investigation within a narrow domain will clarify the key issues and will provide the right frame for generalization. Whatever may be, the analyses contained in this book should appear in the broader landscape of a more general theory, that remains, and will remain probably for some time, overdue!

The book has four parts, the contents of which can be now introduced.

3.1   Part 1: Sunspot Fluctuations around a Steady State: The Case of Simple OLG Models

The first three chapters of the book, which come under the subtitle "Sunspot Fluctuations around a steady state: the case of simple OLG models," have, most unsurprisingly for the first two that are coauthored with Costas, a direct connection with Azariadis's 1981 contribution.

"Prophéties créatrices et Persistance des théories," published in *La Revue Economique* in French in September 1982, and translated here as "Creative Prophecies and Persistence of Theories," elaborates on the quoted initial contribution along three different directions. First, in the model under scrutiny, the assumption that agents have intertemporally separable preferences is relaxed. Second, and more important, the paper proposes a methodology, based on the Poincaré-Hopf index theorem, that will turn out particularly fruitful for exhibing Sunspot Equilibria in dynamical models. It should be noted that this methodology, contrarily to the linearization procedure sketched above, exploits the nonlinearities of the model. Here, it allows to characterize a subset of sunspot phenomena, that is, of Markovian matrices that trigger stochastic equilibria. Third, the paper discusses the exogenous beliefs that drive the agents' actions: why sunspot rather than moonspots? And can different self-fulfilling beliefs coexist in a given society?

The second chapter, "Sunspots and Cycles," presents a slightly improved version of the Poincaré-Hopf methodology previously introduced and a more careful examination of its results. But its main emphasis, as the title suggests, is on the connections between SSE and deterministic periodic solutions (cycles), which were being intensively studied at that time (see, e.g., Grandmont 1985). After stressing easy, although apparently unnoticed, continuity connections (SSE close to deterministic cycles), the chapter establishes that, "generically" in the considered OLG model, SSE do exist if and only if cycles (of order two) exist. This is a surprising result: Mathematically, it clearly exploits the one-dimensionality of an appropriate reduced form of the problem. No general n-dimensional counterpart is known, although I suspect that one interesting weaker result is not entirely hopeless.

The third chapter, "One Stationary Sunspot Equilibria of Order k," with P. A. Chiappori (1989), examines an abstract version of the OLG model, basically a one-dimensional one-step forward looking model. The chapter develops from a more axiomatic basis the Poincaré-Hopf procedure and fully characterize the properties of the spectrum of Markov matrices that are candidates to sustain SSE.

3.2   Part 2: Fluctuations between Two Steady States in Lucas-like Models

A clear distinctive feature of the three chapters of the previous part with respect to other literature is the effort put into characterizing the stochastic processes that trigger selfulfilling prophecies. In spite of the opposite option often taken in related literature, such a characterization seems a natural objective, at least if stochastic equilibria are viewed as possibly sustaining a positive theory of economic phenomena. Another related point, indeed a key point of the philosophy in the background of all the essays in the first part of the book, may be made at this stage. Sunspot equilibria, rather than being large fluctuations trigerred by nothing, may probably be better viewed as large fluctuations (overreactions) triggered by small or even tiny variations of intrisinc variables. Sunspot equilibria are *limits*, when the intrinsic noise tends to zero, of "overreactions equilibria." Extrinsic multiplicity can also be viewed as the limit case of a more standard intrinsic multiplicity phenomenon.

If this latter point is to be taken seriously, the candidate sunspot phenomena are not equally likely; some of them are better than others, because they are more "focal" (and the more focal are not necessarily those with a stationary probabilistic structure). There is one such focal candidate in the celebrated Lucas (1972) model: It is the stochastic process that governs money supply. Indeed, the next chapter of this book, "Expectations, Indeterminacy and the Non-neutrality of Money: An Example" (Chiappori and Guesnerie 1991a), derives analytically, in a special case of the model, besides the so-called Lucas solution, an infinity of sunspot solutions (triggered by the money supply stochastic process) of Lucas functional equation. The paper is admittedly technical: The argument relies on the computation of the solution expressed under the form of a rather complex power series, but it also conveys a simple economic intuition on the *heterodox* sunspot solutions.

The results of the chapter call for two criticisms, the consideration of which is the subject of the next chapter, "Rational Random Walks" by Chiappori and Guesnerie (1993).

First, the logic of the heterodox solutions stressed before has to be better understood. We show that they belong, in fact, to a class of rational expectations solutions that we call *heteroclinic solutions* because the associated trajectories oscillate between two different steady states, and for the existence of which we exhibit general necessary conditions. The second objection to the heterodox solutions of Lucas is the fact that they do not generate, but for the so-called Lucas solution, a time invariant stationary probability distribution on the states of the system. This is quite true, but the paper qualifies this objection by appealing to the *continuity* argument alluded to earlier: If the money supply has a small (as tiny as it may be) intrinsic effect on the system, then the heterodox solutions perhaps appear as overreactions equilibria, but they have the same probabilistic status as the extension of the Lucas solution, whose referential status is now called into question.

Both papers, hence, provide somewhat spectacular instances of a stylized world in which two opposite monetary theories—one is Keynesian-like, the other one monetarist-like—can be alternatively "true" or more exactly self-fulfilling.

3.3   Part 3: Endogenous N-dimensional Fluctuations

The next two chapters deal with the same subject in an abstract one-step forward model but whose state variables are n-dimensional rather than one-dimensional.

"Stationary Sunspot Equilibria in an N-commodity World" (1986) provides, in this framework, a number of conditions for the existence of cycles and sunspot equilibria that significantly extend results known for the one-dimensional case. The connections between cycles and sunspots are, however, now more delicate to elucidate: In particular, the possible multiplicity of spot equilibria adds new mechanisms of self-fulfillment that differ from those exhibited in one-dimensional models, where such multiplicity cannot occur.

"Sunspot Fluctuations around a Steady State: The Case of Multi-dimensional, one-step Forward Looking Economic Models" (1992) focuses attention on the special class of equilibria generating small fluctuations around a steady state and on the characteristics of the underlying stochastic process. The argument relies on linearization, but the validity of linearization is based here on a rather delicate bifurcation argument, which allows a complete characterization and classification of the equilibria. The higher generality of the model allows us to stress both the power and the limits, as well as the difficulties, of the linearization argument.

3.4   Part 4: Variations and Extensions

The topics of the first seven chapters are almost exclusively concerned with the description of stochastic rational expectations equilibria that fall under the heading "endogenous fluctuations." The last three contributions broaden the scope of the previous parts in three directions.

The chapter with M. Woodford, "Stability of Cycles with Adaptive Learning Rules" (1991) explores, in OLG-type models, the conditions of success of "evolutive learning," when the learned equilibrium is periodic. It provides, within the class of the simple adaptive learning rules under consideration, a full characterization (necessary and sufficient conditions) of the local convergence of the algorithm.

Previous articles exclusively dealt with one-step forward looking models, when better applications, which are now pursued (Benhabib and Farmer 1999), may be offered by systems with memory. Naturally, the findings obtained from simpler cases, as well as the research agenda that has been implemented here, are likely to provide useful guidelines for more complex situations.

The existence of Sunspot Equilibria in systems with memory is the subject of the chapter coauthored with J. Dávila, "Sunspot Equilibria in Systems with Memory: An Introductory Presentation." It presents the results obtained in Dávila's Ph.D thesis (Dávila 1994, 1997) that concern stochastic equilibria of a particular kind, those looking like the simple *quasi-cycles* displayed in one-step forward looking models.

Finally, "Theoretical Tests of the Rational Expectations Hypothesis in Economic Dynamical Models" (1993) attempts to present a picture of the research on rational expectations infinite horizon equilibria that gives a broad perspective on the chapters in this book as well as a connection with the companion book mentioned above.

I would finally like to thank all my coauthors, in particular Costas Azariadis and Pierre-André Chiappori, who have respectively contributed to two and three joint papers, Julio Dávila, who has allowed me to reproduce our unpublished presentation, Pierre-Yves Geoffard, and Mike Woodford. Working with them was most enjoyable; they certainly can take credit for whatever the merit the present book has, but, as the book is my own enterprise, they should not be blamed for its shortcomings!

Notes

1. This literature often tends to label itself literature on Rational Expectations: It may deserve the label, although with some qualifications: it has no valid claim to exhaustivity. Indeed, this segment of the literature is a tiny segment of the Rational Expectations literature in the standard meaning of the word, that is, rooted in the Muthian tradition.

2. Note, however, that this creates some problems with Muth's initial justification: "The REH is nothing else than he extension of the rationality hypothesis to expectations." If there are several REE, which one is more rational?

3. The missing constant terms are respectively the dividend and the current nominal money stock. These terms determine the "fundamental" solution, whereas we are interested here in the "bubble" solution (we use here the terminology of Blanchard and Fisher 1989). Strictly speaking, a "bubble" reflects the difference between an asset price and the present value of the relevant stream.

4. The argument is quite simple. It has been long understood that in an economy in which consumers had convex preferences, randomization of allocations based on "extrinsic" noise was undesirable (Caspi 1974). Now, consider a world in which extrinsic and intrinsic noise, the one that concerns the fundamentals, do coexist. The Arrow-Debreu equilibrium, which involves complete markets and hence all insurance markets, is Pareto efficient and hence, because of the previous remark, immune to randomization by extrinsic noise.

5. A contrario, and because all the ingredients of the theorem are required for its proof, the statement makes clear that, outside the context of the Arrow-Debreu model, general equilibrium predictions may be sensitive to the somewhat arbitrary selection of "extrinsic" noise, which depends on beliefs, not fundamentals. (See, e.g., Guesnerie and Laffont 1989).

6. In particular, some markets (options markets, for example) can serve as proxies of the powerful insurance markets à la Arrow-Debreu. But this is another subject on which present theory is unsufficient.

7. Again, the insurance objection may have been taken too seriously, but Azariadis also mentions the argument that markets against sunspots should be so numerous that their occurrence is unlikely. For a discussion of this issue when extrinsic uncertainty is contractible, see, however, Guesnerie and Woodford 1992.

8. It may be argued that the fact that the situation occurs in the simple OLG model only in the case of a sufficiently backward-bending labor supply curve restricts the empirical relevance of the theory for monetary theory; we come back to that later.

I

Sunspot Fluctuations
around a Steady State:
The Case of Simple
Overlapping Generations
Models

1

Creative Prophecies and the Persistence of Theories

Costas Azariadis and
Roger Guesnerie

1 Introduction

A creative or self-fulfilling prophecy can be roughly defined as follows: in a temporal context, it is a forecast (image of tomorrow) that influences (today) and determines the conditions of its own fulfillment (tomorrow).[1] The interest roused by this perplexing phenomenon spans the social sciences. In sociology, Boudon (1979) records already bygone examples of study in this area. In economics, the theme is a recurring one. Rational expectations constitute conjectures which are generally self-fulfilling. The dynamic equilibrium of plans, prices and price expectations depicts situations of perfect forecast where realizations and expectations are closely connected.[2] Following J.-P. Dupuy (1982), one would reinterpret the concepts of static prices and quantities equilibrium used in the formalized models of economic theory as creative prophecies.

If the theme of self-fulfilling prophecy isn't new in economic analyses, one singular dimension has, it seems, been identified in a recent article (entitled "self fulfilling prophecies") by C. Azariadis (1981b). Azariadis develops a suggestion originally made by K. Shell (1978) who, departing from the purely deterministic model, had mentioned that beliefs in the influence of purely exogenous random phenomena ("sun spots") on price levels could effectively trigger stochastic prices whose movement corroborated the initial belief. This conjecture, whose validity has been demonstrated through a series of examples in Azariadis's article cited above, is striking by the arbitrary, and even somewhat perverse, nature of the initial "prophecy." Assuming a correlation between a price and a natural stochastic phenomenon in a world where there is no "intrinsic" uncertainty introduces a source of variations that may be termed "extraneous" according to Azariadis.[3] Even if the conceptual split with more conventional phenomena is difficult to pinpoint, the mechanism by which, in previously cited examples, forecasts affect realizations seems to involve several new aspects. In it, we can see the example of a theory that, though in a certain sense arbitrary, creates the conditions of its own validation, hence, an example of interaction between the *representations* and the *facts* which seem to be particularly worthy of interest.

This chapter proposes to pursue further Azariadis's reflections in that direction. After having been shown when and in what sense the theory by which prices and sunspots are correlated can be factually validated, one wonders if two different "theories," both initially arbitrary, can coexist without being called into question by the observed evolutions therein. Even if the model we employ has characteristics that render it particularly useful for the theoretical study of monetary phenomena (on this point see Cass and Shell 1980), it is more an illustration or a parable that we seek to develop here than a theory of dynamic monetary economy. This chapter will present no detailed economic implications of the results. Rather, it will show that the appearance of the phenomena discussed is neither certain nor impossible, but that the cases where they may be produced are in no way pathological in regard to the traditional behavioral hypotheses of economic theory. Finally, by using powerful tools that allow wide possibilities of extension, we will underline the potential generality of the analysis more that the simplifications which in certain cases can sustain intuition.

This chapter is organized as follows:

In the first part, we will describe the basic model. It is a very simple version of the overlapping generations model formerly introduced by Samuelson (1958). The main properties of this model are well understood today, in particular since the work of Balasko and Shell (1981). The quick reminder that we will present only aims at aiding readers in recollecting, or at least in familiarizing themselves with, the characteristics of the model that are useful in our analysis.

In the second part, we will again take on the results of Azariadis (1981b), which establish the permanence of the "theory of prices correlated with sunspots," while thoroughly examining and generalizing them.

In the third part, we will suppose that society is divided into two subpopulations. The agents of the first category believe in a sunspot/price level correlation, while those of the second believe in a moonspot/price level correlation. We will show that these theories can constitute self-fulfilling prophecies; that is, they generate a stationary stochastic rational expectations equilibrium that, in a sense, validates them statistically. Nonetheless, we will argue that this coexistence resists only criteria of weak validation, and that the two "theories" would be destroyed by the observations of a sophisticated and skeptical econometrician.

2　The Model

This is the specific version of the overlapping generations model already used by Azariadis.

The agents live for two periods. In the first, they are "young" and possess a unit of time. They share the available time between leisure L and labor 1-L. Labor is a constant returns to scale activity that enables the creation of the final good. This good is demanded only by the "old." At each period, a certain amount of money per person is available, say one unit.

Money here has a simple function: It allows the agents to transfer the value of the period of their youth, when they are producers but don't need to consume, to the period of their old age, when they do consume. The decision of each generation depends on the prices of the good (in terms of money) in the first period (where the agents are the sellers) and in the second period (where they are the buyers).

The decision of a young agent in t period could thus be formalized as the solution to the following maximization problem:

$$\text{Max}\, U(C_{t+1}, L_t)$$

$$p_{t+1} C_{t+1} \leq p_t (1 - L_t)$$

where p_t is the good price in period t, where the price of the money is 1, C_{t+1} is the good consumption in period $t + 1$, and L_t is the leisure consumption in period t (production therefore is $1 - L_t$).

The solution to the preceding leads to a decision of labor supply (supposed to be unique), which is dependent solely on the ratio p_t/p_{t+1}.

We note that $y_t \overset{def}{=} 1 - L_t = s(p_t/p_{t+1})$.

A *perfect foresight equilibrium* is associated with the infinite series $(.. y_t^*, C_t^*, .) (., p_t^*, ..)$, such as:

$$y_t^* = s(p_t^*/p_{t+1}^*) \tag{2.1}$$

$$y_t^* = C_t^* \tag{2.2}$$

$$p_t^* C_t^* = 1 \tag{2.3}$$

The first condition gives labor supply in period t as a function of the relative prices of t and $t + 1$. The latter is transformed into production and according to the second condition equals consumption. The third condition indicates that the total amount of money (per person) held by the "old" is used to buy goods.

We could also summarize (1), (2), (3), under the form:

$$\frac{1}{p_t^*} = s(p_t^*/p_{t+1}^*)$$ (2.4)

where $\frac{1}{p_t^*}$ is the demand of goods from the "old" in period t and $s(p_t^*/p_{t+1}^*)$ is the (indirect) supply of goods from the "young" in period t.

Now, we will examine the nature and characteristics of such perfect foresight equilibria.

First, we consider the number $\bar{p}$ defined by $\frac{1}{\bar{p}} = s(1)$. The sequence $p_t^* = \bar{p}$ constitutes a stationary deterministic equilibrium. In order to exhibit equilibria that are not stationary, it is useful to first consider the case where $s(\cdot)$ is an increasing function: If the (relative) renumeration of labor in period t increases, labor supply increases, as well as the planned consumption for the second period. In this case we sometimes say that leisure and consumption are "gross substitutes."

Let's start from $p_0^* > \bar{p}$ and try to construct a p_t^* series by the "ascending" method. The candidate p_1^* in period 1 should satisfy $\frac{1}{p_0^*} = s\left(\frac{p_0^*}{p_1^*}\right)$ and as $\frac{1}{p_0^*} < \frac{1}{\bar{p}}$; it follows that $s\left(\frac{p_0^*}{p_1^*}\right) < s(1)$ and therefore that $p_1^* > p_0^*$. Starting from $p_0^* > \bar{p}$, we can generate step by step a p_t^* series that will increase and increasingly move away from the stationary equilibrium $\bar{p}$. On the contrary, we cannot generate an infinite series according to this same principle starting from $p_0^* < \bar{p}$.[4]

Let us now consider the case in which s is a decreasing function, at least in a neighborhood of $\bar{p}$ (consumption and leisure can then be considered "gross complements").

The reasoning of the ascending construction can be taken up again and, on the condition that we limit ourselves to an area where s is growing, we have:

$$p_0^* > \bar{p} \Rightarrow \frac{1}{p_0^*} < \frac{1}{\bar{p}} \Rightarrow p_1^* < p_0^*$$

Likewise $p_0^* < \bar{p}$ implies $p_1^* > p_0^*$ and so on.

We can study the behavior of the series since p_0^* is fairly close to $\bar{p}$ when we consider the linear system.

$$\frac{1}{p_t} - \frac{1}{\bar{p}} = s' \cdot \left(\frac{p_t}{p_{t+1}} - 1 \right)$$

Setting $\alpha_t = \dfrac{1}{p_t} - \dfrac{1}{\bar{p}}$, simple calculations lead to:

$$\alpha_{t+1} = \frac{\alpha_t^2}{s'} + a_t \left[\frac{1}{\bar{p}s'} \right] + 1$$

This linear system α_t converges to zero whenever:

$$1 \geq \frac{1}{\bar{p}s'} + 1 \geq -1$$

In other words, as soon as $\bar{p}s'$, which is nothing else than the elasticity of function $s(\alpha)$ at the point $\alpha = 1$, is inferior to $-\frac{1}{2}$.

Here we note that the economic theory of consumption doesn't allow a choice between successively envisioned hypotheses for function s since the decision of the agents superimposes an income effect and a substitution effect, normally of opposite direction. In summary we emphasize that

i) There exists an infinity of (deterministic) perfect foresight equilibria. Among them, only one exists that is stationary.

ii) equilibria that are not stationary may have very diverse characteristics.

ii)α) if s is an increasing function, we can construct an increasing explosive sequence starting from p_0 greater than $\bar{p}$. (We then have a chronic inflation path.)

ii)β) If s is a decreasing function, starting from any p_0 sufficiently close to $\bar{p}$, we can construct a series converging asymptotically toward $\bar{p}$ (with regard to the temporal process, then, the stationary equilibrium is asymptotically stable).

ii)γ) In the case where s is alternatively increasing and decreasing, we can construct series with very different characteristics: series with cyclical characters or even chaotic series with "strange" behavior.[5]

3   Prices Correlated with Sunspots

Here we will again take up the model of Azariadis, modifying it slightly with the aim of significantly generalizing the conclusions.

In regard to section 1, we introduce an exogenous uncertainty tied to a natural phenomenon (for example, sunspots). We assume that there are two states of nature (in the strictest sense of the word) a, b, one of which appears in each period. Their appearances are correlated in time. Specifically, we suppose that the subjacent stochastic process is Markovian. Therefore it is described by the four numbers $\pi(a|a)$ (probability of a tomorrow, if a today. $\pi(b|a)$, (probability of b tomorrow if a today), $\pi(a|b)$, $\pi(b|b)$, which verify:

$$\pi(a|a) + \pi(b|a) = 1 \qquad (3.1)$$

$$\pi(a|b) + \pi(b|b) = 1 \qquad (3.2)$$

We will call π^a the vector $(\pi(a|a), \pi(b|a))$[6] π^b the vector $(\pi(a|b), \pi(b|b))$.

We also will note that the above probability law is not subjective but "objective."

Let us suppose that *all* the agents of the economy believe that there exists a relationship between sunspots and actual prices. We will show that there is a *stationary stochastic equilibrium* that validates the beliefs. More precisely a *stationary stochastic equilibrium perfectly correlated with "sunspots"* assumes the existence of two numbers p_a, p_b such that if a (resp. b) appears in a given period, the equilibrium price of that period is p_a (resp. p_b).

The following scenario sustains the concept: The agents observe a (resp. b) (at t); they anticipate future prices p_a and p_b with the probabilities given by the vector π^a (resp. π^b) (at t) and determine, keeping these anticipations in mind, their supply curve. The confrontation of supply and demand effectively triggers the emergence of p_a (resp. p_b) as the equilibrium price.

In order to give a formal definition of the concept, let us consider the problem of determining the labor supply of the "young" consumer who believes in the sunspot "theory" in the following sense: when a appears, the price is p_a, when b appears, the price is p_b.

His decision results from the solution to the following maximization program (p_t being fixed):

$$\operatorname{Max} E\, U(C_{t+1}, y_t)$$

$$\tilde{p}_{t+1} C_{t+1} \leq p_t y_t$$

E designates the symbol of expected value, $\tilde{p}_{t+1}$ is the random variable that takes the value p_a with probability $\pi(a|a)$ (resp. $\pi(a|b)$) and p_b with probability $\pi(b|a)$ (resp. $\pi(b|b)$), if one observes a (resp. b).

If a is observed (resp. b), labor supply depends on p the current price, p_a, p_b, the expected prices and π^a the probability vector (resp. π^b). Under standard assumptions, labor supply is uniquely defined and is designated by $s_a(p, p_a, p_b, \pi^a)$ (resp. $s_b(p, p_b, p_a, \pi^b)$).

We can then formally define a *stationary stochastic equilibrium with rational expectations and completely correlated to sunspots* as being associated with two numbers p_a and p_b, $p_a \neq p_b$ that satisfy:

$$s_a(p_a, p_a, p_b, \pi^a) = \frac{1}{p_a} \tag{3.3}$$

$$s_b(p_b, p_b, p_a, \pi^b) = \frac{1}{p_b} \tag{3.4}$$

The equations (3.3) and (3.4) are supply equals demand equations and reflect the fact that p_a and p_b clear the market, when a and b, respectively, occur.

In such a equilibrium, the conjectures made by the agents indeed hold the status of creative or "self-fulfilling" prophecies. The agents' beliefs in such an equilibrium is sufficient to engender it and its realization creates conditions for perpetuating the initial belief, and for its eventual validation in the future.

We will return to the study of functions s_a and s_b for which we will rewrite more completely the program of which $s_a(p, p_a, p_b, \pi^a)$ is a solution.

$$\text{Max } \pi_1^a U(C_{t+1}^a, y_t) + (1 - \pi_1^a) U(C_{t+1}^b, y_t)$$

$$p_a C_a^{t+1} \le p y_t$$

$$p_b C_b^{t+1} \le p y_t$$

with $\pi_1^a = \pi(a|a)$.

$s_b()$ solves an analogous program with b replacing a throughout (and vice versa) and $\pi_1^b = \pi(b|b)$.

Note:

$$S_a(p_a, p_b) = s_a(p_a, p_a, p_b)$$

$$S_b(p_b, p_a) = s_b(p_b, p_b, p_a)$$

The functions s_a, s_b, S_a, S_b have the following properties:

$$s_a(p, p', p') = s_b(p, p', p') \ \forall p, p'$$

This is obvious because neither tomorrow's prices nor today's behavior are dependent on a and b.

$$\frac{\partial S_a}{\partial p_a} = -\frac{p_b}{p_a}\frac{\partial S_a}{\partial p_b}; \frac{\partial S_b}{\partial p_b} = -\frac{p_a}{p_b}\frac{\partial S_b}{\partial p_a}$$

$S_a(p_a, p_b)$ solves the program above where p is equal to p_a; it results that S_a is homogeneous to degree zero and therefore

$$p_a\frac{\partial S_a}{\partial p_a} + p_b\frac{\partial S_a}{\partial p_b} = 0.$$

To these two properties, we will add an assumption by which labor supply is bounded away from zero by a number $\varepsilon > 0$ (possibly depending on π^a). Though it does not derive from consumption theory in its most general form, this assumption seems fairly anodyne.

• H

$\exists \varepsilon > 0$, such that:

$$s_a(p_a, p_a, p_b, .) > \varepsilon, \forall p_a, p_b$$

$$s_b(p_b, p_b, p_a, .) > \varepsilon, \forall p_a, p_b$$

Finally, we note that the continuity of the functions considered is obtained if, for example, the utility function is strictly concave. It is also clear, for the same reasons as those put forward above for function s, that consumption theory involves no a priori restriction on the sign of the derivatives of functions s_a, s_b with respect to their arguments.

Let us consider then the compact subset K of $\mathbb{R}^2_+$:

$$K = \left\{(p_a, p_b) \middle| 0 \le p_a \le \frac{1}{\varepsilon}, 0 \le p_b \le \frac{1}{\varepsilon}\right\}$$

Let us define the function φ by:

$$\varphi_1(p_a, p_b, .) = \frac{1}{s_a(p_a, p_a, p_b)}$$

$$\varphi_2(p_a, p_b, .) = \frac{1}{s_b(p_b, p_b, p_a)}$$

Taking H into account, φ is a continuous application of K into itself, which therefore has a fixed point.

Nevertheless this does not suffice for deriving the existence of a "stochastic equilibrium completely correlated to sunspots." Indeed, we already know that $p_a = p_b = \overline{p}(s.t.\ s(1)) = \dfrac{1}{\overline{p}}$ is a fixed point of φ (the only possible one with $p_a = p_b$). It is therefore necessary to show that the map φ has *several* fixed *points*.

To this purpose, let us consider the vector field ψ defined in K by:

$$\psi_a(p_a, p_b) = 1 - p_a S_a(p_a, p_b)$$

$$\psi_b(p_a, p_b) = 1 - p_b S_b(p_a, p_b)$$

Under the previous assumtion, for α and α' small enough,

$$\psi_a\left(\frac{1}{\alpha}, p_b\right) < 0, \forall p_b \leq \frac{1}{\alpha'}$$

$$\psi_b\left(p_a, \frac{1}{\alpha'}\right) < 0, \forall p_a \leq \frac{1}{\alpha}$$

Elsewhere for $p_a = 0$, $p_b = 0$, ψ_a is positive and ψ_b is positive.

It follows that the field of ψ vectors "points inward" (constructing a diagram may help).

Let us compute the determinant Δ associated with the function ψ at any given point.

$$\Delta = \begin{vmatrix} -p_a \dfrac{\partial S_a}{\partial p_a} - S_a & -p_a \dfrac{\partial S_a}{\partial p_b} \\[2mm] -p_b \dfrac{\partial S_b}{\partial p_a} & -p_b \dfrac{\partial S_b}{\partial p_b} - S_b \end{vmatrix}$$

$$\Delta = S_a S_b + S_a p_b \frac{\partial S_b}{\partial p_b} + S_b p_a \frac{\partial S_a}{\partial p_a}$$

$$\Delta = 1 + \frac{p_b}{S_b} \frac{\partial S_b}{\partial p_b} + \frac{p_a}{S_a} \frac{\partial S_a}{\partial p_a}$$

Still, calling ε_a and ε_b elasticities of the functions of "pseudo" supply S_a and S_b with respect to p_a and p_b, respectively:

$$\Delta = \varepsilon_a + \varepsilon_b + 1$$

But then, all the conditions for applying Poincaré-Hopf's index theorem (see Milnor 1965) are met. Taking into account the topological nature of the rectangle K, the degree of the mapping ψ is necessarily minus one. It follows that a sufficient condition for more than one equilibrium, besides the $p_a = p_b = \bar{p}$ equilibrium is that $\bar{\varepsilon}_a + \bar{\varepsilon}_b + 1 < 0$, where $\bar{\varepsilon}_a$, $\bar{\varepsilon}_b$ are the elasticities in $\bar{p}$ of the functions S_a and S_b.

We can summarize the argument in the following proposition:

PROPOSITION 3.1   If the sum of elasticities $\bar{\varepsilon}_a$, $\bar{\varepsilon}_b$ associated with functions S_a and S_b in $\bar{p}$ is smaller than -1, there exists at least one stochastic equilibrium completely correlated with sunspots.

As it is, the proposition is not totally conclusive. It is certainly intuitive that the condition $\bar{\varepsilon}_a + \bar{\varepsilon}_b + 1 < 0$ can be verified for configurations of nonpathological preferences and therefore for a group of "nonzero-measure" economies. We would nonetheless hope to relate the condition that concerns the pseudo functions S_a, S_b to the primitive data of the problem and, in any case, to the deterministic supply function s.

This exercise will not be presented in detail, though the reader desiring further information can refer to Azariadis and Guesnerie 1982b. Nonetheless, returning to the program that defines the functions s_a, s_b, the reader can imagine the intuitive validity of the formulas that relate $\bar{\varepsilon}_a$, $\bar{\varepsilon}_b$ to $\bar{\varepsilon}$, the elasticity of the function $s(\cdot)$ at point 1, namely:

$$\bar{\varepsilon}_a = (1 - \pi(a/a))\bar{\varepsilon},$$

$$\bar{\varepsilon}_b = (1 - \pi(b/b))\bar{\varepsilon}$$

It follows that, if $\bar{\varepsilon} < 0$, the condition of the above proposition is equivalent to:

$$\pi(a/a) + \pi(b/b) \leq 2 + 1/\bar{\varepsilon}$$

We see then, that as soon as $\bar{\varepsilon} < -\frac{1}{2}$, it is possible to find strictly positive numbers $\pi(a|a)$, $\pi(b|b)$ satisfying the condition; in other words, there can then exist natural phenomena that generate stationary stochastic equilibria. It is notable that the sufficient condition given here makes that property appear from the moment that the deterministic sequence of perfect foresight equilibria becomes asymptotically locally stable. The reader will also note that the formula shows that a bad correlation between the appearance of a today and a tomorrow or of b today and b tomorrow favorably affects the appearance of stochastic equilibria "correlated to sunspots."

A more thorough discussion of these points goes beyond the purpose of this chapter.

We will conclude this section with four remarks.

Remark 1. The condition given here is a sufficient one. It is not necessary; stochastic equilibria can exist in an economy where this condition is not verified.

Remark 2. From the moment there is one stationary stochastic equilibrium, in fact there are necessarily two, according to the index theorem. In this model, equilibria of this type necessarily appear in pairs (their number being even).

Remark 3. The relation between the results obtained here and those that were found by Azariadis (1981b) is somewhat complex and we will not discuss it in detail. Let us simply note the difference in the adopted approaches: Azariadis's first article looked for, within a resticted class of utility functions, a Markov matrix of a natural phenomenon apt to generate stochastic equilibria. Our reasoning here considers an exogenously given Markov matrix and any class of utility functions.

Remark 4. In order to prepare the generalization of the following section, the argument was presented in the most abstract way it could be. Indeed, the functions S_a and S_b being homogeneous to degree zero, we could have written the problem in terms of the one-dimensional variable $\alpha = \frac{p_a}{p_b}$. The existence of an equilibrium correlated with sunspots corresponds to the case where the graph of the function of excess demand cuts the axis of α at the deterministic equilibrium through an angle, such that, taking into account the boundary conditions, it must cut it at least two more times.

4   Theory in Dispute: Sunspots or Moonspots?

Now we will complicate the preceding model by supposing that the population is divided into two categories of equal size. The first is made up of agents who observe sunspots and consider their effects on price levels. Those of the second category observe another natural phenomenon (at the exclusion of the first); let's say moonspots. The sunspots appear (*a*) or don't appear (*b*). There are likewise two possibilities to be observed with moonspots (*c*) and (*d*). The appearance of *a* or *b* is governed by the Markovian process described earlier associated with vectors π^a, π^b. In similar fashion, the natural states *c* and *d* are determined by a Markovian process, which for simplification we suppose to be independent of the first. This process is described by the probablity vectors $\pi^c = (\pi(c|c), \pi(d|c))$ and $\pi^d = (\pi(c|d), \pi(d|d))$.

The temporal structure of the decisions is fairly analogous to the one envisioned in the preceding model. In period *t* the two subpopulations of "young" observe the two natural phenomena considered. On the market, they submit their *supply curve*, which reflects their expectations. The equilibrium prices emerge from the confrontation between the supply curves and the global demand curve $\left(\text{which is } \dfrac{1}{p}\right)$.

The observation of the moon or sun leads the agents to adopt two different "theories," both stationary.

The stochastic theory founded upon sunspots, which is adopted by the agents who observe sunspots, is the following:

• if a occurs, the prices are governed by a probability law associated with distribution μ_a,

• if b occurs, the prices are governed by a probability law associated with distribution μ_b.

The stochastic theory founded on moonspots is similar; c, d replace a, b, and μ_c, μ_d replace μ_a, μ_b. For reasons we will explain later, the distributions considered will be of finite support and with precisely two values.

Let us emphasize at this stage that:

1) The theories envisioned are stationary theories that do not explicitly depend on time.

2) Observation, which triggers the anticipations of the natural state tomorrow and therefore of tomorrow's price that it induces, affects the supply curve. On the other hand, the expectation on today's price that observation may determine has no effect on the supply curve.

3) The "theories" are macroeconomic theories clearly very worn. They rely on no analysis of behavior but rather on observations that an exterior omniscient observer would judge to have no relation to objective facts. Let us note, however, that each group observes only one of the two natural phenomena and, not being able to explain the price fluctuations that necessarily engender adhesion of the other group to a stochastic theory, it is rightful for each

group to seek a correlation between prices subject to fluctuations (of which one part is, at any rate, inexplicable) and an observable phenomenon.

Now let us consider the decision problem of the agent who believes in the influence of the sun on price levels when he observes a in period t. The key parameter is the probability distribution of tomorrow's prices, which is obtained by composition of the probabilities π^a and of the distributions μ_a, μ_b. We will label it Λ^a with $\Lambda^a = \pi(a|a)\mu_a + \mu(b|a)\mu_b$, or again, in short form $\Lambda^a = \pi^a \otimes (\mu_a, \mu_b)$.

The maximization program of the agent is then:

$$\text{Max}\, E(U(C_{t+1}, y_t))$$

$$\tilde{p}_{t+1}\, C_{t+1} \leq p_t\, y_t$$

where the expectation is taken with respect to Λ^a, the distribution of the random variable p_{t+1}.

The solution to this program is noted $y_t = s_a(p_t, \Lambda^a)$.

We would likewise define s_b, and for the followers of the lunar theory s_c and s_d.

The concept of *stochastic equilibrium which weakly validates the theories* becomes more specific. It will consist of probability distributions conditional to the observations μ_a, μ_b, μ_c, μ_d such that the equilibrium prices resulting from expectations formed from Λ_a, Λ_b posses distributions conditional to a, b, c, d, which are stationary and given by μ_a, μ_b, μ_c, μ_d, Let us immediately note that such a equilibrium does not exist for distributions that are not of finite support: In effect when a and c occur, for example, the supply curves of the two types of agents are determined and there can't be a finite number of equilibrium prices. Therefore it is natural to limit oneself to the case where only four equilibrium prices, corresponding to the couples of observations ac, ad, bd, bd, can appear. We will call them p_1, p_2, p_3, p_4.

In this case, the program of maximization in the case of the occurrence of a, for an agent who believes in the sun, can be written more explicitly:

$$\text{Max} \sum \lambda_i^a U(C_{t+1}^i, y_t)$$

$p_{t+1}^i C_{t+1}^i \leq p_i y_t,\ i = 1, 2, 3, 4$

And its solution is noted: $y_t = s_a(p_t, \ldots p_{t+1}^i, \ldots, \Lambda^a)$.

A stationary stochastic equilibrium that weakly validates the theory can be formally defined as a sequence (p_1, p_2, p_3, p_4) such that

(1) $s^a(p_1, p_1, \ldots, p_4, \Lambda^a) + s^c(p_1, p_1, \ldots, p_4, \Lambda^c) = \dfrac{2}{p_1}$

(2) $s^a(p_2, p_1, \ldots, p_4, \Lambda^a) + s^d(p_2, p_1, \ldots, p_4, \Lambda^d) = \dfrac{2}{p_2}$

(3) $s^b(p_3, p_1, \ldots, p_4, \Lambda^b) + s^c(p_3, p_1, \ldots, p_4, \Lambda^c) = \dfrac{2}{p_3}$

(4) $s^b(p_4, p_1, \ldots, p_4, \Lambda^b) + s^d(p_4, p_1, \ldots, p_4, \Lambda^d) = \dfrac{2}{p_4}$

where Λ^a, Λ^b, Λ^c, Λ^d are the probability vectors:

$\Lambda^a = (\pi(a|a)\pi(c),\ \pi(a|a)\pi(d),\ \pi(b|a)\pi(c),\ \pi(b|a)\pi(d))$

$\Lambda^b = (\pi(a|b)\pi(c),\ \pi(a|b)\pi(d),\ \pi(b|b)\pi(c),\ \pi(b|b)\pi(d))$

$\Lambda^c = (\pi(c|c)\pi(a),\ \pi(d|c)\pi(a),\ \pi(c|c)\pi(b),\ \pi(d|c)\pi(b))$

$\Lambda^d = (\pi(c|d)\pi(a),\ \pi(d|d)\pi(a),\ \pi(c|d)\pi(b),\ \pi(d|d)\pi(b))$

$\pi(a)$, $\pi(b)$ and $\pi(c)$, $\pi(d)$ being the stationary limit probabilities of states a and b in the two Markovian processes.

$(\pi(a) + \pi(b) = 1,\ \pi(c) + \pi(d) = 1)$

The stationary stochastic equilibrium leads then to the following evolutions.

For the agents who "believe in the sun," when a occurs, the equilibrium prices are either p_1 or p_2 with the stationary probabilities in time $\{\pi(c),\ \pi(d)\}$ (it is the distribution μ_b of the general approach). This sunspot/price correlation combines with the sunspot today, sunspot tomorrow correlation in such a way that observation affects conjecture of tomorrow's prices—whose conditional laws a and b are indicated by Λ^a and Λ^b—and therefore the supply curve.

By the same token, the agents who "believe in the moon' have the following theories: if c *occurs*, the prices are p_1, p_3 with probabilities $\pi(a)$, $\pi(b)$; if d occurs, the prices are p_2, p_4, still with probabilities $\pi(a)$, $\pi(b)$.

The theories are weakly validated in the following sense:

• the conjectures on the (two) possible values of the prices that are conditional to natural events are confirmed by these facts;

• in the long term, the frequency of the appearances confirms the stationary laws foreseen by the theory.

The theories, in a certain sense confirmed by the facts, are not, however, strongly validated: There exist correlations between the prices today and the prices tomorrow that can be observed by an econometrician and are not foreseen.

The weakness of the validation criteria is doubtless exaggerated by the stylization of the model (simplemindedness of the mechanisms and of the two groups being completely ignorant of their respective beliefs and observations). In a complex universe where the agents have the possibilities of limited calculation, it seems legitimate that they turn their attention by priority toward the verification of the points that the theory to which they adhere indicates to them as essential rather than to the analysis of numerous other facts that are not pertinent from the point of view of his explanatory system. Notable on this subject are the analogies between our concept of weak validation and the one which according to Popper, applies to physical theories (Popper 1959).

Two questions will be briefly examined:

· Does a stochastic equilibrium exist that weakly validates the theory?

· Does a stochastic equilibrium exist that would strongly validate i (in a way we will specify)?

The answer to the first question relies on a reasoning highly analogous to that of the preceding paragraph.

The left hand side of (1), (2), (3), (4), will be called S_1 $(p_1, \ldots, p_4)$, S_2 $(p_1, \ldots p_4), \ldots$ respectively. As previously, we can show that the functions are homogeneous of degree zero.

Assuning that a lower bound of S_1, S_2, S_3, S_4 is a number $\varepsilon > 0$, one can deduce that the vector field $\psi = \left\{ -S_1 + \dfrac{2}{p_1}, -S_2 + \dfrac{2}{p_2}, \right.$

$\left. -S_3 + \dfrac{2}{p_3}, -S_4 + \dfrac{2}{p_4} \right\}$ defined on a sufficiently large parallelepiped of $\mathfrak{R}^4$, is "pointing inward."

Considering then the straightforward solution to (1), (2), (3), (4) given by $p_1 = p_2 = p_3 = p_4 = \bar{p}$, we will call Δ the determinant of the jacobian of ψ at point $\overline{P} = (\bar{p} \ldots \bar{p})$ and we will conclude in the same manner as previously.

PROPOSITION 4.1   A condition sufficient for the existence of a stochastic equilibrium weakly validating the theory is that:

$$\Delta = \begin{vmatrix} -\dfrac{\partial S_1}{\partial p_1} - \dfrac{2}{p_1^2} & \dfrac{\partial S_1}{\partial p_2}, & \dfrac{\partial S_1}{\partial p_3}, & \dfrac{\partial S_1}{\partial p_4} \\ \ldots & \ldots \end{vmatrix}$$

evaluated in $\overline{P}$ be strictly positive.

It is fitting here, as in the preceding paragraph, to transform the above expression in eliciting as much as possible the primitive elements of the problem. Our objective here is not to go into thorough economic interpretation; the result, such as it is, highlights the possibility of the appearance of stochastic equilibria weakly validating the two theories under hypotheses that are not pathological.

Returning to the problem of strong validation, we must note that there is a clear correlation between the prices today and the prices tomorrow that is different from that which the agents see through their theories. Indeed, if p_1 occurs, the "true" conditional probability of p_1 tomorrow is not $\pi(a|a)\,\pi(d)$ but $\pi(a|a)\,\pi(d|d)$. The only way to account for this correlation is to condition the forecasts of price tomorrow on the prices observed yesterday (in the basic formalization, the prices today are not available at the moment that the supply curve is announced). The only correlation pertinent to the analysis is therefore the one which relates the prices yesterday with the prices tomorrow: The reader will easily establish the conditional probabilities, the formulas being slightly more complicated than those shown above.

At period t, instead of two events a, b, eight can present themselves to the consumer who "believes in the sun": $a^1, a^2, \ldots, a^4, b^1,$ $\ldots, b^4$. For the consumer who "believes in the moon" the same would occur. This implies 16 profiles of different behaviors and hence 16 different possible equilibrium prices and contradicts the initial hypothesis of four equilibrium prices unless, of course, the 16 events that determine 16 different behavior functions lead to four equilibria. This is unlikely to occur. In other words, "generically" there doesn't exist a stationary stochastic equilibrium with a finite number of equilibrium prices that strongly validates the theory (in the sense that the correlation between the prices yesterday and those tomorrow would be correctly understood by the agents). Nonetheless we nust note that, if we admit that the agents correctly anticipate the day's prices before presenting their supply curve, they can learn the characteristics of the process that determines moonspots by observing the correlations between the prices today and the prices tomorrow. There could well be, then, an equilibrium strongly validating the two theories, but it would be reduced to the stationary stochastic equilibrium eventually obatined if all the agents believe in the "union" of the two theories (by observing at the same time the moon and the sun).

5 Conclusion

We will conclude by briefly discussing the schematic framework of the generational model used in this study.

The temporal vision of the phenomenon adopted here is undeniably useful. A certain repetition is necessary for the emergence of stationary "beliefs." The theme of learning, of which we have only scratched the surface, but which is fundamental, of course requires a dynamic approach. And bringing to light these relationships between the appearance of stochastic equilibria and the asymptotic convergence of sequences of deterministic equilibria raises ticklish questions whose essential dimension is temporal.

Nevertheless, we must forcefully emphasize that, in essence, the analyses conducted in this chapter persist outside the specific framework of the generational model, even with a short temporal horizon. The effect of beliefs on conjectures is susceptible to being "self-fulfilling" today, even if the contradiction of the forecasts tomorrow render improbable the perpetuity of the initial belief. The mechanisms engaged under the circumstances identified here, are likely to have wide applicatrility.

Notes

1. We thank for their useful comments made during various seminars: H. Atlan, J. P. Dupuy, B. Wallisper, and G. Weisbuch.

2. See, for example, Radner (1972) and Guesnerie and Jaffray (1974).

3. For Azariadis (1981b) as for others here, sunspots constitute a useful metaphor for approaching the purely psychological problems of economic decision and for

attempting to explain the phenomena of panics, apparently unconnected with objective facts, of which economic history offers spectacular examples.

4. Symmetrically, we could have $p^*_{t+1} < p^*_t$ for all candidate series, but the procedure would have to stop without result, since we can neither converge towards a price limit (or else we would have a different stationary equilibrium), nor go beyond one for the inverse of the price.

5. On this point see R. Day (1980). The question of the pertinence of these perfect foresight equilibria for a positive theory naturally arises. Thus, it is completely improbable that the agents can correctly anticipate a chaotic series. Stationary equilibria or certain cyclical equilibria are more natural solutions. The question leads us towards the study of the agents' learning mechanisms and their eventual convergence. This indisputably important point is only mentioned here for memory (see, still, M. Bray [1982]).

6. π^a, π^b both belong to the simplex of R^2 denoted S^2.

2   Sunspots and Cycles

Costas Azariadis and
Roger Guesnerie

I   Introduction

Models of rational expectations (Lucas (1972), Radner (1979), Grossman and Stiglitz (1976)) typically determine prices on the basis of the intrinsic data of an economy—preferences, endowments, production sets. Price uncertainty in this framework is merely a reflection of randomness in the underlying intrinsic structure itself, and is not affected by "extrinsic" uncertainty, i.e., by events unrelated to economic "fundamentals."

From recent work undertaken in the framework of the overlapping generations model (Shell (1977), Azariadis (1981b), Cass and Shell (1983)) we know now that we can construct examples of rational expectations equilibria with random prices and no intrinsic uncertainty. The randomness of these prices is due entirely to the beliefs that individuals hold about their environment. If these beliefs are shared by everyone, price randomness may be self-fulfilling and will not of necessity dissipate, even asymptotically, as individuals accumulate more observations. We call this phenomenon a "sunspot" equilibrium.

The meaning of sunspot equilibria is still open to interpretation. One may view "sunspots" as a convenient label for a host of psychological factors (animal spirits, fears, Bayesian learning theories, etc.) that are unrelated to the preferences, endowment or

production set of any individual, and yet come to influence the forecasts and actions of economic decision-makers. And the reading of
economic historians may suggest that these factors have some pertinence for the explanation of phenomena like the Dutch tulip
mania in the seventeenth century and the Great Depression in our
own. Whatever it may denote, the concept of sunspot equilibrium
seems to be of central importance for a thorough understanding of
rational expectations as an equilibrium construct. The general
purpose of this chapter, which follows a previous attempt by Azariadis and Guesnerie (1982), is to contribute towards the clarification
of that construct, and especially of rational expectations equilibria
in non-linear dynamic economics.

More precisely, we seek completely to characterize a limited class
of sunspot equilibria (stationary ones of order two, i.e. with two
possible events or states of nature) in a simple overlapping generation (OLG) model of identical households that consume a
single produced good. This rather modest objective deserves some
comment.

The study of rational expectations equilibria in *linear* systems
has borne fruit only recently, through the work of Taylor (1977),
Shiller (1978), and Gouriéroux, Laffont and Montfort (1982). The
economics of the *non-linear* case is bound to be more complex;
the present state of the mathematical theory of non-linear systems
suggests, moreover, that it may be wise to begin with problems of
low dimension.

Sunspot phenomena, of course, are not necessarily dynamical;
the related concept of "correlated equilibrium" (see Maskin and
Tirole (1985)), for instance, does not require the passage of time. But
these ideas make more sense when stable beliefs are supported as
long-run equilibria of an open-ended economy like ours. Furthermore, the simple OLG model has been prominent in the recent
revival of dynamical macroeconomics, of which one example is the
work of Grandmont (1985). We choose, in other words, to study an

economy whose perfect foresight equilibria are well understood, and that understanding includes periodic equilibria.

Stationarity in its extended sense is important for two reasons: because stable beliefs are likely to be the asymptotic outcome of many well-defined learning processes; and because understanding stationary sunspot equilibria is a prerequisite towards understanding dynamical sunspot phenomena.

Our first result (Theorem 1) expresses formally a rather straightforward connection between sunspots and cycles. We continue with a sufficient condition (Theorem 2) for the existence of sunspot equilibria. This condition, which bears upon the stochastic characteristics of extrinsic uncertainty and the shape of the saving function, describes a class of economies in which sunspot equilibria exist. As it turns out, the same condition implies local asymptotic stability of the golden rule and existence of periodic equilibria of order 2. The reasons for this connection are elucidated in Theorem 3 which describes how stationary equilibria bifurcate to sunspot equilibria.

These results led us to investigate in greater depth the relationship between sunspot equilibria and cycles. The connection exhibited is surprisingly strong: Theorem 4 asserts that cycles of order 2 exist, if and only if, sunspot equilibria with two states exist.

Which of our results will survive in a more general model? The issue is taken up in the concluding section. All we need say here is that extensions from two to more than two natural events or from one to more than one type of household require relatively straightforward modifications of the methodology presented here; extensions to more than one physical commodity are the subject of a paper by Guesnerie (1986); and examples of non-stationary sunspot equilibria are provided in the appendix to this chapter as well as in a related work by Peck (1987).

II Perfect Foresight

The framework we shall be using is the overlapping generations model of fiat money with production, a simple reinterpretation of the related pure-exchange model examined by Samuelson (1958), Gale (1973) and others. Our results would not change in any essential way if we focused instead on pure exchange; we retain production here in order to preserve uniformity with earlier research on sunspots and cycles.

Time extends from one to infinity; at discrete points in time $t = 1$, $2, \ldots,$ a fixed-size generation of identical individuals appears, lives for two periods, "youth" and "old age," and dies at $t + 2$. Consumption occurs only in old age, production takes place only in youth. Each member of generation t is endowed with $e_1 > 0$ units of divisible leisure in youth, $e_2 > 0$ units of a single, perishable consumption good in old age. The only exception from this pattern is the very first generation that is born "old" at $t = 1$: each member of it is endowed with e_2 units of the consumption good and one unit of fiat "money," i.e., of an intrinsically worthless paper asset that will be the sole store of value in our economy.

Each member of the young generation may use a constant-returns-to scale technology to transform $n \in [0, e_1]$ units of his own leisure into $y \leqq n$ units of the perishable consumption good in order to purchase the store of value and finance in old age consumption in excess of e_2. The entire stock of the paper asset is then held by the old, provided it has positive value. All individuals are price takers and possess perfect foresight about future prices.

Individuals have preferences over intertemporal bundles. The utility of an individual born at t depends, first, upon the leisure he gives up at t or, equivalently, upon the amount of good he offers, y_t; second, upon his consumption c_{t+1} at $t + 1$. The utility function denoted $u(c_{t+1}, y_t)$ is assumed to be monotone, twice continuously differentiable and strictly concave. We assume throughout this paper that consumption and leisure are (strict) *normal goods* and that young individuals would choose positive savings if confronted with a zero real rate of interest.

Community excess demand for the consumption good in period t is the sum $x_t - y_t$ of excess demands by the old (x_t) and by the young $(-y_t)$. In this simple model, x_t necessarily equals the purchasing power, $1/p_t$, of existing fiat money balances, so that one may define aggregate excess demand to be

$$D(p_t, p_{t+1}) = 1/p_t - s(p_t/p_{t+1}) \tag{1}$$

where

$$s(R) = \arg \max_{0 \leq y \leq e_1} u(e_2 + Ry, y) \tag{2}$$

is the savings function of the representative household.

A *competitive equilibrium with perfect foresight* is associated with a sequence $(p_t)_{t=1}^{\infty}$ of non-negative prices that satisfies $D(p_t, p_{t+1}) = 0$ for all t; or, equivalently, with a sequence $(m_t)_{t=1}^{\infty}$ of real money balances satisfying $D(1/m_t, 1/m_{t+1}) = 0$, where $m_t = 1/p_t$ by definition. Finding equilibria with perfect foresight is equivalent to "solving" the difference equation $D(p_t, p_{t+1}) = 0$ either backward or forward. A backward solution has the form $m_t = f(m_{t+1})$ and a forward one is of the form $m_{t+1} = \phi(m_t)$, where f and ϕ are known maps.

Of particular interest to this paper is the notion of periodicity. We call the sequence $(p_t)_{t=1}^{\infty}$ a *periodic competitive equilibrium of order k* (or *k-cycle*) if $p_t = p_{t+k}$ for $t = 1, 2, \ldots$ and $k \geq 2$ while $p_t \neq p_{t+j}$ for all integers j in the interval $(0, k)$.

We state below without proof two useful results on competitive equilibria in general and on periodic equilibria in particular. Proposition 1 is well known and may be found, for example, in Cass Okuno and Zilcha (1979); Proposition 2 is due to Grandmont (1985).

PROPOSITION 1   If the individual's indifference map satisfies standard boundary assumptions and if consumption and leisure are

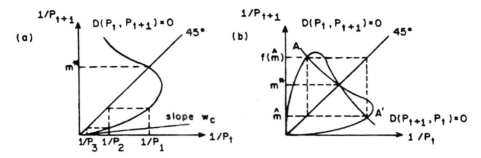

Figure 2.1

normal goods, then a backward-looking competitive equilibrium exists and it is unique. In addition, if the current price is not "too small," a forward-looking competitive equilibrium exists as well but is not necessarily unique.

PROPOSITION 2   If the monetary stationary equilibrium is locally dynamically stable, then a 2-cycle exists.

Figure 2.1 illustrates: a competitive equilibrium is the sequence $(p_1, p_2, p_3, \ldots)$ in panel (a); the alternating price sequence $(1/\hat{m}, 1/f(\hat{m}), 1/\hat{m}, \ldots)$ in panel (b) is a two-cycle.

III   Stationary Sunspot Equilibria

Sunspot equilibria are rational expectations equilibria that are perfectly correlated with extraneous events or with factors other than the preferences, endowment and production set of any individual. Equilibria of this type are not necessarily stationary. We provide in the appendix an example of dynamical sunspot equilibria in which the impact of sunspots dissipates over time. Here we are only interested in stationary sunspots, for we wish to understand how the set of stationary equilibria is enlarged by the sunspot hypothesis. A natural complement of the present study would be to investigate how the set of *non-stationary* perfect-foresight equilibria is enlarged by the inclusion of sunspots, but that is outside the scope of this essay.

The event we are considering now is characterized by two values: either sunspot activity (a) or absence of sunspot activity (b). The occurrence of a and b is governed by a Markov process with the following stationary transition probability matrix

$$\Pi = \begin{pmatrix} \pi_{aa} & \pi_{ba} \\ \pi_{ab} & \pi_{bb} \end{pmatrix}. \tag{3}$$

For $i = a, b$ and $j = a, b$, an element π_{ij} of this matrix denotes the probability that sunspot activity will be i tomorrow given that it is j today.

Suppose now that all agents in the economy believe in a perfect and stationary correlation of future prices with sunspot activity: in other words, all individuals forecast future price to be $p = \phi(i)$, for $i = (a, b)$, if i occurs tomorrow. Loosely speaking, a stationary sunspot equilibrium is a rational-expectations equilibrium in which the forecast is validated by actual price behavior. Before we proceed to define stationary sunspot equilibrium (SSE), we collect some useful properties of the savings function z, the rational expectations counterpart of the perfect-foresight savings function s.

LEMMA 1   The function

$$z(R, \pi) = \arg \max_{0 \leq y \leq e_1} [\pi u(e_2 + y, y) + (1 - \pi)u(e_2 + Ry, y)]$$

is single-valued, continuous and such that $z(R, 0) = s(R)$ for all R, and $z(1, \pi) = s(1)$ for all π. Furthermore, $z(R, \pi)$ lies between $s(R)$ and $s(1)$ for all R and π; also $z(R, \hat{\pi})$ lies between $z(R, 0)$ and $z(R, \pi)$ if $\hat{\pi} < \pi$.

The single-valuedness and continuity of z comes from the strict concavity and continuity of the consumer's maximand w.r.t. y. The remainder of this lemma follows once we write down the first-order conditions and differentiate w.r.t. π. The key result here is that z is a simple deformation of s, with which it coincides when $\pi = 0$.

LEMMA 2   Let $\eta(R, \pi)$ be the wage elasticity of savings under stochastic beliefs w.r.t. the real wage R, evaluated at (R, π). Then $\eta(1, \pi) = (1 - \pi)\varepsilon(1)$ for all π, where $\varepsilon(R)$ is the corresponding elasticity of savings under perfect foresight.

To prove this statement, one derives an expression for $\varepsilon(1)$ by differentiating w.r.t. R the first-order conditions for the two consumer problems (perfect foresight, rational expectations), evaluating the resulting two expressions at $R = 1$, and comparing.

Having defined the function z, we are now in a position to define formally stationary sunspot equilibria.

DEFINITION   A stationary sunspot equilibrium (SSE) is a quadruple $(p_a, p_b, \pi_{aa}, \pi_{bb})$ of positive numbers such that π_{aa} and π_{bb} lie in the open interval $(0, 1)$; $p_a \neq p_b$; and the excess demand for the consumption good is zero for each current state, i.e.

$$D^a \equiv 1/p_a - z(p_a/p_b, \pi_{aa}) = 0 \tag{4a}$$

$$D^b \equiv 1/p_b - z(p_b/p_a, \pi_{bb}) = 0. \tag{4b}$$

As a matter of convenient terminology, we say that a SSE $(p_a, p_b, \pi_{aa}, \pi_{bb})$ is a *SSE with respect to a given* (exogenous) *matrix* Π if the numbers π_{aa}, π_{bb} in our definition are diagonal elements of the matrix Π. This definition accords with the informal one proposed earlier. If event a (respectively b) occurs in the present period, p_a (respectively p_b) is actually the equilibrium price by equation (4a) and (4b). The beliefs $p_a = \phi(a)$, $p_b = \phi(b)$ are then self-fulfilling.

Note also that the definition requires both $p_a \neq p_b$ and $0 < \pi_{aa} < 1$, $0 < \pi_{bb} < 1$. If $p_a = p_b$, a SSE degenerates to a stationary equilibrium of the golden-rule type (See Lemma 1).[1] Another type of degeneracy obtains when certain transitions are ruled out in the matrix Π. In particular when $\pi_{aa} = 0$, $\pi_{bb} = 0$, the occurrence of event a (respectively b) today ensures the occurrence of b (respectively a) tomorrow. In other words, the equilibrium prices p_a and p_b necessarily succeed each other. A SSE then degenerates into a 2-cycle, as can be seen formally from Lemma 1 and equations (4a) and (4b): *two-cycles thus appear as limiting sunspot equilibria associated with a 2×2 degenerate matrix Π that has zeros in the diagonal.*

As a direct consequence of this limiting argument we have the following result.

THEOREM 1 (Sunspot equilibria in the neighbourhood of two-cycles). In an economy that admits a periodic equilibrium of order two, there is generically a neighbourhood $v(\overline{\Pi})$ of the 2×2 matrix $\overline{\Pi}$ such that a SSE exists w.r.t. every Π in $v(\overline{\Pi})$.

A proof of this statement is left to the reader. It is, however, fairly intuitive and follows immediately from standard transversality theorems if the economy is identified with a sufficiently differentiable savings function. We shall reexamine the connection between sunspots and cycles more precisely in the sequel. For the time being we call *regular*[2] a periodic equilibrium of order 2 if it satisfies the conclusions of Theorem 1.

IV   An Existence Theorem for SSE

To investigate the existence of stationary sunspot equilibria, we put $w = p_a / p_b$ and define the following single-valued function

$$F(w, \pi_{aa}, \pi_{bb}) = wz(w, \pi_{aa}) - z(1/w, \pi_{bb}). \tag{5}$$

A SSE exists if, ond only if, F has a positive root $w \neq 1$ for some $\pi_{aa} \in (0, 1)$ and $\pi_{bb} \in (0, 1)$. This is so because any SSE satisfying (4a) and (4b) for some $p_a \neq p_b$, also satisfies $1/w = z(w, \pi_{aa})/z(1/w, \pi_{bb})$, and therefore $F(\cdot) = 0$. Moreover, for any positive root $w \neq 1$ of F, we can find two positive numbers, p_a and p_b, such that (4a) and (4b) hold true.

Useful properties of the function F are collected in Lemma 3.

LEMMA 3   The function $F(w, \pi_{aa}, \pi_{bb})$ is continuous for every (w, π_{aa}, π_{bb}) with $w > 0$. For each (π_{aa}, π_{bb}) it has the following properties:

(i) $F(1, \pi_{aa}, \pi_{bb}) = 0$

(ii) $F \to \infty$ as $w \to \infty$.

(iii) For w small enough, $F(w, \pi_{aa}, \pi_{bb}) < 0$

(iv) If w is a root of $F(w, \pi_{aa}, \pi_{bb})$, then $1/\hat{w}$ is a root of $F(w, \pi_{bb}, \pi_{aa})$.

Proof   Parts (i) and (iv) are straightforward. Part (ii) derives from the fact that $z(w, \pi)$ is between $s(1)$ and $s(w)$ (see Lemma 1), and from standard boundary assumptions on individual behaviour, i.e., $ws(w) \to +\infty$ as $w \to \infty$. To prove (iii), we rewrite F as $w[z(w, \pi_{aa}) - (1/w)z(1/w, \pi_{bb})]$, and we note that, because of (ii), the term in brackets tends to $-\infty$ as $w \to \infty$, so that F becomes negative for small w. ||

With the assistance of Lemma 3 we may now attempt to answer two related questions. First, what can we say about the set of 2×2 transition probability matrices for which a SSE exists? Second, can we find sunspot equilibria in the neighbourhood of stationary perfect-foresight equilibria?

We begin by evaluating at $w = 1$ the derivative of the function F w.r.t. w. From Lemma 1 we obtain

$$\partial_w F(1, \pi_{aa}, \pi_{bb}) = s(1)[1 + \eta(1, \pi_{aa}) + \eta(1, \pi_{bb})]. \tag{6}$$

This combines with Lemma 2 to yield

$$\partial_w F(1, \pi_{aa}, \pi_{bb}) < 0 \quad \text{if } (2 - \pi_{aa} - \pi_{bb})\varepsilon(1) < -1. \tag{7}$$

A direct implication of (7) is

THEOREM 2 (Sufficient conditions for the existence of a two-state SSE)[3]   Suppose that the utility function satisfies regularity assumptions on differentiability, concavity and boundary behaviour. Then a sufficient condition for the existence of a sunspot equilibrium with respect to a given Markovian transition probability matrix Π is

$$\varepsilon(1) < 0, \quad \pi_{aa} + \pi_{bb} < 2 - \frac{1}{|\varepsilon(1)|}. \tag{8}$$

Proof Note first that $\varepsilon(1) \geq 0$ violates (8), and also that $F(1, \pi_{aa}, \pi_{bb}) = 0$. Given the boundary properties of F established in Lemma 3, the inequality $\partial_w F < 0$ is sufficient to ensure that F has at least one pair of roots other than $w = 1$. ‖

Since this proof nowhere assumes that $\pi_{aa} > 0$, $\pi_{bb} > 0$, it applies directly to the existence of 2-cycles. The outcome is stated as Corollary 1 which merely restates Proposition 2.

COROLLARY 1 If $\varepsilon(1) < -\frac{1}{2}$, then there exists a periodic equilibrium of order 2.

The identity of Corollary 1 and Proposition 2 is based on the fact that $\varepsilon(1) < -\frac{1}{2}$ is equivalent to local dynamic stability of the monetary stationary equilibrium.

Theorem 2 identifies a subset of the set of all two-state transition probability matrices for which there exist SSE. This subset is marked by the shaded area in Figure 2.2, where $K = 2 - 1/|\varepsilon(1)|$. The whole

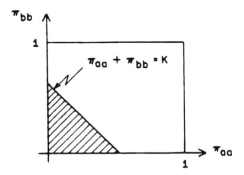

Figure 2.2

set of those matrices coincides with the unit square, and the origin represents the degenerate matrix associated with periodic two-cycles.

One thing that Theorem 2 *does not* assert is that the existence of SSE somehow depends on the $\pi_{aa} + \pi_{bb}$. As we shall see later, such a claim can only be made strictly on the borderline of the subset shaded in Figure 2.2, and approximately in the neighbourhood of that borderline.

V   SSE in the Neighbourhood of the Deterministic Stationary Equilibrium

To grasp some of the implications of Theorem 2, we look at sunspot equilibria in the neighbourhood of the line $\pi_{aa} + \pi_{bb} = K$ in Figure 2.2. When $\pi_{aa} + \pi_{bb}$ decreases passing through K, $\partial_w F$ is first strictly positive, then vanishes and becomes strictly negative. The passage through zero of the derivative of F implies for that function what mathematicians call a bifurcation. We characterize that bifurcation in

THEOREM 3   Consider the one-dimensional bissectrix of the (π_{aa}, π_{bb}) plane crossing P the line $\pi_{aa} + \pi_{bb} = K$ at some point C. Then the graph of $w = p_a/p_b$ as a function of the curvilinear abscissa along p has the shape of a "pitchfork" bifurcation, with only one equilibrium before point C and three equilibria after.

Let us begin by noticing that the qualitative features of the graph will be somewhat similar along a "transversal" path and along a diagonal path with $\pi_{aa} = \pi_{bb}$. Along this latter path, because of the symmetry property of F in Lemma 3, the function F bifurcates as suggested by Figure 2.3(a). An elementary proof would show that two zeros arbitrarily close to 1 necessarily exist on one side of the bifurcation, and would use the implicit function theorem at these zeros. It is simpler to note that Thom's classification

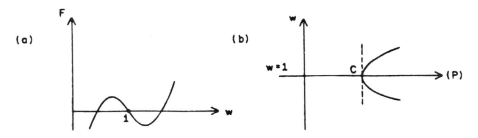

Figure 2.3

theorem applies here (since all vector fields on R are gradient vector fields): given the parameter space and symmetry properties, we have a cusp catastrophe and the section of the cusp manifold is of the pitchfork type because 1 is invariant here.

An alternative method, suggested in Woodford's survey of over-lapping generations (1984), employs an approximation argument to arrive at sufficient conditions like Theorem 2. We propose below an approximation that is less formal and, we hope, more intuitive than Woodford's.

Using equation (1) we expand the excess demand function of perfect foresight about the stationary price level p^*. Putting $x_t = p_t - p^*$ one obtains

$$\varepsilon(1)x_{t+1} - [1 + \varepsilon(1)]x_t = 0. \tag{9}$$

Local dynamic stability here corresponds, as we already know, to $|1 + 1/\varepsilon(1)| < 1$ or, equivalently, to $\varepsilon(1) < -\frac{1}{2}$.

In the rational-expectations case we define $x_a = p_a - p^*$, $x_b = p_b - p^*$ where (p_a, p_b) are sunspot prices. Then we use Lemma 2 to linearize the system consisting of equations (4a) and (4b) to:

$$(1 + \pi_{ab}\varepsilon(1))x_a - \pi_{ab}\varepsilon(1)x_b = 0 \tag{10a}$$

$$\pi_{ba}x_a - (1 + \pi_{ba}\varepsilon(1))x_b = 0. \tag{10b}$$

Intuitively, sunspot equilibria close to the stationary deterministic equilibrium obtain when this system has non-zero solutions in (x_a, x_b), i.e., if

$$\pi_{ab}\varepsilon(1)/[1+\pi_{ab}\varepsilon(1)]=[1+\pi_{ba}\varepsilon(1)]/\pi_{ba}\varepsilon(1) \tag{11}$$

or, equivalently, if

$$\pi_{ab}+\pi_{ba}=-1/\varepsilon(1). \tag{12}$$

We note again that $\pi_{ab} + \pi_{ba} = 2$ (equivalently, $\pi_{aa} + \pi_{bb} = 0$) requires that $\varepsilon(1) = -\frac{1}{2}$ if equation (12) is to hold. Degenerate transition probability matrices of the form $\pi_{aa} = \pi_{bb} = 0$ admit sunspot equilibria in the neighbourhood of the deterministic stationary date if that stationary state possesses borderline dynamic stability.

VI   Sunspot vs. Periodic Equilibria

The central result of this section is

THEOREM 4   Given standard assumptions on preferences and strict normal goods, a two-state stationary sunspot equilibrium exists if, and only if, a regular deterministic periodic equilibrium of order two exists.

Proof   A regular deterministic equilibrium is by definition one for which Theorem 1 holds. Hence, the "if" part of Theorem 4 is tautologically true. The reciprocal is not obvious.

Assume accordingly that there exists a sunspot equilibrium, i.e., three positive numbers $(\overline{w}, \pi_{aa}, \pi_{bb})$ such that $\pi_{aa} < 1$, $\pi_{bb} < 1$ and $F(\overline{w}) = \overline{w}z(\overline{w}, \pi_{aa}) - z(1/\overline{w}, \pi_{bb}) = 0$. We shall demonstrate that a deterministic 2-cycle necessarily exists. To that end, we define the sets $\Omega_1 = [w|s(w) \geqq s(1)]$, $\Omega_2 = [w|s(w) \leqq s(1)]$ and prove successively the following four statements:

(S1) $\psi(w) \equiv wz(w, \pi_{aa}) < s(1)$ for $w < 1$.

(S2) There is no $w > 1$ such that $w \in \Omega_1$ and $F(w) = 0$.

(S3) There is no $w > 1$ such that $1/w \in \Omega_2$ and $F(w) = 0$.

(S4) If $F(\bar{w}) = 0$ for some $\bar{w} > 1$, than $\bar{w}s(\bar{w}) - s(1/\bar{w}) \leq 0$.

(S1) For the first statement, we note from Lemma 1 that $s(w) \geq z(w, \cdot) \geq s(1)$ in Ω_1, and $s(w) \leq z(w, \cdot) \leq s(1)$ in Ω_2. Therefore, if $w \in \Omega_2$, then $z(w, \cdot) \leq s(1)$ and $\psi(w) = wz(w, \cdot) \leq ws(1) < s(1)$ for any $w < 1$. If $w \in \Omega_1$, on the other hand, then $s(1) \leq z(w, \cdot) \leq s(w)$ by Lemma 1 and the definition of Ω_1; therefore $\psi(w) \leq ws(w)$. However, our normality assumption implies that $ws(w)$ is an increasing function of w, i.e., $ws(w) < s(1)$ for $w < 1$. Hence $\psi(w) < s(1)$ for $w \in \Omega_1$ s.t. $w < 1$. This completes the proof of (S1).

(S2) $F(w) = 0$ implies $z(w, \pi_{aa}) = (1/w)z(1/w, \pi_{bb})$. For $w > 1$, the right-hand side of this equality is smaller than $s(1)$, which implies $z(w, \pi_{aa}) < s(1)$ for $w < 1$, or $s(w) < s(1)$. By definition, this cannot happen for any $w \in \Omega_1$, and the proof of (S2) is complete.

(S3) This is shown in the same manner as (S2).

(S4) From (S2) we have that $\bar{w} \in \Omega_2$ and $z(\bar{w}, \cdot) > s(\bar{w})$; hence $\bar{w}z(\bar{w}, \cdot) > \bar{w}s(w)$. From (S3), on the other hand, it follows that $1/\bar{w} \in \Omega_1$, so that $z(1/\bar{w}, \cdot) \leq s(1/\bar{w}, \cdot) \leq s(1/\bar{w})$ and $-z(1/\bar{w}, \cdot) > -s(1/\bar{w})$. Hence, (S2) and (S3) together yield $F(\bar{w}) > \bar{w}s(\bar{w}) - s(1/\bar{w})$, which completes the proof of (S4).

Having proved the preliminary statements, we make two additional observations. First, from the symmetry of the roots of F noted previously, we assume without loss of generality that the root $\bar{w}$ of $F(w)$ *exceeds unity* (possibly after inverting a and b). Second, the function $ws(w) - s(1/w)$ becomes positive as $w \to +\infty$.

Therefore, the continuous function $ws(w) - s(1/w)$ is non-positive at $\bar{w} > 1$, and becomes strictly positives as $w \to +\infty$; it will have at least one finite real root greater than unity. ‖

The reader should notice that the proof only uses the fact that z is "between" $s(w)$ and $s(1)$ in the sense of Lemma 1. A shorter proof obtains if we rely on the fact that $\eta(w, \pi)$, the wage-elasticity of z, exceeds minus one (see note 4). It follows from this property that $wz(w, \cdot)$ is increasing in w, and points 2 and 3 follow more immediately. However, as the above proof shows, this specific property of z is not actually needed. The main proof is more open to generalization. In fact, careful inspection of that proof suggests that Theorem 4 can be strengthened as follows:[5]

THEOREM 4′ Suppose preferences satisfy standard assumptions and strict normality. If a SSE exists relative to the matrix with diagonal elements (π_{aa}, π_{bb}), then a SSE also exists for every matrix with diagonal elements $(\hat{\pi}_{aa}, \hat{\pi}_{bb})$ such that $\hat{\pi}_{aa} < \pi_{aa}$ and $\hat{\pi}_{bb} < \pi_{bb}$.

Proof As in Theorem 4, except that (S4) must now be replaced by (S4′): $F(\bar{w}, \pi_{aa}, \pi_{bb}) = 0$ for some $\bar{w} > 1$ implies that $F(\bar{w}, \hat{\pi}_{aa}, \hat{\pi}_{bb}) < 0$ for $\hat{\pi}_{aa} < \pi_{aa}$ and $\hat{p}_{bb} < \pi_{bb}$. The rest of the argument still applies because of Lemma 2. ‖

According to this result, the set of matrices associated with SSE is connected and its frontier, although not of necessity a straight line as in Figure 2.2, does slope downward. Behind Theorems 4 and 4′ lies the same intuition that explains two-cycles in Figure 2.1(b).

A two-cycle requires that, for some wage rate, the income effect of a wage change should outweigh the substitution effect by a sufficient margin. Transition probability matrices with infinitesimal diagonal elements do not alter by much the relative strength of substitution and income effects. Therefore, the continuity of savings behaviour implies that a SSE exists whenever a two-cycle does.

Suppose, on the other hand, that a SSE exists for some transition probability matrix Π and that $\varepsilon(1) < 0$. Then Lemma 2 says that, if we reduce the size of diagonal elements in Π, we strengthen the income effect of a wage change relative to the substitution effect and facilitate the existence of stationary sunspot equilibria. An extreme point of this process is when the diagonal elements vanish altogether and we obtain a deterministic two-cycle.

VII Conclusions

We review here the main results from earlier sections and discuss the prospects for generalizing each of them. The summary relies heavily on the diagrams of Figure 2.4; each panel in that figure graphs the SSE price ratio w against a one dimensional parameter—say, $\pi = \pi_{aa} + \pi_{bb}$ for simplicity—that stands for the transition probability matrix Π.

Theorem 1, depicted in panel (a), says that the two broken-line branches exist for any 2-cycle. This theorem is a formal elaboration of a simple idea which, to the best of our knowledge, does not appear in the literature antedating the present paper. The existence of sunspot equilibrium in the neighbourhood of periodic cycles

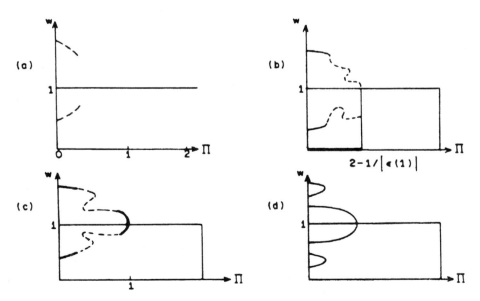

Figure 2.4

is potentially a very general property, holding for n-dimensional systems (i.e., for n physical commodities) in which expectations look one period forward and for cycles of any order k.

Theorem 2, on the other hand, means that the graph is non-empty above the thick line of panel (b). The principle of the method used for proving Theorem 2 is quite general. The argument based on the slope of the tangent is, in fact, a one-dimensional version of the Poincaré-Hopf theorem. A generalization of that sufficient condition to n-dimensional systems is obtained in a forthcoming paper of Guesnerie (1986).

The same methodology applies in generalizing theorems 2 and 3 to cycles of order k, either in one-or multi-dimensional systems. We note, meantime, that the existence of sunspots of order k follows generically from the existence of sunspots of order 2.[6] Let us sketch here the argument for passing from $k = 2$ to $k = 3$. Consider a SSE of order 2 associated with two events a and b. Then add to these a third event c such that the probability of passage from a to c is zero, the one from b to c is also zero, and the probability of passing from c to c is unity. If (p_a, p_b) are equilibrium prices in a SSE of order 2, and p^* is the equilibrium price at the stationary monetary equilibrium, then clearly the vector (p_a, p_b, p_c) is a "degenerate" SSE of order 3 if $p_c = p^*$. Perturbing slightly the transition probability matrix will yield a regular SSE of order 3.

Panel (c) demonstrates the bifurcation studied in Theorem 3. The pitchfork, or transcritical, aspect of that bifurcation seems to be a characteristic of the bifurcation for sunspots of order 2, even in more general systems. However, sunspots of higher order have necessarily more complex bifurcations. Finally, panel (d) provides one possible illustration of the details that Theorems 4 and 4′ add to our knowledge of sunspot equilibria. We note, nevertheless, that the one-dimensional parametrization of transition probability matrices wastes some information on the set of matrices compatible with stationary sunspot equilibria.

Appendix: Two Examples of Dynamic Sunspot Equilibrium

Example 1 (Sunspot equilibrium is a lottery on multiple temporary equilibria) Suppose the offer curve bends backward, i.e., the forward-looking solution to $D(p_t, p_{t+1}) = 0$ is not unique. Then there exist equilibrium price sequences $(p_1, p_2, \ldots)$ and $(p_1, p_2, \ldots)$ such that $p_2 \neq p_2^1$. Furthermore, it must be the case that $y = 1/p_1$ maximizes both $u(p_1y/p_2 + e_2, y)$ and $u(p_1y/p_2^1 + e_2, y)$ over the interval $[0, e_1]$. It follows that the same value of y maximizes over the same interval the function $\pi u(p_1y/p_2 + e_2, y) + u(p_1y/p_2^1 + e_2, y)$ for any arbitrary $\pi \in [0, 1]$. Therefore, a third equilibrium price sequence $(p_1, \tilde{p}_2, \ldots)$ exists, where $\tilde{p}_2$ is a random variable with realizations $\tilde{p}_2 = p_2$ w.p. $\pi; = p_2^1$ w.p. $1 - \pi$.

Example 2 (Multiple temporary equilibria are not necessary for the existence of dynamical sunspot equilibria) Suppose now that endowments are $e_1 > 0$, $e_2 = 1$, and preferences are given by $u = c_{t+1} - (1/2)y_t^2$. Then, in perfect foresight, the savings function equals p_t/p_{t+1}, and excess demand is $D(p_t, p_{t+1}) = 1/p_t - p_t/p_{t+1}$. An equilibrium price sequence (p_t) exists for each $p_t \geq 1$, and it is unique; at $p_t = 1$ we support the golden-rule allocation.

With extraneous uncertainty, individuals maximize expected utility conditional on price and other observations. Specifically, saving now equals $p_t E(p_t^{-1}|I_t)$, where I_t is the conditioning information for t, and excess demand is

$$d(p_t, I_t) = 1/p_t - p_t E(p_{t+1}^{-1}|I_t). \tag{13}$$

We introduce now two arbitrary numbers $\theta \in (0, 1)$ and $q_1 > 1$, and define two infinite scalar sequences $(q_t)_{t=2}^{\infty}$ and $(\pi_t)_{t=2}^{\infty}$ recursively from

$$q_{t+1} = q_t^2/\theta, \quad \pi_{t+1} = \frac{1-\theta}{q_t^2 - \theta}. \tag{14}$$

Since $q_{t+1} > q_t$ and $q_1 > 1$, we have $q_t > 1$ for $t = 1, 2, \ldots$, and $\pi_t \in (0, 1)$ for $t = 2, \ldots$.

One verifies easily that the sequence $(\tilde{p}_t)_{t=2}^{\infty}$ of random variables with realizations

$$p_t = p_{t-1} \quad \text{if } p_{t-1} = 1 \tag{15}$$

$$p_t = \begin{cases} q_t & \text{w.p.} \quad 1 - \pi_t \\ 1 & \text{w.p.} \quad \pi_t \end{cases}, \quad \text{if } p_{t-1} \neq 1$$

constitutes a sunspot equilibrium, that is, satisfies $d(p_t, I_t) = 0$. By construction, the sequence $(\tilde{p}_t)$ converges to the golden rule with some probability $Q > 0$, and to autarky with probability $1 - Q$.

Notes

1. The golden rule is typically defined in connection with stationary consumption optima in growth problems: at $m = m^*$, stationary ordinal utility $u(e_2 + m, m)$ attains a maximum. See Phelps (1961).

2. Note that this definition is not standard. Regular equilibria in the usual sense are regular in our sense but the converse is not necessarily true.

3. Another equivalent sufficient condition of SSE equilibria has been given in Azariadis and Guesnerie (1982b), where condition (8) is also stated without complete proof. See Spear (1984) for a similar result.

4. It is easy to conclude in fact that $\eta(w, \pi) > \eta(w, 0)$, which itself is greater than -1.

5. We are grateful to an anonymous referee for suggesting this extension.

6. This would not be true of deterministic cycles. It is therefore possible, as Woodford (1984) points out, for higher-order SSE to exist even though the corresponding periodic cycle does not.

3   On Stationary Sunspot Equilibria of Order *k*

Pierre-André Chiappori and
Roger Guesnerie

1 Introduction

This chapter is devoted to the study of stationary sunspot equilibria in a one-dimensional, one-step forward-looking dynamical system. Such dynamical systems describe economies, indexed by time, in which the state variable at time *t* is one-dimensional and the relevant forecasting horizon of the agents is of one period. Although many relevant economic questions with time dimensions cannot be captured within such an elementary structure, a number of simple variants of the popular overlapping-generations model do fit this framework. Other examples of the relevance of the simplified structure under scrutiny, outside of the overlapping-generations class of model, include the model described by Woodford (1988).

The attention to one-dimensional, one-step forward-looking systems is justified not only by possible economic relevance but also by simplicity and exemplarity. The study of stationary sunspot equilibria in more complex systems—for example by Guesnerie (1986) or Woodford (1986)—should benefit from progress in the understanding of stationary sunspot equilibria (SSE) in one-dimensional, one-step forward-looking systems.

Our point of view in this chapter has two characteristics that should be emphasized. First, in the line of Guesnerie (1986), we describe the system through an abstract excess-demand function; we formulate axiomatically a certain number of requirements, which are minimal for the theory and which should result, in more specific versions of the model, from the conclusions of consumer or producer theory. This abstract description of the system is justified, in our opinion, by its simplicity and generality. Second, we take a specific line of investigation that differs from other approaches in the literature. Such a line, which in its techniques as well as its perspectives can be traced back to the work of Azariadis and Guesnerie (1982a, 1986), leads to emphasizing the stochastic properties of the singular, extrinsic (in the sense of Shell, 1977, and Cass and Shell, 1983) sunspot process on which beliefs are based. Other approaches using different techniques lead to existence results of SSE (around the stationary state in Woodford, 1986, or of global nature in Grandmont, 1986) in which the stochastic pro-perties of the sunspot process are neither directly nor necessarily completely apprehended. Naturally, the various competing per-spectives and techniques are complementary rather than opposing. We do think, however, that what could be termed the Azariadis–Guesnerie perspective, which is taken here, is well adapted to a full understanding of some important features of the sunspot phenomenon.

The plan of this chapter is as follows: In Section 2 we describe the model, and in Section 3 we apply the Poincaré–Hopf argument, first introduced by Azariadis and Guesnerie (1982a) for the existence of stationary sunspot equilibria, to the abstract system under con-sideration. Specifically, considering systems with a unique "inde-terminate" stationary equilibrium, we extend to sunspots of order k the sufficient conditions previously obtained for sunspots of order 2 in a simple OG framework. In particular, we characterize a broad class of Markov matrices that are associated with sunspots of order k. The set of SSE of order k is considered from a differential view-point in Section 4; we show that, in some sense, "many" sunspot equilibria of strict order k do exist "close to" sunspots of order $k -$ 1. Section 5 introduces a few results on the bifurcations of the system near the stationary state and gives brief indications on the route for obtaining local counterparts of the global results obtained in Section 3.

2 The Model

a Excess Demand under Certainty

The basic model is a very simple variant of Guesnerie (1986). We define an abstract, deterministic, one-dimensional system through a mapping:

$Z: \mathbb{R}_+ \times \mathbb{R}_+ \to \mathbb{R}$.

Here, $Z(p_t, p_{t+1})$ can often (but not necessarily) be interpreted as the excess demand for the unique good when present price (in terms of money) is p_t and the (perfectly foreseen) future price is p_{t+1}. Under the (perfect foresight) dynamics described by Z, perfect foresight equilibria are defined by

$\forall t, Z(p_t, p_{t+1}) = 0$.

In particular, a stationary equilibrium is a price $\bar{p}$ such that

$Z(\bar{p}, \bar{p}) = 0$.

The equations describing the evolution of the usual overlapping-generation (OG) model with a representative consumer define a one-dimensional, one-step forward-looking system of the kind we are considering. The system may have one or several stationary equilibria (or steady states). Often, as in the next section, we shall assume that it has only one (as is the case for the simple OG model with representative consumer and no government expenditures).

From Z, we can define a vector field ZZ over $\mathbb{R}_+$ by

$$ZZ: (p_1, p_2) \rightarrow [Z(p_1, p_2), Z(p_2, p_1)].$$

b   Uncertainty and Sunspots

Assume now that expectations are stochastic. Tomorrow the price can take any of k different values $p_{t+1}^1, \ldots, p_{t+1}^k$ with respective probabilities $\pi^1, \ldots, \pi^k$. The excess demand of the system can still be defined; but now it is a mapping,

$$\tilde{Z}^k: \mathbb{R}_+^{k+1} \times S^{k-1} \rightarrow \mathbb{R},$$

where S^{k-1} is the simplex in $\mathbb{R}^k$. In words. $\tilde{Z}^k$ is a function of present price p_t, future prices $p_{t+1}^1, \ldots, p_{t+1}^k$, and probabilities $\pi^1, \ldots, \pi^k$ (with $\Sigma_\ell \pi^\ell = 1$). Again, $\tilde{Z}^k$ can easily be derived from consumers' utilities in a usual OG context. In what follows, we shall assume that Z and $\tilde{Z}^k$ are *smooth* (of class C^2) for all $k \in \mathbb{Z}$.

We now come to the definition of a *stationary sunspot equilibrium* *(SSE)*. The intuition is the following. Consider a random exogenous Markovian phenomenon with k different states; it is described by $k \times k$ Markov matrix M. Let M_ℓ denote the ℓth line of M; that is, $M_\ell = (m_{\ell 1}, \ldots, m_{\ell k})$, where $m_{\ell s}$ is the probability of being tomorrow in state s, given that the present state is ℓ. In particular,

$$\sum_s m_{\ell s} = 1, \quad \text{for each } \ell.$$

Associated with M is a price vector $p = (p_1, \ldots, p_k)$ of $\mathbb{R}_+^k$. Suppose that the agents in the economy believe that the price of the unique good in period t will be p_ℓ if and only if the exogenous process is in state ℓ at that date. Under such a "theory," the *present* state of process brings information on the *future* price of the good; namely, if the present state is ℓ, then the probability of the price being p_s tomorrow is exactly $m_{\ell s}$. That is, under this theory, the present excess demand will be $\tilde{Z}^k(p_\ell, p, M_\ell)$. Now we say that the vector p is an SSE associated with the matrix M if this theory is self-fulfilling; that is, if, given the agents' behavior, the price that clears the market when the process is in state ℓ is exactly p_ℓ, as predicted.

This leads to the following formal definition. First, we define the mapping

$$\hat{Z}^k: \mathbb{R}_+^k \times \mathfrak{M}_k \to \mathbb{R}^k$$

by $\hat{Z}^k(p, M) = [\tilde{Z}^k(p_1, p, M_1), \ldots, \tilde{Z}^k(p_k, p, M_k)]$, where $\mathfrak{M}_k$ is the set of $(k \times k)$ Markov matrices. In words, the ℓth component of $\hat{Z}^k$ is the excess demand when present price is p_ℓ and the process is in state ℓ. Now we have the following.

DEFINITION 1 A pair (p, M), for which the components $(p_1, \ldots, p_k)$ of p are not all identical, define an SSE of cardinal k if $\hat{Z}^k(p, M) = (0, \ldots, 0)$.

In the same way, *local* SSE are defined as follows.

DEFINITION 2 The economy exhibits local SSE (of cardinal k) around the steady state if, for any neighborhood $\mathfrak{N}$ of $(\bar{p}, \ldots, \bar{p})$, there exists a SSE (p, M) such that $p \in \mathfrak{N}$.

In words, we speak of local SSE when SSE exists in any, however small, neighborhood of the steady state.

Note that we have defined the *cardinal* of the SSE as the number of components of p. Now, the number of *different* components in p will be called the *order* of the SSE. Note that, from Definition 1, the order of a SSE is at least 2.

c   Basic Axioms

A number of requirements are in order. First, we need some consistency axioms that describe the relationship between excess demands under certainty and uncertainty. We shall state a few regularity assumptions concerning the "certain" excess demand Z at the stationary state. In what follows, the partial mapping $\hat{Z}^k(\cdot, M)$, for given M, is denoted $\hat{Z}^k_M(\cdot)$.

(i) Quantity Consistency (A1)

Assume that $p_{t+1} = (p^1_{t+1}, \ldots, p^k_{t+1})$ is such that $p^i_{t+1} = p^j_{t+1}$ (with $i < j$). Define $p'_{t+1} \in \mathbb{R}^{k-1}$ by

$$p'_{t+1} = p^{-j}_{t+1} = \left(p^1_{t+1}, \ldots, p^i_{t+1}, \ldots, p^{j-1}_{t+1}, p^{j+1}_{t+1}, \ldots, p^k_{t+1}\right).$$

Then $\tilde{Z}^k$ depends only on the probability distribution of the p_{t+1}; that is, for any p_t and any $\pi \in S^{k-1}$,

$$\tilde{Z}^k(p_t, p_{t+1}, \pi) = \tilde{Z}^{k-1}(p_t, p'_{t+1}, \pi'),$$

with $\pi' \in S^{k-2}$ equal to $(\pi^1, \ldots, \pi^i + \pi^j, \ldots, \pi^{j-1}, \pi^{j+1}, \ldots, \pi^k)$.

In particular, if $p^j_{t+1} = p$ for all j, then whatever π,

$$\tilde{Z}^k(p_t, p_{t+1}, \pi) = Z(p_t, p).$$

(ii) Consistency of Derivatives (A2)

$\forall \pi$, $\forall \bar{p}_{t+1} = (\bar{p}, \ldots, \bar{p})$, we have

$$\frac{\partial \tilde{Z}^k}{\partial p_t}(p_t, \bar{p}_{t+1}, \bar{\pi}) = \frac{\partial Z^k}{\partial p_t}(p_t, \bar{p}),$$

and $\forall \ell$, we have

$$\frac{\partial \tilde{Z}^k}{\partial p^\ell_{t+1}}(p_t, \bar{p}_{t+1}, \bar{\pi}) = \bar{\pi}_\ell \cdot \frac{\partial Z}{\partial p_{t+1}}(p_t, \bar{p}).$$

(iii) Boundary Assumptions (A3)

(A3a) Consider the rectangle $R = [b_t, B_t] \times [b_{t+1}, B_{t+1}]$ in $\mathbb{R}^2_+$. For b_t, b_{t+1} small enough and B_t, B_{t+1} large enough, ZZ, considered as a vector field over R^2, points inward.

(A3b) For any given Markov matrix M, consider the rectangle $\tilde{R} = \Pi^k_{\ell=1} [b^\ell_{t+1}, B^\ell_{t+1}]$ in $\mathbb{R}^k_+$. For $b^1_{t+1}, \ldots, b^k_{t+1}$ small enough, and

$B_{t+1}^1, \ldots, B_{t+1}^k$ large enough, $\hat{Z}_M^k$, considered as a vector field over $\tilde{R}$, points inward.

These axioms generalize in a straightforward way those in Guesnerie (1986). We see that (A1) essentially says that $\tilde{Z}$ depends only on the probability distribution of future *prices* (and not of the sunspot per se). In particular, whenever the future price is known *with certainty* to be p_{t+1}, then $\tilde{Z}^k$ and Z coincide. Incidentally, an immediate consequence of (A1) is that $\tilde{Z}_M^k[\bar{p}] = 0$, where $\bar{p} = [\bar{p}, \ldots, \bar{p}]$ is a stationary state, for all M. When future price is certain, the derivatives of Z and $\tilde{Z}^k$ with respect to present price p_t must also coincide; this is the meaning of the first relation in (A2), which, incidentally, could simply be deduced from (A1). Also consider, at the margin of this certainty situation, an infinitesimal change dp_{t+1}^ℓ in p_{t+1}^ℓ. Because this introduces only an infinitesimal uncertainty, the change is equivalent to a *sure* change of magnitude $\bar{\pi}^\ell \cdot dp_{t+1}^\ell$ (i.e., the *expected value* of the initial change, hence the second relation in (A2)). Last, (A3a) is a standard boundary assumption, and (A3b) is its unsurprising extension to stochastic forecasts.[1]

It must be stressed that the consistency properties (A1) and (A2) are derived (as the reader can check) from utility maximization, in the context of an usual OG model with representative consumer; no specific assumption is needed upon utilities apart from strong quasiconcavity and sufficient differentiability. However, they hold true in more general frameworks. Note, for instance, that they are preserved by aggregation of individual demands; hence, they do *not* require, in fact, anything like a representative consumer.

We now state a regularity assumption.

(iv)   Generic Regularity of a Stationary Equilibrium (GR)
In a stationary equilibrium $\bar{p}$, we have

$$\frac{\partial Z}{\partial p_{t+1}}(\bar{p}, \bar{p}) \neq 0,$$

$$\frac{\partial Z}{\partial p_t}(\bar{p}, \bar{p}) + \frac{\partial Z}{\partial p_{t+1}}(\bar{p}, \bar{p}) \neq 0,$$

$$\frac{\partial Z}{\partial p_t}(\bar{p}, \bar{p}) - \frac{\partial Z}{\partial p_{t+1}}(\bar{p}, \bar{p}) \neq 0.$$

It is clear that if Z is extracted from a "rich" enough set, (GR) is generic (hence, the terminology), A more precise meaning of the genericity assumption can be given in more specific models (e.g., representative consumer and finite number of consumers); this task is left to the reader.

In what follows, we shall note Z_1 (respectively, Z_2) for $(\partial Z / \partial p_t)$ $(\bar{p}, \bar{p})$ [respectively, $(\partial Z / \partial p_{t+1})$ $(\bar{p}, \bar{p})$]. A first remark is that the boundary assumption (A3a), together with uniqueness of stationary equilibrium, determines the sign of $Z_1 + Z_2$.

RESULT 1   Assume (A3a). If the stationary equilibrium $\bar{p}$ is unique and regular (in the sense of GR), then

$Z_1 + Z_2 < 0.$

Proof   An elementary proof is the following. Consider the mapping

$z: \mathbb{R}_+ \to \mathbb{R},$

$p \to Z(p, p) \overset{def}{=} z(p).$

Then (A3a) implies $z(p) > 0$ if p is "small enough" and $z(p) < 0$ if p is "large enough." Also,

$$\frac{dz}{dp}(p) = \frac{\partial Z}{\partial p_t}(p, p) + \frac{\partial Z}{\partial p_{t+1}}(p, p).$$

Assume (dz/dp) $(\bar{p})$ = $Z_1 + Z_2 > 0$. Then the boundary properties imply that the equation $z(p) = 0$ has two solutions in addition to $\bar{p}$

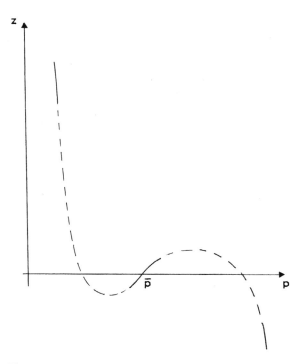

Figure 3.1

(one smaller that $\underline{p}$ and one greater than $\bar{p}$). So there must exist at least three stationary equilibria, which is a contradiction. ∎

The idea of the proof is summarized by Figure 3.1.

The conclusion given here is nothing but a particular case of a powerful result in differential topology, the Poincaré–Hopf theorem. Since the general version of the theorem will be used later, it may be useful to give a very simplified presentation of the basic argument. Let S be a manifold with boundaries of $\mathbb{R}^n$, and z a smooth vector field on S with regular, isolated zeros; assume that z points inward at all boundary points of S. If $\bar{p}$ is a zero of z, define the index $i(p)$ of z at $\bar{p}$ by

$i(p) = +1$ if $\Delta_p z(\bar{p}) > 0$,

$i(p) = -1$ if $\Delta_p z(\bar{p}) < 0$,

where $\Delta_p z(\bar{p})$ is the Jacobian determinant of z in $\bar{p}$.

The Poincaré-Hopf theorem then implies that the sum of the indices at the zeros of z is a topological invariant of S; in particular, if does not depend on the particular choice of vector field. Moreover, if S is diffeomorphic to a disk of dimension k, then this sum is equal to $(-1)^k$.

How does this result apply here? Take $S = (b, B)$, defined as in (A3a), so that the vector field z points inward at the boundary points. Because $k = 1$, the sum of the indices at the zeros of z must be (-1). But, in this one-dimensional case, the index at p is simply the sign of $(dz/dp)(p)$. If $(\partial z/\partial p)(\bar{p}) > 0$, then the index at $\bar{p}$ is $+1$; so there must be at least two other zeros, with index (-1) [and possibly an equal number of zeros with indices $(+1)$ and (-1)], which is a contradiction.

Of course, this argument can be generalized to any $k \geq 1$. Let $\bar{p}$ be a zero of z, such that the sign of the Jacobian determinant $\Delta_p z(\bar{p})$ is $(-1)^{k+1}$. Then there must be at least two other zeros with index $(-1)^k$. This argument will be used extensively in the next section.

3   Existence of SSE of Cardinal k

In this section we state sufficient conditions for a (given) Markov matrix of dimension k to be associated with an SSE. The conditions generalize those obtained by Azariadis and Guesnerie (1982a) for matrices of dimension 2 (associated with sunspots of order 2). More precisely, Azariadis and Guesnerie show, in the context of the simple OG model, that if

1 the wage elasticity of savings (under perfect foresight) at the stationary equilibrium $\in$ is lower than $-\frac{1}{2}$; and

2 the 2×2 matrix

$$M = \begin{pmatrix} m_{11} & m_{12} \\ m_{21} & m_{22} \end{pmatrix}$$

satisfies $m_{12} + m_{21} > -1/\epsilon$, then there exists an SSE associated with M.

Using the same techniques (which rely basically upon the Poincaré–Hopf theorem), we show that condition 1 and an equivalent version of condition 2 apply to $(k \times k)$ matrices for any $k \geq 2$.

a   Preparation Lemmas

The forthcoming results rely upon some technical preliminaries that are gathered here in four lemmas. In what follows, we denote by $\bar{p} = (\bar{p}, \ldots, \bar{p})$ the stationary state of the model and by $\Delta \hat{Z}_M^k(p)$ the Jacobian determinant of $\hat{Z}_M^k$ in $p = (p_1, \ldots, p_k)$.

LEMMA 1   Assume that there exists a unique stationary equilibrium and that the boundary assumptions (A3) are fulfilled. If a Markov matrix M' is such that

$$(-1)^k \Delta \hat{Z}_{M'}^k(\bar{p}) < 0, \tag{1}$$

then there exists an SSE (p, M') where $p \in \mathbb{R}^k$.

Proof   Lemma 1 says that the index of $\hat{Z}_M^k$ at $\bar{p}$ is $(-1)^{k+1}$. This implies from the Poincaré–Hopf theorem that the equation $\hat{Z}_{M'}^k(p) = 0$ has at least two solutions other than $\bar{p}$; these must be SSE associated with M'.   ∎

Thus the existence of SSE can be deduced from the sign of $\Delta \hat{Z}_M^k(\bar{p})$. The next step is to compute this determinant; this task can easily be performed using the consistency axioms (A1) and (A2) and the generic regularity condition (GR).

LEMMA 2   Assume that (A1), (A2), and (GR) are fulfilled. Then, for any Markovian matrix M,

$$\Delta \hat{Z}_M^k(\bar{p}) = (Z_2)^k \operatorname{Det}\left(M + \frac{Z_1}{Z_2} I\right), \tag{2}$$

where I is the $(k \times k)$ identity matrix.

Proof   The generic term $\hat{z}_{ij}$ of the Jacobian matrix of $\hat{Z}_M^k$ at $\bar{p}$ is

$$\hat{z}_{ij} = \frac{\partial \tilde{Z}^k}{\partial p_{t+1}^j}(\bar{p}, M_i) + \delta_i^j \frac{\partial \tilde{Z}^k}{\partial p_t}(\bar{p}, M_i),$$

where $\delta_i^j = 1$ if $i = j$, and 0 otherwise.

It follows from (A2) that

$$\Delta \hat{Z}_M^k(\bar{p}) = \begin{vmatrix} Z_1 + m_{11}Z_2 & \cdots & m_{1k}Z_2 \\ \vdots & & \vdots \\ m_{k1}Z_2 & \cdots & Z_1 + m_{kk}Z_2 \end{vmatrix}.$$

Since, from (GR), $Z_2 \neq 0$, this relation can be written as

$$\Delta \hat{Z}_M^k(\bar{p}) = (Z_2)^k \operatorname{Det}\left(M + \frac{Z_1}{Z_2} I\right). \qquad \blacksquare$$

A first consequence is that relation (1) cannot hold unless $|Z_1/Z_2| \leq 1$ [note that (GR) then implies a strict inequality]; also, the set of Markov matrices satisfying (1) for a given value of Z_1/Z_2 can be characterized in the following way:

LEMMA 3   Assume the uniqueness of stationary equilibrium, boundary condition (A3), and genericity condition (GR).

(i) If $|Z_1/Z_2| > 1$, then, for any Markov matrix M,

$$(-1)^k (Z_2)^k \operatorname{Det}\left(M + \frac{Z_1}{Z_2} I\right) > 0. \tag{3}$$

(ii) Suppose that $|Z_1/Z_2| < 1$. Let M be a Markov matrix; assume that (Z_1/Z_2) is not an eigenvalue of M. Then the relation

$$(-1)^k (Z_2)^k \mathrm{Det}\left(M + \frac{Z_1}{Z_2} I \right) < 0 \tag{4}$$

holds if and only if the number of real eigenvalues of M, inferior to $-Z_1/Z_2$, is odd.

Proof From Result 1 of Section 2, the assumptions imply that $Z_1 + Z_2 < 0$. Now, a first remark is that relation (3) must hold for $M = I$. Otherwise, from Lemma 1, there would exist an SSE associated with I; but, clearly, this would contradict uniqueness of stationary equilibrium. Assume, now, that $|Z_1/Z_2| > 1$. Suppose that there exists a matrix that does not satisfy (3). Then, from the previous remark, the mapping

$$M \to \mathrm{Det}\left(M + \frac{Z_1}{Z_2} I \right)$$

must change its sign over the (connected) set of Markov matrices; hence, there exists a Markov matrix $\overline{M}$ such that Det $[\overline{M} + (Z_1/Z_2)I] = 0$. This implies that $\overline{M}$ has an eigenvalue equal to (Z_1/Z_2), which is a contradiction because all eigenvalues of a Markov matrix are within the unit circle. To the contrary, suppose that $|Z_1/Z_2| < 1$. Clearly, Det $[M + (Z_1/Z_2)I]$ is a polynomial $P(x)$ of degree k in $x = -Z_1/Z_2$; the real roots of this polynomial are nothing but the real eigenvalues of M. Now, the sign of $P(x)$ depends only on the position of x with respect to the real roots of P and, more precisely, on the *parity* of the number of real roots of P below x. In particular, for any given k, the sign of the left-hand side (l.h.s.) of (4) depends only on whether the number of real eigenvalues of M, below $-Z_1/Z_2$, is even or odd.

Last, let us prove that this number must be odd. Indeed, suppose the contrary. Because the only (multiple) eigenvalue of I is 1, this implies that the number of eigenvalues of I below $-Z_1/Z_2$ is zero (i.e., an even number). So (4) holds for I, which is a contradiction to the preceding remarks.

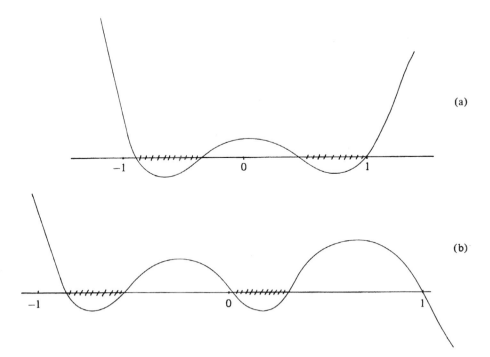

(a)

(b)

Figure 3.2

Of course, the fact that the number of eigenvalues below $-Z_1/Z_2$ must be odd can also be checked directly. Assume, first, that k is even. Then $(Z_2)^k$ is positive, so Poincaré–Hopf (PH) applies if Det $[M + (Z_1/Z_2)I] < 0$. But the characteristic polynomial of M is of even degree, which implies that the number of roots under $-Z_1/Z_2$ must be odd (Figure 3.2a).

Assume, now, that k is odd. If Z_2 is negative, then also $(Z_2)^k$, and PH again requires Det $[M + (Z_1/Z_2)I] < 0$. The characteristic polynomial of M is of odd degree. It is negative for "high" values of $-Z_1/Z_2$, specifically for $-Z_1/Z_2 > 1$; but this is excluded by Result 1. So we need the number of eigenvalues of M below $-Z_1/Z_2$ to be odd (Figure 3.2b). Last, the case with k odd *and* Z_2 positive is ruled out because Result 1 implies $-Z_1/Z_2 > 1$ for that case.   ∎

Incidentally, a by-product of this proof is that the PH characterization does not apply unless $Z_2 < 0$; indeed, $Z_2 > 0$ and $Z_1 + Z_2 < 0$ implies that $|Z_1/Z_2| > 1$. In words, excess demand is "backward-bending" at $\bar{p}$ in the sense that an increase in future price decreases today's excess demand.

A last question is whether the set of Markov matrices satisfying (4), when $|Z_1/Z_2| < 1$, is nonempty. The answer is positive.

LEMMA 4   If $|Z_1/Z_2| < 1$, then there exist $(k \times k)$ Markov matrices M, such that $\Delta\hat{Z}_M(\bar{p}) < 0$.

Proof   From Lemma 3, it is sufficient to show that, given any real number $x(= -Z_1/Z_2)$ in $(-1, 1)$, there exists a Markov matrix M such that the number of eigenvalues of M below x is odd. Now, take any $-1 < \lambda_1 < x$, and any $\lambda_2, \ldots, \lambda_{k-1}$ such that $1 \geq \lambda_i > \text{Max}(x, 0)$, $i = 2, \ldots, k - 1$. The Markov matrix

$$M = \begin{pmatrix} (\lambda_1+1)/2 & (1-\lambda_1)/2 & 0 & \cdots & 0 \\ (1-\lambda_1)/2 & (1+\lambda_1)/2 & 0 & \cdots & 0 \\ 1-\lambda_2 & 0 & \lambda_2 & \cdots & 0 \\ \vdots & & & \cdots & \\ 1-\lambda_{k-1} & 0 & 0 & \cdots & \lambda_{k-1} \end{pmatrix}$$

has exactly one eigenvalue below x (namely, λ_1).   ∎

b   The Result

The economic substance of the preceding results can be summarized as follows:

PROPOSITION 1   Assume that there exists a unique stationary equilibrium, and that conditions (A1), (A2), (A3) and (GR) are fulfilled. If

$$\left|\frac{Z_1}{Z_2}\right| < 1, \tag{5}$$

then for any Markov matrix M having an odd number of eigenvalues below $-Z_1/Z_2$, there exists a price vector p such that (p, M) is an SSE. In particular, since the set of such matrices is nonempty, (5) is a sufficient condition for the existence of SSE.

Two remarks may help in understanding this result.

Remark 1   Suppose $k = 2$; then

$$M = \begin{pmatrix} m_{11} & m_{12} \\ m_{21} & m_{22} \end{pmatrix}$$

has two eigenvalues, namely, 1 and $\lambda = m_{11} + m_{22} - 1 = 1 - m_{21} - m_{12}$. Thus an SSE is associated with M if

$$m_{12} + m_{21} > 1 + \frac{Z_1}{Z_2}, \tag{6}$$

that is, loosely speaking, if the process changes its state with a "high enough" probability (a result in the spirit of Azariadis and Guesnerie). In fact, we shall see that in the usual one-dimensional OG model, (6) is identical to the Azariadis–Guesnerie's relation.

Remark 2   It can easily be checked that Proposition 1 applies to matrices of cycles of even order. Indeed, the eigenvalues of a $(\ell \times \ell)$ cycle matrix are the ℓ roots of unity. In particular, if ℓ is even, then the matrix has exactly two real eigenvalues, 1 and -1, so the sufficient conditions of Proposition 1 are fulfilled. Note, however, that the SSE associated with a $(\ell \times \ell)$ cycle matrix is not necessarily a cycle of order ℓ; it may be degenerate, in the sense that the corresponding price vector p has identical components. This aspect will be investigated in Section 4.[2]

c   Application: the One-Dimensional OG Model

Let us apply this result to the usual, one-dimensional OG model. Here "young" people only work (and save their wage through money holdings with a zero interest rate), and "old" people consume only their wealth. We can assume that the total quantity of money is 1, so total demand at period t is 1 in nominal terms and $1/p_t$ in real terms. Also, under perfect foresight, the young peoples' supply (or savings) is a function s of real wage p_t/p_{t+1} (i.e., the nominal wage today p_t deflated by the price of the consumption goods tomorrow p_{t+1}). So the excess demand under certainty is

$$Z(p_t, p_{t+1}) = \frac{1}{p_t} - s\left(\frac{p_t}{p_{t+1}}\right).$$

The reader can easily check that, under standard assumption on preferences, assumptions (A1) – (A3) are fulfilled. Hence,

$$\frac{\partial Z}{\partial p_t} = -\frac{1}{p_t^2} - \frac{1}{p_{t+1}} s'\left(\frac{p_t}{p_{t+1}}\right),$$

$$\frac{\partial Z}{\partial p_{t+1}} = \frac{p_t}{p_{t+1}^2} s'\left(\frac{p_t}{p_{t+1}}\right).$$

As the stationary equilibrium is characterized by

$$Z(\bar{p}, \bar{p}) = \frac{1}{\bar{p}} - s(1) = 0,$$

then

$$\bar{p} = \frac{1}{s(1)}$$

and

$$Z_1 = -s(1)^2 - s(1)s'(1),$$

$$Z_2 = s'(1)s(1).$$

Thus,

$$-\frac{Z_1}{Z_2} = \frac{s(1)}{s'(1)} + 1 = 1 + \frac{1}{\in(1)},$$

where $\in (1)$ is the wage elasticity of savings (or of labor supply).

The condition $|Z_1/Z_2| < 1$ gives $\in (1) \le -\frac{1}{2}$. This is merely the usual condition of local indeterminacy of the stationary equilibrium. Note that, in particular, $s'(1)$ must be negative: the labor supply curve is backward bending. A consequence is that Z_2 must be negative.

Last, assume $k = 2$ (Azariadis–Guesnerie case). Then condition (6) gives

$$m_{12} + m_{21} > 1 + \frac{Z_1}{Z_2} = -\frac{1}{\in (1)},$$

which (as predicted) is exactly the Azariadis–Guesnerie result.

4   The Local Structure of the Set of SEE: A Differential Viewpoint

The previous results exhibit sufficient conditions for the existence of SSE of cardinal k. However, nothing has been said so far on the order of those SSE. Clearly, the SSE might be degenerate in the sense that the associated price vector has (at least) two identical components; in this case, its order is less than k.

In this section, we investigate the structure of the set of degenerate SSE. We show that under some regularity assumptions "almost all" SSE are nondegenerate; specifically, the set of SSE of order k is shown to be, locally, an open, dense subset of the set of SSE of cardinal k. In other words, an SSE (p, M) can of course be degenerate, but in that case there exist nondegenerate SSE arbitrarily close to (p, M).

The tools used in this section are borrowed from differential topology. This approach is very natural because an SSE is defined as a zero (with nonidentical components) of the smooth mapping $\hat{Z}^k$. That is, the set of SSE of cardinal k is included in the set

$$E^k = \{(p, M) \in \mathbb{R}_+^k \times \mathfrak{M}_k / \hat{Z}^k(p, M) = 0\};$$

and for any (p, M) in E^k, either (p, M) is an SSE or $p_1 = \ldots = p_k = \bar{p}$ from the assumptions made above.

However, our approach is local rather than global. The reason is that E^k is *not*, in general, a manifold (globally). To see this, suppose that the conditions of Proposition 1 are fulfilled. Then there exists a matrix $\bar{M}$ such that

$$\Delta \hat{Z}^k_{\bar{M}}(\bar{p}) = 0.$$

A direct consequence of consistency axioms (A1) is that, at $\bar{p}$, $\hat{Z}^k$ does *not* depend on M:

$$\forall M, \forall i, \tilde{Z}^k(\bar{p}, M^i) = Z(\bar{p}, \bar{p}) = 0.$$

This implies that $(\bar{p}, \bar{M})$ is a singular point and consequently that 0 is a singular value of $\hat{Z}^k$. In fact, it will be shown in the next section that $(\bar{p}, \bar{M})$ is a *bifurcation* of the system: Local SSE appear in any neighborhood of $(\bar{p}, \bar{M})$. So the structure of E^k, in a neighborhood of $(\bar{p}, \bar{M})$, is not diffeomorphic to $\mathbb{R}^n$ for some n. We shall argue, however, that, generically over the excess demand $\tilde{Z}^k$, the *local* structure of E^k around any (p, M) is that of a smooth manifold, at least if $p_i \neq \bar{p}$ for all i; in particular, the usual tools can be applied locally.

a Preparation Lemmas

We first introduce the notion of a *regular* sunspot.

DEFINITION A point (p, M) in E^k is regular if it is a regular point of the mapping $\hat{Z}^k$.

Here, *regular* is intended in the usual sense: The derivative $D\hat{Z}^k$ at (p, M) must be onto $\mathbb{R}^k$. Technically, (p, M) is regular if one can extract, from the $(k \times k^2)$ matrix $D\hat{Z}^k$, a nonzero determinant of order k.[3]

If $(p, M) \in E^k$ is regular, then the structure of E^k around (p, M) is very simple:

LEMMA 5   Assume $(p, M) \in E^k$ is regular and that M is within the interior $\overset{\circ}{\mathfrak{M}}_k$ of $\mathfrak{M}_k$. For any "small enough" open neighborhood U of (p, M), $E^k \cap U$ is a smooth manifold of dimension $k^2 - k$.

Proof Since $\hat{Z}^k$ is smooth, for U small enough, any point in U is regular. In particular, 0 is a regular value for the restriction of $\hat{Z}^k$ to U. Then, from the inverse image theorem (see Milnor, 1965), $E^k \cap U$ is a smooth manifold of U. Last, $\hat{Z}^k$ maps $U \subset \mathbb{R}_+^k \times \mathfrak{M}_k$ in $\mathbb{R}^k$, and $\mathfrak{M}_k$ is a manifold (with boundaries) of dimension $k^2 - k$; so the dimension of U is $k + (k^2 - k) - k = k^2 - k$.   ∎

We now consider the case of degenerate SSE. Define

$$E_{ij}^k = \{(p, M) \in E^k \text{ s.t. } p_i = p_j\}.$$

An SSE in E_{ij}^k is degenerate in the sense that the price in state i is the same as in state j. Thus, though there are k possible *states* for the sunspot, there are only (at most) $(k - 1)$ possible *prices*. Because excess demand depends only on *prices*, this suggests that an SSE in E_{ij}^k should be "similar" (in a sense to be defined) to some SSE of cardinal $(k - 1)$, with well-chosen transition probabilities.

This intuition can be developed in a (slightly) more technical way. To simplify notation, we assume that $i = 1, j = k$. Let (p, M) be an SSE in E_{1k}^k. By definition, it satisfies

$$\tilde{Z}^k(p_1; p, M_1) = 0,$$

$$\tilde{Z}^k(p_i; p, M_i) = 0, \quad i = 2, \ldots, k-1,$$

$$\tilde{Z}^k(p_k; p, M_k) = \tilde{Z}^k(p_1; p, M_k) = 0.$$

Now, the idea is to construct an SSE of cardinal $(k - 1)$—say (q, N)—by "melting" states 1 and k of the initial SSE (p, M), thus reducing the number of states. Obviously, $q = (p_1, \ldots, p_{k-1})$. Also, to define the ith row of matrix N, for $2 \leq i \leq k - 1$, we proceed as follows:

i The transition probabilities between i and j ($2 \leq j \leq k - 1$) are unchanged:

$n_{ij} = m_{ij}, \quad 2 \leq i \leq k - 1, 2 \leq j \leq k - 1.$

ii Any transition between state i and either state 1 or state k (in the SSE of cardinal k) is equivalent to a transition between i and 1 (in the SSE of cardinal $k - 1$); hence,

$n_{i1} = m_{i1} + m_{ik}, \quad 2 \leq i \leq k - 1.$

It can easily be checked that, from the consistency axiom (A1),

$\tilde{Z}^{k-1}(q^i; q, N_i) = \tilde{Z}^k(p^i; p, M_i) = 0 \quad \text{for } 2 \leq i \leq k - 1.$

However, there are two possible ways to define the first line of N. Take, for instance,

$n_{11} = m_{11} + m_{1k} \quad \text{and} \quad n_{1i} = m_{1i}, \quad 2 \leq i \leq k - 1.$

Then,

$\tilde{Z}^{k-1}(q_1; q, N_1) = \tilde{Z}^k(p_1; p, M_1) = 0.$

But, $n'_{11} = m_{k1} + m_{kk}$ and $n'_{1i} = m_{ki}$ ($2 \leq i \leq k - 1$) also gives

$\tilde{Z}^{k-1}(q_1; q, N'_1) = \tilde{Z}^k(p_1; p, M_k) = \tilde{Z}^k(p_k; p, M_k) = 0.$

In summary, from matrix M we can, by adding the kth column to the first, construct exactly k vectors of S^{k-2}—say $N_1, \ldots, N_k$—such that $\tilde{Z}^{k-1}(q_i; q, N_i) = 0$ ($2 \leq i \leq k - 1$) and

$\tilde{Z}^{k-1}(q_1; q, N_1) = \tilde{Z}^{k-1}(q_1; q, N_k) = 0.$

In particular, if

$$N = \begin{pmatrix} N_1 \\ N_2 \\ \vdots \\ N_{k-1} \end{pmatrix} \quad \text{and} \quad N' = \begin{pmatrix} N_k \\ N_2 \\ \vdots \\ N_{k-1} \end{pmatrix},$$

both N and N' are $(k-1) \times (k-1)$ Markov matrices, and both (q, N) and (q, N') are SSE of cardinal $(k-1)$.

At this point, it is natural to extend the notion of regularity to degenerate SSE. The argument just developed suggests the following definition.

DEFINITION   An SSE (p, M) in $E_{1,k}^k$ is regularly degenerate if the vector $(q, N_1, \ldots, N_k)$ is a regular point of the mapping $\Psi_{1,k}^k$ defined by

$$\Psi_{1,k}^k : \mathbb{R}_+^{k-1} \times (S^{k-2})^k \to \mathbb{R}^k,$$
$$(q, N_1, \ldots, N_k) \to [\tilde{Z}^{k-1}(q_1; q, N_1), \ldots,$$
$$\tilde{Z}^{k-1}(q_{k-1}; q, N_{k-1}), \tilde{Z}^{k-1}(q_1; q, N_k)].$$

The extension of this definition to any E_{ij}^k is immediate.

The following consequence obtains:

LEMMA 6   Let $(p, M) \in E_{ij}^k$ be regularly degenerate. Then,

(i) (p, M) is regular (in the sense of regularity for points in E^k);

(ii) (q, N) and (q, N') (defined as before) are regular in E^{k-1}.

Proof   The proof of (i) is immediate because from the consistency axioms, the Jacobian matrix $D\Psi_{1,k}^k$ at $(q, N_1, \ldots, N_k)$ is a submatrix of $D\hat{Z}^k$ at (p, M). In particular, if the former is of full rank, so is the latter. For (ii), note that the Jacobian matrix $D\hat{Z}^{k-1}$ in (q, N) is identical to $D\Psi_{1,k}^k$ without its last row. If the latter is onto a neighborhood of zero in $\mathbb{R}^k$, the former is onto a neighborhood of zero in $\mathbb{R}^{k-1}$. The same argument applies to (q, N').   ∎

It can be noted, incidentally, that the properties (i) and (ii) of Lemma 6 are necessary but not sufficient. In other words, the property of regular degeneracy is stronger than regularity of (p, M) (for the mapping defining SSE of cardinal k) and of both (q, N) and (q, N') (for the mapping defining SSE of cardinal $k - 1$).[4] However, as we shall argue later, it is not "much" stronger.

As previously, the regular degeneracy property gives information on the local structure of E_{ij}^k. Specifically, we can show the following:

LEMMA 7 Let $(\mathring{p}, \mathring{M}) \in E_{ij}^k$ be regularly degenerate, where $\mathring{M}$ is interior to $\mathfrak{M}_k$. Then there exists an open neighborhood U' of $(\mathring{p}, \mathring{M})$, such that the set $\bar{E}^k$ of nondegenerate SSE in $E^k \cap U'$ is an open, dense subset of $E^k \cap U'$.

In other words, if $(\mathring{p}, \mathring{M})$ is regularly degenerate, then in any "small" neighborhood of $(\mathring{p}, \mathring{M})$ there exists a nondegenerate SSE; in fact, almost all SSE near $(\mathring{p}, \mathring{M})$ are nondegenerate.

Proof Because $(\mathring{p}, \mathring{M})$ is regular, $E^k \cap U'$ is a smooth manifold of dimension $k^2 - k$; and the set of nondegenerate SSE is obviously open in this manifold.

Now, consider the mapping φ:

$$\mathbb{R}_+^{k-1} \times \mathfrak{M}_k \to \mathbb{R}^k,$$

$$(q, M) \to [\tilde{Z}^{k-1}(q_1; q, N_1), \ldots, \tilde{Z}^{k-1}(q_{k-1}; q, N_{k-1}), \tilde{Z}^{k-1}(q_1; q, N_k)],$$

where N is constructed from M as explained before. Pose $\mathring{q} = (\mathring{p}_1, \ldots, \mathring{p}_{k-1})$ and $(\mathring{p}, \mathring{M})$ is a regular point of φ. Because $\tilde{Z}^{k-1}$ is smooth, there exists a neighborhood V of $(\mathring{q}, \mathring{M})$ in which all points are regular; in particular, 0 is a regular value of the restriction of φ to V. A consequence is that $\varphi^{-1}(0)$ is a smooth manifold of dimension $k^2 - k - 1$; moreover, $\varphi^{-1}(0)$ is locally diffeomorphic to $E_{1,k}^k$ [consider the mapping $(q, M) \to (q, q_1, M)$]. Because $E_{1,k}^k$ is locally diffeomorphic to $\mathbb{R}^{k^2-k}$, thus, for a small enough U', the complement $\bar{E}_{1,k}^k$ of $E_{1,k}^k$ in $E^k \cap U'$ is dense in $E^k \cap U'$.

The same argument applies to $\bar{E}_{i,j}^k$ for all i, j. Finally,

$$\bar{E}^k \cap U' = \bigcap_{i,j \leq k} \bar{E}_{i,j}^k$$

is dense, as a finite intersection of dense subsets.   ■

b   The Main Result

We can now prove the main result.

DEFINITION   An SSE (p, M) in E^k is strongly regular

(i) if it is regular,

(ii) if it is degenerate (then it is regularly degenerate).

PROPOSITION 2   Let (p, M) be a strongly regular SSE with M interior to $\mathfrak{M}_k$. There exists an open neighborhood U of (p, M) in $\mathbb{R}_+^k \times \mathfrak{M}_k$ such that

(i) $E^k \cap U$ is a smooth manifold of dimension $k^2 - k$; and

(ii) the set of nondegenerate SSE in U is a dense, open subset of $E^k \cap U$.

Proof   The proof of (i) is a direct consequence of Lemmas 5 and 6. Moreover, if (p, M) is degenerate, then (ii) is implied by Lemma 7. If (p, M) is nondegenerate, note that the set of nondegenerate SSE is open; thus, for U small enough, every SSE in U is nondegenerate.   ■

In other words, assuming strong regularity, one can characterize the local structure of the set of SSE of cardinal k. Under this hypothesis, E^k is locally diffeomorphic to $\mathbb{R}^{k^2-k}$; in particular, SSE of cardinal k exist in any neighborhood of (p, M). Moreover, almost all of these SSE are of order k.

Finally, Lemmas 5–7, as well as Proposition 3, consider only matrices that are interior to $\mathfrak{M}_k$. However, the same arguments apply to the boundary of $\mathfrak{M}_k$, the only difference being that the manifolds mentioned would become, in that case, manifolds with boundaries. The transposition is left to the interested reader.

It must be clear, from previous remarks that not all points in E^k are strongly regular; for instance, $(\bar{p}, M)$ is not regularly degenerate, whatever M. This suggests defining the following set:

$$\sum{}^k = \{(p, M) \in E^k \text{ s.t.} \forall i, p_i \neq \bar{p}\}.$$

Now, a natural question is the following: Are the SSE in Σ^k strongly regular? We conjecture that the answer is positive, at least, generically. Naturally, giving a precise meaning (and proof) to this conjecture would require additional work. Particularly, it is likely to require a systematic use of transversality theory, a mathematical investment that may look excessive in our context. An informal support to the conjecture can, however, be obtained as follows. Consider the equations $\hat{Z}^k(\bar{p}, M) = 0$ or $\hat{Z}^{k-1}(q, N) = \hat{Z}^{k-1}(q, N') = 0$, and replace them by $\hat{Z}^k(p, M) = \epsilon$, $\hat{Z}^{k-1}(q, N) = \epsilon'$, $\hat{Z}^{k-1}(q, N') = \epsilon''$, with $\epsilon \in \mathbb{R}^k$ and $\epsilon', \epsilon'' \in \mathbb{R}^{k-1}$. From Sard's theorem, for almost all $(\epsilon, \epsilon', \epsilon'')$, *all* solutions to these equations are regular. This suggests that even if the conjecture is not true for some given $\tilde{Z}$, it should become true after any slight change in $\tilde{Z}$.

Moreover, the conjecture, even if only the weakest form we can think of is true, has several interesting consequences. We shall briefly mention three of them.

1. Consider an economy with SSE of order $k - 1$. From any such SSE (q, N) with $q \neq \bar{p}$ for all i, it is easy to construct an SSE of cardinal k [take $p_i = q_i$ for $i \leq k - 1$, $p_k = p_1$; define M_i ($i \leq k - 1$) by $m_{i1} = m_{ik} = n_{i1}/2$, and $m_{ij} = n_{ij}$ otherwise; then pose $M_k = M_1$]. When this SSE is regularly degenerate, Proposition 2 then implies that SSE of order k exist in any neighborhood. By induction, this suggests that, generically over $\tilde{Z}$, if an economy admits an SSE (q, N) of order 2, with $q_1, q_2 \neq \bar{p}$, then it admits SSE of any order. In particular, from Proposition 2, consider an economy such that $|Z_1/Z_2| < 1$; generically, this economy exhibits sunspots of any order.

2. Let M be a Markov matrix in $\overset{\circ}{\mathfrak{M}}_k$ such that (p, M) is in Σ^k for some $p \in \mathbb{R}^k_+$. Consider the canonical projection from E^k to $\mathfrak{M}_k$:

$(p, M) \to M$.

From Sard's theorem, the set of singular values of this (trivially smooth) mapping is null. Hence, for almost all SSE matrices M, the projection is locally *onto*. Since (p, M) is regular, both E^k and $\mathfrak{M}_k$ have, locally, the structure of $k^2 - k$ manifolds; so the projection is, locally, a diffeomorphism. Hence, for almost all M, all matrices in a (small enough) neighborhood of M are sunspot matrices; and almost all of them are associated with SSE of order k.

3. Assume that (p, M) is an SSE, where M is a $(k \times k)$ cycle matrix. As mentioned before (p, M) is not necessarily a cycle of order k because the price vector p may be degenerate. However, we know from the remarks above that in any small neighborhood of (p, M), there exist SSE of order k. The fact that SSE of order k can be found arbitrarily close to (p, M) can be expressed in probabilistic terms: For all T and $\epsilon > 0$, there exists an SSE of order k such that the probability of observing, during T period, a deviation from a purely cyclical behavior, is less than ϵ. In particular, *if the stationary state is indeterminate, then for any even integer k, our conjecture implies the existence of SSE of order k arbitrarily close (in the sense just defined) of cycles of order k.*

5 "Local" Sunspots: the Bifurcation Viewpoint

Existence theorems of Section 3 rest upon local as well as global restrictions of the excess-demand function under consideration. The nature of the local restrictions suggests that they are valid in a broad class of economic problems covered by our model. The global properties—that is, the boundary assumptions and the uniqueness of the stationary state—are likely to be more restrictive. For example, the reader is invited to check that, in the simple OG model, the introduction of government expenditures à la Sargent (1984) at the same time creates a second stationary state and invalidates our boundary conditions (at least as a condition bearing on the whole domain of prices).

Our global results do rest upon the global assumptions we have just recalled. However, these global results have local counterparts that are bifurcations results. This fact is not surprising if one remembers that the local considerations of bifurcation theory and the global viewpoint of the Poincaré–Hopf theorem refer to a similar core of mathematical arguments.

We do not intend to provide a full development of the bifurcations point of view here. We want only to provide some insights on the local counterparts of our global results, restricting ourselves to formal support only from existing results (i.e., Guesnerie, 1986).

Let us note first that we are considering bifurcations in the space of Markov matrices and *not* in the space of economies—that is, again with the point of view of Azariadis and Guesnerie (1986) rather than the point of view of Grandmont (1989).

Consider then a one-dimensional family of ($k \times k$) Markov matrices indexed by a parameter α, and compute

$$\text{Det}\left[M(\alpha) + \frac{Z_1}{Z_2} I \right] = \Psi(\alpha).$$

The bifurcations are bifurcations from the stationary state (with price $\bar{p}$, $\bar{p}$, ...) toward stationary SSE that are local sunspots in the sense of definition 2. Such bifurcations are associated with the fact that the Jacobian of the mapping $p \to p - \hat{Z}(p, M(\alpha))$ in $\bar{p}$ has an eigenvalue equal to +1 (the other ones being outside the unit circle). But the fact that $I - D\hat{Z}$ has an eigenvalue of 1 is itself equivalent to the fact that $D\hat{Z}$ is singular, that is (from Lemma 2), to the fact that $\Psi(\alpha) = 0$. The bifurcations we are looking for will thus occur at a point $\bar{\alpha}$, around which $\Psi(\alpha)$ changes its sign.

The following result provides an example of a bifurcations statement toward SSE of order 2.

PROPOSITION 3   Consider a stationary state, and let Z_1, Z_2 be the derivatives of the deterministic excess-demand function, as previously defined, at this stationary state.

Now consider a one-dimensional family of (2×2) Markov matrices $M(\alpha)$ and a number $\overline{\alpha}$ such that

(i) $m_{12}(\overline{\alpha}) + m_{21}(\overline{\alpha}) = 1 + \dfrac{Z_1}{Z_2}$;

(ii) $\dfrac{\partial(m_{12} + m_{21})(\alpha)}{\partial \alpha}\bigg|_{\alpha=\overline{\alpha}} > 0.$

Then, for any neighborhood N of $(\overline{p}, \overline{p})$ in $\mathbb{R}^{2n}$, there exists a $\alpha \neq \overline{\alpha}$ such that N contains a vector $p(\alpha)$ such that $[p(\alpha), M(\alpha)]$ is an SSE.

Proof   This statement is a special case of theorem 4 in Guesnerie (1986). To see that, it is enough to check that all the conditions of the theorem are fulfilled, note that the matrix B of the general theorem reduces to the one-dimensional matrix $-Z_2/Z_1$ whose unique eigenvalue is $-Z_2/Z_1$.   ∎

The reader should notice that the preceding statement applies to any stationary equilibrium when the system has several of them. For example, in the simple OG model, it signals bifurcations matrices at the Samuelsonian stationary point with backward-bending labor supply when the bifurcation is the one studied in Azariadis and Guesnerie (1986). But in the OG model with government expenditures, the statement signals local sunspots in the neighborhood of the high inflation stationary state, even when labor supply is not backward-bending; a fact well in line with the more global analysis of this situation found in Grandmont (1986) as well as with the previous example of Farmer and Woodford (1983). The bifurcations toward SSE of order k could be pursued along the lines suggested;

it is clear, for instance, that local SSE (of any order) cannot exist around the stationary state unless $|Z_1/Z_2| \leq 1$. Here we shall note only that the bifurcations result of Proposition 3, together with the results of Section 4, imply, at least generically, the existence of local sunspots of any order in the neighborhood of any stationary state such that $|Z_1/Z_2| < +1$. Again this fact is compatible with the (more precise) insights obtained from a different perspective by Grandmont (1986b) in the (more specific) context of the OG model with one representative consumer.

6 Conclusion

We have been concerned with stationary sunspot equilibria in one-dimensional, one-step forward-looking economic systems. The first examples of such SSE have been provided by Azariadis (1981) and Farmer and Woodford (1983). Elements of theory of such a phenomenon, initially brought forth by Azariadis and Guesnerie (1982a, b, 1986) and Spear (1984) have been completed by further works of Grandmont (1986), Peck (1988), and Woodford (1986). This chapter, building on the initial contributions, adds another stone.

The issue of existence of SSE in one-dimensional, one-step forward-looking dynamic systems should not be considered as settled. It is outside the scope of this chapter to write a list of unresolved questions (some arise directly from out earlier comments). We should like, however, to point out that when sunspot beliefs are based on time-independent processes that are somewhat less well-behaved than the one we considered here (such as the processes of money supply in Lucas-type models, which are Markovian but do not admit an invariant distribution), the study of (time-independent) sunspot equilibria raises mathematical issues that are extremely different from those coming into the picture here (see Chiappori and Guesnerie, 1991a, 1993). If one considers that such exogenous processes are economically important, then the present study, together with its predecessors, does not exhaust our understanding of sunspot equilibria of economic relevance, even in the simplest (one-dimensional, one-step forward-looking) framework.

Notes

1. That assumption holds, for example, in the simple OG model without government expenditures. For a more comprehensive discussion of the boundary assumption as well as of the others, the reader can refer to Guesnerie (1986).

2 In fact, in many situations it is necessarily the case that our sufficient conditions signal only *degenerate* cycles because no cycle of order k exists (cf. the general theory of cycles in one-dimensional systems).

3. As an illustration, consider for any Markov matrix M the point $(\bar{p}, M)$; then $(\bar{p}, M)$ is in E^k, and $D_M \hat{Z}^k(\bar{p}, M) = 0$. This $(\bar{p}, M)$ is regular if and only if $D_p \hat{Z}^k(\bar{p}, M)$ is of full rank; that is, if and only if $\Delta \hat{Z}_M^k(\bar{p}) \neq 0$.

4. As an example, assume that (p, M) is such that

$D_p \hat{Z}^k(p, M)$ is of rank k,

$D_q \hat{Z}^{k-1}(q, N)$ and $D_q \hat{Z}^{k-1}(q, N')$ are of rank $(k-1)$,

$D_M \hat{Z}^k(p, M)$ is of rank zero (i.e., locally, $\hat{Z}^k$ does *not* depend on transition probabilities).

Then (i) and (ii) are fulfilled; however, $D\Psi_{1,k}^k$ has only $(k-1)$ nonzero columns (i.e., $D_q \Psi_{1,k}^k$ is of rank $(k-1)$ and $D_{N^1}, \ldots, {}_{N^k} \Psi_{1,k}^k$ is of rank zero), so it cannot be locally *onto*. For instance, the reader can check that, for any matrix M, $(\bar{p}, M) \in E^k$ is degenerate but not regularly degenerate though (i) and (ii) may perfectly be fulfilled.

II

Fluctuations between Two Steady States in Lucas-like Models

4

The Lucas Equation, Indeterminacy, and Non-Neutrality: An Example

Pierre-André Chiappori and Roger Guesnerie

Lucas' model (1972) has received widespread and deserved attention from the economic profession. His influential message rests upon the analysis of a stylized model. Stationary equilibria of this model ("rational expectations equilibria," in Lucas' terminology) are identified with functions which are solutions of a functional equation. The study of this functional equation, which is at the heart of Lucas' analysis, is the subject of the present article.

Our study has three main purposes:

First, we consider the only model (to the best of our knowledge) in which an explicit analytical solution of the Lucas model has been exhibited, namely the model used in the pedagogical presentation of Azariadis (1981a). In this simplified framework, as well as in a more general setting, the basic functional equation has a unique solution within the class of functions which are linear in one of the observable variables, the past-period money supply. Removing the restriction to this class of linear (in money) solutions, we exhibit other solutions, still under analytical form. The first objective of this study is thus to attempt a more comprehensive study of the Lucas equation in a specific case accessible to computation.

A second objective, of independent interest, is to propose a method for the resolution of functional equations arising from the theory of rational expectations, which is (again to the best of our knowledge) original in the economic literature. This method is conceptually natural—the solution is expressed under the form of a power series—but analytically difficult.

Third, our example provides another illustration of the possible indeterminacy of rational-expectations equilibria—an illustration which has, as we shall argue, original features. To this point let us mention that we exhibit a one-dimensional family of solutions in which the Lucas solution is a limit case of a zero value for the indexing parameter. We can also already note that all solutions but the Lucas solution are nonlinear in past money and invalidate the special version of money neutrality imbedded in the Lucas solution.

Naturally, we hope that the text reflects the influence of Frank Hahn's demanding requirements and intellectual flair on our own production. At least, the content of the text is not, we believe, foreign to Hahn's preoccupations. He repeatedly insisted on the need for a better assessment of the theoretical foundations of the thought of the new neoclassical school, and he contributed substantially (Hahn 1982, 1988a, 1988b) to the clarification of this field. The present text attempts to provide some additional thoughts on this issue.

1 The Lucas–Azariadis Model

Lucas considers a Samuelsonian overlapping-generations economy, in which the "old" generation only consumes. Total labor supply from the young is θy, where y is the labor supply of a representative young producer and θ is a random coefficient associated with a real shock in the economy. Demand from the old generation, which only holds money, equals mx/p, where mx is the money stock (the product of m—previous money stock—and x—a monetary shock). Moreover, θ and x satisfy $\mathbb{E}(x) = \mathbb{E}(\theta) = 1$.

Azariadis' simplifying assumption is that the utility function of the representative consumer is

$$U = c' - \frac{1}{2}y^2, \tag{1}$$

where c' is future consumption. (Note that "young" people do not consume.) When young agents choose their labor supply, future consumption may be random; then they maximize

$$E(U/I) = E(c'/I) - \frac{1}{2}y^2,$$

where I denotes the information available at that date.

Since future consumption is simply $c' = ypx'/p'$, every interior solution to the maximization problem of the typical goods supplier satisfies

$$y = E\left[\frac{px'}{p'} \bigg/ I\right], \tag{2}$$

the expectation being taken conditionally on present information I.

Lucas and Azariadis assume that I is the current equilibrium price p, so the market-equilibrium condition is

$$E\left[\frac{px'}{p'} \bigg/ p\right] = \frac{mx}{\theta p}. \tag{3}$$

At this point, the basic idea in Lucas' paper is to define an equilibrium price to be a *function* $p(m,x,\theta)$. The agent's expectations will be said to be rational if (3) is satisfied—that is, if

$$E\left[\frac{p(m,x,\theta) \cdot x'}{p(mx,x',\theta')} \bigg/ p(m,x,\theta)\right] = \frac{mx}{\theta p(m,x,\theta)}. \tag{4}$$

An important property of (4) is the following:

LEMMA 1 (Lucas 1972)   For any solution of (4),

$$\frac{x_1}{\theta_1} \neq \frac{x_2}{\theta_2}$$

implies

$$p(m, x_1, \theta_1) \neq p(m, x_2, \theta_2).$$

Proof Suppose $p(m, x_1, \theta_1) = p(m, x_2, \theta_2)$. Then (4) immediately implies

$$\frac{x_1}{\theta_1} = \frac{x_2}{\theta_2}.$$

Note, however, that the reciprocal of lemma 1 does *not* hold in general. For any solution of (4), the equilibrium price reveals the shock ratio $z = x/\theta$ (lemma 1), but it might well reveal "more" than z. In other words, there might exist solutions of (4) in which different values of x and θ are associated to the *same* ratio $z = x/\theta$, but to *different* equilibrium prices $p(m, x, \theta)$. (See Lucas 1983.)

An immediate consequence of this point is that equation (4) cannot be solved under this most general form. Following Lucas' erratum (1983), we shall restrict our attention to a special subclass of solutions—namely, to the function p, which can be written in the form

$$p(m, x, \theta) = \psi(m, z) \text{ with } z = x/\theta. \tag{5}$$

In this case, (4) becomes

$$E\left[\frac{\psi(m, z) x'}{\psi(mx, z')} \middle/ \psi(m, z)\right] = \frac{mx}{\theta \psi(m, z)}. \tag{6}$$

Under this restriction, a consequence of lemma 1 is that each solution of ψ of (6) defines a one-to-one correspondence between prices and shock ratios. This, in turn, shows that the expectation in (6) can equivalently be taken conditionally on z, i.e., that solutions of (6) are solutions to

$$E\left[\frac{\psi(m, z) x'}{\psi(mx, z')} \middle/ z\right] = \frac{mx}{\theta \psi(m, z)}. \tag{7}$$

However, a solution of (7) is a solution of (6) if and only if it meets the condition stated in lemma 1—i.e., if $z_1 \neq z_2$ implies $\psi(m, z_1) \neq \psi(m, z_2)$.

Defining

$$\varphi(m,z) = \frac{mz}{\psi(m,z)} \quad (= \text{per capita labor supply})$$

leads to the *Lucas-Azariadis equation*:

$$E\left[\frac{\theta'}{\theta}\varphi(mx,z')/z\right] = [\varphi(m,z)]^2. \tag{8}$$

The above discussion shows that any solution of (8) that satisfies lemma 1 will be a solution of (6), and hence of (4). It is then a rational expectation, or a self-fulfilling theory. The remaining of the paper is devoted to the study of a family of solutions to the basic functional equation (8).[1]

2 Solutions to the Lucas–Azariadis Equation

The Lucas–Azariadis Solution

Lucas and Azariadis solve (8) under the following additional hypothesis:

(H) $\varphi(m,z)$ does not depend on m.

Note that (H) implies that the price $p = \psi(m,z)$ is proportional to m. That is, (H) can be understood as a neutrality-like assumption: the component m of the money stock, which is common knowledge when the agents make their decision, has no real effect.

PROPOSITION 1 (Lucas, Azariadis)   Under hypothesis (H), the *unique* solution of equation (8) is

$$\varphi(m,z) = u_0\sqrt{\chi_0(z)},$$

where

$$\chi_0(z) = E\left[\frac{1}{\theta}\Big/z\right]$$

and

$$u_0 = E[\theta'\sqrt{\chi_0}(z')].$$

Proof   Under (H), equation (8) becomes

$$E[\theta'\varphi(z')] \cdot E\left[\frac{1}{\theta}\Big/z\right] = \varphi(z)^2.$$

Since $E[\theta'\varphi(z')]$ is a constant, $\varphi(z)$ must be of the form $u_0 \cdot \chi_0^{1/2}(z)$; then the computation of u_0 is straightforward.

The Existence of a Non-Lucas Solution

Lucas' uniqueness result of proposition 1 relies on the neutrality hypothesis (H). Note, however, that (H) does *not* stem from Lucas' definition of rational expectations; rather, it appears as a totally independent assumption. A natural question is whether equation (8) admits solutions that do not satisfy (H).

We now show, from an example, that the answer is positive. Assume that the distributions of x and θ are log normal, with respective densities

$$f_x(t) = \frac{1}{t\sigma\sqrt{2\pi}}\exp\left[-\frac{1}{2\sigma^2}\left(\mathrm{Log}\, t + \frac{\sigma^2}{2}\right)^2\right]$$

and

$$f_\theta(t) = \frac{1}{t\mu\sqrt{2\pi}}\exp\left[-\frac{1}{2\mu^2}\left(\mathrm{Log}\, t + \frac{\mu^2}{2}\right)^2\right],$$

where σ and μ are positive parameters.[2] Note that these densities satisfy Lucas' requirement that $E(x) = E(\theta) = 1$.

The basic idea, at that point, is to look for a solution of (8) that can be written in the form[3]

$$\varphi(m,z) = \sum_{k=0}^{\infty} a_k(z)m^{-\lambda k},$$ (9)

where λ is a real positive number to be determined. The complete construction requires four steps.

Step 1: Necessary Condition   For a function (5) to be a solution of (4), we must have

$$\sum_{k=0}^{\infty} E\left\{\frac{\theta'}{\theta} a_k(z')m^{-\lambda k}x^{-\lambda k}\Big|z\right\} = \sum_{k=0}^{\infty}\sum_{i=0}^{k}[a_i(z)a_{k-i}(z)]m^{-\lambda k}.$$ (10)

With the factors of $m^{-\lambda k}$ identified on both sides, the (infinite) following set of conditions obtains:

$$E\left(\frac{\theta'}{\theta} a_0(z')|z\right) = a_0^2(z),$$ (11)

$$E\left(\theta' a_1(z')\frac{x^{-\lambda}}{\theta}|z\right) = 2a_0(z)a_1(z),$$ (12)

$$E\left(\theta' a_k(z')\frac{x^{-\lambda k}}{\theta}|z\right) = \sum_{i=0}^{k} a_i(z)a_{k-i}(z), \quad k \geq 2.$$ (13)

Step 2: A Solution of (11) and (12)   We already know the solution of (11), since it is nothing else than the Lucas–Azariadis solution. Equation (12) can be written

$$E\{\theta' a_1(z')\} \cdot E\left\{\frac{x^{-\lambda}}{\theta}|z\right\} = 2a_0(z)a_1(z).$$

Conforming with previous notation, we write

$$E\left\{\frac{x^{-\lambda}}{\theta}|z\right\} = \chi_\lambda(z).$$

Then $a_1(z)$ must be of the form

$$\frac{K_1\chi_\lambda(z)}{a_0(z)}.$$

From equation (12), we have

$$K_1 = \frac{1}{2} E\{\theta' a_1(z')\} = \frac{K_1}{2} E\left\{\frac{\theta' \chi_\lambda(z')}{a_0(z')}\right\}.$$

K_1 can be any arbitrary real number (in the following, we shall take it positive), provided that

$$E\left\{\frac{\theta' \chi_\lambda(z')}{a_0(z')}\right\} = 2.$$

Using (11), this is equivalent to

$$E\left\{\frac{\theta' \chi_\lambda(z')}{\sqrt{\chi_0(z')}}\right\} = 2E(\theta' \sqrt{\chi_0}(z')). \qquad (14)$$

For $\lambda = 0$, the left-hand side of (14) equals $E\{\theta' \sqrt{\chi_0}(z')\}$, which is smaller than the right-hand side. We show now that for λ large enough, the left-hand side becomes bigger than the right-hand side. For the sake of simplicity, we use the lognormal assumption to prove this property (but it holds under more general assumptions on the distribution).

With the lognormal distribution, it can be shown that

$$E\left(\frac{x^s}{\theta} \middle| z\right) = A^{s^2 - 4s + 3} z^{\alpha s + \beta}, \qquad (15)$$

with

$$A = \exp\left\{\frac{\mu^2 \sigma^2}{2(\mu^2 + \sigma^2)}\right\},$$

$$\alpha = \frac{\sigma^2}{\mu^2 + \sigma^2},$$

and

$$\beta = \frac{\mu^2}{\mu^2 + \sigma^2} = 1 - \alpha,$$

and that

$$E\{z'^{\alpha s+\beta/2}\theta'\} = BC^{s^2-s},$$

with

$$B = \exp\left\{-\frac{\mu^2}{8}\frac{\mu^2+2\sigma^2}{\mu^2+\sigma^2}\right\}$$

and

$$C = \exp\left\{\frac{\sigma^4}{2(\mu^2+\sigma^2)}\right\}.$$

It follows that

$$
\begin{aligned}
E\left\{\frac{\theta'\chi_\lambda(z')}{\sqrt{\chi_0(z')}}\right\} &= \frac{A^{\lambda^2}+4\lambda+3}{A^{3/2}}E\left\{\frac{\theta'z'^{-\alpha\lambda+\beta}}{(z')^{\beta/2}}\right\}\\
&= A^{\lambda^2+4\lambda+3/2}E\{\theta'z'^{-\alpha\lambda+\beta/2}\}\\
&= A^{\lambda^2+4\lambda+3/2}BC^{\lambda^2+\lambda}
\end{aligned}
$$ (16a)

and

$$E\{\theta'\sqrt{\chi_0}(z')\} = A^{3/2}E\{\theta'z'^{\beta/2}\} = A^{3/2}B.$$ (16b)

For λ large enough, obviously

$$A^{\lambda^2}\cdots BC^{\lambda^2}\cdots > A^{3/2}B.$$

Furthermore, here, there is a unique $\lambda_0 > 0$ for which equation (14) holds. It is defined by

$$A^{\lambda_0^2+4\lambda_0}C^{\lambda_0^2+\lambda_0} = 2.$$

So the log-normality assumption leads to

$$a_0(z) = A^3Bz^{\beta/2} \stackrel{def}{=} u_0z^{\beta/2}$$ (17)

and

$$a_1(z) = u_1z^{-\alpha\lambda_0+\beta/2},$$ (18)

where u_1 is an arbitrary (non-negative) real number.

Step 3: A Solution of (13)   Now we come back to the general term. Equation (13) can be written as

$$2a(z)a_k(z) = K_k \chi_{\lambda_0 k}(z) - \sum_1^{n-1} a_i(z)a_{k-i}(z),\tag{19}$$

where

$$K_k = E(\theta' a_k(z')).\tag{20}$$

We first show, by induction, the following:

LEMMA 1   Take $a_0(z)$ as defined in (17), choose an arbitrary u_1, and compute $a_1(z)$ as in (18). Then, any solution to equations (19) and (20) for $k \geq 1$ is of the form

$$a_k(z) = u_k z^{-\alpha\lambda_0 k + \beta/2},$$

where u_k is positive. Furthermore, u_k is of the form $\zeta_k u_1^k$.

Proof   Note first that $a_0(z)$ and $a_1(z)$ actually have the form assumed here. Now assume that the property is true for $2, \dots, k-1$; we show that it is true for k. Note first that (19) writes down

$$2a_0(z)a_k(z) = K_k A^{\lambda_0^2 k^2 + 4\lambda_0 k + 3} z^{-\alpha\lambda_0 k + \beta} - \left(\sum_{i=1}^{k-1} u_i u_{k-i}\right) z^{-\alpha\lambda_0 k + \beta}$$

or

$$a_k(z) = \frac{1}{2A^3 B}\left[K_k A^{\lambda_0^2 k^2 + 4\lambda_0 k + 3} - \left(\sum_{i=1}^{k-1} u_i u_{k-i}\right)\right] z^{-\alpha\lambda_0 k + \beta/2}.$$

This shows that $a_k(z) = u_k z^{-\alpha\lambda_0 k + \beta/2}$. It remains to show that $u_k > 0$. From (20), K_k is determined by

$$K_k = \left(\sum_1^{k-1} u_i u_{k-i}\right)\frac{C^{\lambda_0^2 k^2 + \lambda_0 k}}{-2A^3 + A^{\lambda_0^2 k^2 + 4\lambda_0 k + 3} C^{\lambda_0^2 k^2 + \lambda_0 k}}.$$

Hence,

$$u_k = \frac{1}{u_0}\left[\frac{\sum_1^{k-1} u_i u_{k-i}}{A^{\lambda_0^2 k^2 + 4\lambda_0 k} C^{\lambda_0^2 k^2 + \lambda_0 k} - 2}\right],\quad k > 1.\tag{21}$$

As announced, u_k is positive since the denominator is strictly positive for $k > 1$. Also, if u_i and u_{k-i} are proportional to $(u_1)^i$ and $(u_1)^{k-i}$, u_k is proportional to $(u_1)^k$. This terminates the induction proof.

Note that (21) uniquely defines the sequence u_k for any given u_1 (and, by the way, that the positivity of u_1 is crucial for the argument).

Step 4 It remains only to show that the series

$$\sum_0^\infty u_k \left(z^{-\alpha\lambda_0 k + \beta/2} \right) m^{\lambda_0 k}$$

converges for any couple $(z,m) \in \mathbb{R}_+^2$. For the sake of notational simplicity, let

$$D(k) = u_0 \left[A^{\lambda_0^2 k^2 + 4\lambda_0 k} C^{\lambda_0^2 k^2 + \lambda_0 k} - 2 \right].$$

Note that for any $\gamma > 1$, $D(k)$ becomes greater at infinity than $k\gamma^{k^{3/2}}$. More precisely, choose some $\gamma > 1$; then

$$\exists K \,|\, \forall k \geq K, D(k) > k\gamma^{k^{3/2}}. \tag{22}$$

Let us then define

$$M = \text{Min} \left(1, \min_{2 \leq k \leq K-1} \frac{D(k)}{k\gamma^{k^{3/2}}} \right). \tag{23}$$

Note that M is strictly greater than zero and that for any $k \leq K$

$$\frac{kM}{D(k)} \leq \gamma^{-k^{3/2}}. \tag{24}$$

Then the following can be shown:

LEMMA 2   If $u_1 < \bar{u}_1 = M/\gamma$, then $u_k < M\gamma^{-k^{3/2}}$, $k \geq 1$.

Proof We proceed by induction, and assume that the property holds true for any u_i, $1 \leq i < k$. Then, in particular, $u_i < M$, $i < k$, and

$$u_k = \frac{\sum_{i=1}^{k-1} u_i u_{k-i}}{D(k)} < \frac{kM^2}{D(k)} \left(= M \frac{kM}{D(k)} \right). \tag{25}$$

If $k > K$, then by (16)

$$\frac{k}{D(k)} < \gamma^{-k^{3/2}}$$

and by (23) $M \leq 1$; hence, $u_k < M\gamma^{-k^{3/2}}$. And if $k \leq K$, the same conclusion follows from (24) and (25). This terminates the proof of the lemma.

Note that the power series we are considering is absolutely dominated by

$$M \sum_0^\infty \gamma^{-k^{3/2}} \left(z^{-\alpha\lambda_0 k + \beta/2} \right) m^{\lambda_0 k},$$

which converges for any z and m. Hence, for some values of u_1, the power series we are considering converges for any z and m. However, this is sufficient for the convergence of the series of *any* u_1, z, and m:

LEMMA 3   If there exists a $u_1^* > 0$ such that the series converges for any z and m, then the series converges for any u_1, m, and z.

Proof Suppose that the power series

$$\varphi^*(z,m) = \sum_0^\infty u_k^* m^{-\lambda_0 k} z^{-\alpha\lambda_0 k + \beta/2},$$

where the u_k^* are deduced from u_1^* by (23), converges for any m and z. Consider the series

$$\overline{\varphi}(z,m) = \sum_0^\infty u_k m^{-\lambda_0 k} z^{-\alpha\lambda_0 k + \beta/2},$$

where the u_k are obtained according to (21), from some $u_1 \neq u_1^*$. Pose $w = u_1^*/u_1$; then, from lemma 1,

$$\forall k, u_k = \frac{u_k^*}{w^k}.$$

Thus,

$$\overline{\varphi}(z,m) = \sum_0^\infty u_k^* \frac{m^{-\lambda_0 k}}{w^k} z^{-\alpha\lambda_0 k + \beta/2}$$

$$= \varphi^*\left(\frac{m}{w^{-1/\lambda_0}}, z\right), \text{ which converges.}$$

We can now recapitulate the conclusion:

Take $u_0 = A^3 B$. Take λ_0 such that

$$A^{\lambda_0^2 + 4\lambda_0} C^{\lambda_0^2 + \lambda_0} = 2.$$

After fixing u_1, compute recursively

$$u_k = \frac{\sum_1^{k-1} u_i u_{k-i}}{u_0\left[A^{\lambda_0^2 k^2 + 4\lambda_0 k} C^{\lambda_0^2 k^2 + \lambda_0 k} - 2\right]}, \quad k > 1.$$

For any $u_1 > 0$, the power series

$$\sum_0^\infty u_k z^{-\alpha\lambda_0 k + \beta/2} m^{-\lambda_0 k}$$

converges toward a positive function $\varphi(m,z)$ which is a solution to the functional equation (8). The limit solution corresponding to $u_1 = 0$ is nothing else than the Lucas solution. We can thus state the following result:

PROPOSITION 2   There exists a continuum S of solutions to equation (8), indexed by a non-negative parameter u_1. All of them are also solutions to equation (6), hence to equation (4). The limit solution corresponding to $u_1 = 0$ is the Lucas–Azariadis solution. For all strictly positive values of u_1, the corresponding solutions do not satisfy (H).

It may be interesting to consider the (limit) case in which there is no real shock. Technically, the random variable θ becomes certain, which corresponds to the condition $\mu = 0$. Then the observation of z fully reveals x; the basic equation (8) becomes

$$\mathop{E}_{x'}[\varphi(mx, x')] = [\varphi(m,x)]^2. \tag{8'}$$

The results of proposition 2 immediately apply to this particular case:

COROLLARY 1   Equation (8′) has a continuum of solutions, indexed by a non-negative parameter u_1. The (limit) solution corresponding to $u_1 = 0$ (i.e., Lucas' solution) is constant. For all other values of u_1, the labor supply strictly decreases with both m and x.

Proof   For $\mu = 0$, we get $A = B = 1$ and $C = e^{\sigma^2/2}$. Lucas' solution, $\bar{\varphi}$, then degenerates to $\bar{\varphi} \equiv 1$. Other solutions are defined, for any given $u_1 > 0$, by

$$\varphi_{u1}(m, z) = \sum u_k (mz)^{-\lambda k},$$

where λ is the positive root of $\lambda^2 + \lambda = (2 \ln 2)/\sigma^2$ and where the u_k are sequentially defined by

$$u_k = \frac{\sum_1^{k-1} u_i u_{k-i}}{C^{\lambda^2 k^2 + \lambda k} - 2}, \quad k > 1.$$

The remainder of the proof is straightforward.

A conclusion is that the real shock—hence, the presence of imperfect transmission of information—is *not* necessary for non-Lucas solutions to exist. (We shall come back, in the conclusion, to the interpretation of this case.) To the contrary, non-Lucas solutions disappear if we assume away the *money* shock ($\sigma = 0$), as the reader may easily check.

3   Lucas versus Non-Lucas Solutions

We shall now compare the "non-Lucas" solutions described in proposition 2 with the (traditional) Lucas–Azariadis one. In what follows, the former (corresponding to $u_1 > 0$) will be referred to as *non-strongly-neutral* solutions. That is, they do not satisfy the (strong) neutrality requirement (H): once a specific solution φ (i.e., a specific self-fulfilling theory) has been chosen, real output along the corresponding trajectory does depend on the first-period quantity of money m, as well as on the shock ratio z. Note, however, that the solutions we derive still satisfy a (weak) form of neutrality: the *set* of solutions is not affected (in real terms when the initial quantity of money is modified).[4]

Qualitative Properties

Let us first consider the qualitative properties of the solutions (Figures 4.1, 4.2).[5]

For "high" values of z and/or m, non-neutral solutions behave as the Lucas one; in particular, both price and labor supply tend to infinity with z. For "low" values of m and z, however, labor supply tends to infinity in the non-neutral solutions, whereas it tends to zero in the Lucas one.

Also, note that for any non-neutral solution, the corresponding price function,

$$\psi(m,z) = mz/\varphi(m,z),$$

is strictly monotonic in z. That is, lemma 1 is satisfied; hence, ψ is a solution of (6).

In particular, it must be stressed that, for *all* solutions (including the Lucas–Azariadis one), labor supply is unbounded; moreover, in non-strongly-neutral solutions, labor supply is bounded away from zero, whereas it is not in the strongly neutral one. From a stochastic viewpoint, since the support of z is $]0, +\infty[$, this means that, in *all* solutions, labor supply may take arbitrarily large values with positive probability. This fact—which, in a sense, contradicts Lucas' (1972) original result—is closely linked to the particular utility function chosen, for convenience, by Azariadis. Again, it must be reminded that Azariadis' paper is (to our knowledge) the only example of analytic resolution of Lucas' equation; in fact, analytical resolution requires a very simplified framework. The fact that labor

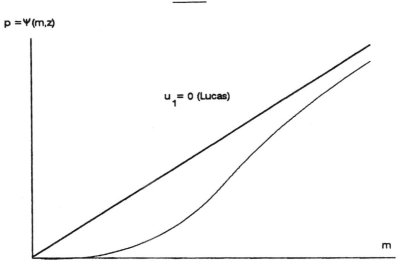

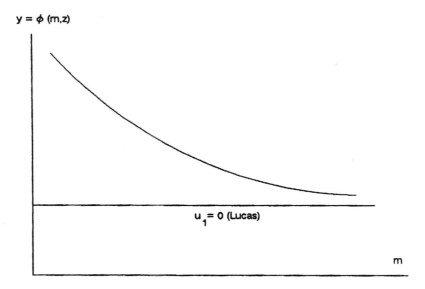

Figure 4.1

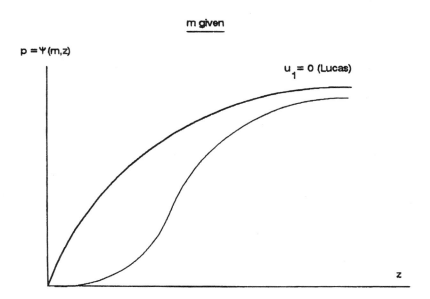

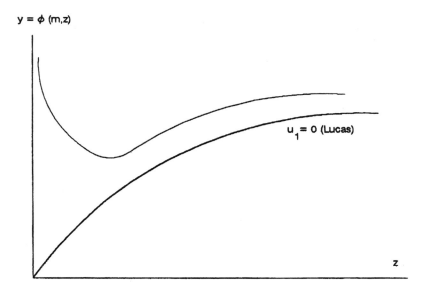

Figure 4.2

supply may become arbitrarily large, unrealistic as it seems, must hence be considered as a "red herring," due to particular functional forms. In Chiappori and Guesnerie 1988, we claim that the present set of solutions only illustrates a more general class, which can be associated to heteroclinic orbits[6] of a dynamical system (which, in turn, is associated to the existence problem). From this point of view, infinite labor supply simply corresponds to a particular stationary point of the system. In particular, in a slightly different context, the existence of *bounded* solutions of this kind can be demonstrated; but an analytical expression, in those cases, seems technically out of reach.

Stochastic Properties

On the other hand, the stochastic behaviors of Lucas and non-Lucas solutions are not identical. Specifically, in Lucas solution, the stochastic process followed by labor supply is uncorrelated through time; i.e., labor supply at data t is totally independent of labor supply at date $t' < t$. In particular, it is (trivially) stationary, in the probabilistic sense. To the contrary, in the non-Lucas solutions described in proposition 2, labor supply at date t depends on money supply at that date; since the money process is autocorrelated, autonomous, and nonstationary in the probabilistic sense,[7] the labor-supply process inherits the same properties. In other words: nonstationarity of labor supply, in our solution, can be seen as an immediate consequence of both Lucas' money process *and* the "strong non-neutrality" hypothesis that labor supply may depend on money stock

Welfare Comparison

It is possible to rank the solutions obtained above from a welfare viewpoint. To be more precise:

PROPOSITION 3   The *ex ante* welfare of each generation is an increasing function of u_1. In particular, any non-neutral solution Pareto dominates the Lucas solution.

Proof   Per capita labor supply during the generation's first period of life is $y = \psi(m,z)$, m being the currently available quantity of money. Total production during the second period is $\theta'\psi(mx,z')$, to be divided among θ agents. Hence, each agent's expected utility is

$$E(U) = E\left[\frac{\theta'}{\theta}\varphi(mx,z')\right] - \frac{1}{2}E\left[\varphi(m,z)^2\right].$$

But the basic functional equation, (8), becomes

$$\underset{\theta',z'}{E}\left[\frac{\theta'}{\theta}\varphi(mx,z')\right] = \varphi(m,z)^2.$$

Taking both sides' expectations with respect to z and θ gives, from a classical property of conditional expectations,

$$\underset{\theta,z,\theta',z'}{E}\left[\frac{\theta'}{\theta}\varphi(mx,z')\right] = \underset{z}{E}\left[\varphi(m,z)^2\right].$$

Hence,

$$E(U) = \frac{1}{2}E\left[\varphi(m,z)^2\right].$$

Since, for any m and z, φ is increasing with respect to u_1 (see the figures), a higher u_1 generates a higher expected utility.

Conclusion

We should briefly compare the achievements of the paper with the objectives stated in the introduction.

Concerning the first objectives, although we have not exhausted the study of the set of solutions of equation (8) in the model under consideration we have indeed exhibited a new class of solutions to the Lucas equation in the specific model under consideration. Naturally these new solutions may be challenged for economic reasons (see the previous section). But as far as existence is concerned, they are relevant and cannot be dismissed *a priori*.

Second, the paper demonstrates that the method of resolution we propose is indeed feasible. It is, however, incomparably more difficult to implement than standard methods of unknown coefficients used in previous studies of linear rational-expectations equations. (See, for example, Broze, Gourieroux, and Szafarz 1985.) Here, an infinity of unknown coefficients must be identified, and it must be shown that the corresponding power series has an adequate radius of convergence[8]; moreover, the difference-of-martingales technique does not apply here, because of the imperfect information component.

Third, and finally, the contribution of the paper to the understanding of the general indeterminacy issue is the subject of further studies. The main question concerns the theoretical status of our "new" solutions. Part of their originality relies upon the analysis they provide of the specific relative influence of real and monetary shocks in heterodox solutions.

Forgetting about real shocks and concentrating on solutions of the form given by corollary 1, one can argue that those are now *sunspot* solutions. The reason is that money, intrinsic in the general model, is now *extrinsic*: it is not a fundamental of the economy, i.e., one of the factors that influence its *real* behavior. Hence, the real effect of money, as described by corollary 1, can be viewed as an example where an extrinsic signal "matters." This is exactly the definition of a sunspot equilibrium. (See Chiappori and Guesnerie 1991b for a presentation.) This interpretation, and specifically the exact status of the particular solutions we find, are examined in Chiappori and Guesnerie 1993.

Some points can, however, be made here.

Our solutions—in the limit case of the absence of real shocks—

have features which make them qualitatively different (for example, in view of the stochastic properties of economic variables) from classical sunspot solutions. They differ from the Azariadis (1981b) and the Azariadis–Guesnerie (1986) solutions (which require backwards-bending labor supply), and from the Farmer–Woodford (1984) solutions (which do not exist in the present model). The findings of Peck (1988), who constructs time-dependent sunspot equilibria converging to autarky with probability 1, have no direct implications for our study.

In Chiappori and Guesnerie 1989 we attempt a partial although reasonably general classification of sunspot solution in one-dimensional, one-step-forward-looking dynamical systems. We identify sunspot solutions with the trajectories—possibly degenerated—of some associated dynamical system. Some of the solutions are indeed associated with a heteroclinic orbit of the system; they are called heteroclinic solutions. It turns out that the solutions computed in the present paper are "sunspot connected" with such solutions; i.e., they coincide with these heteroclinic solutions when the intrinsic noise disappears. In view of that, the controversial issue of a possibly infinite labor supply is a somewhat red herring: heteroclinic trajectories going to plus infinity are nothing more than particular heteroclinic trajectories.

Acknowledgment

We are indebted to J.-M. Grandmont for helpful comments.

Notes

1. J.-M. Grandmont has pointed out to us that the set of *all* solutions to this equation could be characterized using the following trick, directly borrowed from the study of linear systems (Broze, Gouriéroux, and Szafarz 1987). Equation (8) can be written as

$$(\theta/\theta') \cdot \varphi(mx, z') = [\varphi(m, z)]^2 + \varepsilon',$$

where ε' satisfies $\mathbb{E}(\varepsilon'/z) = 0$. Then solving this new functional equation in φ, for an arbitrary ε, provides us with a general solution of (8). Of course, the power-series method described in the paper can clearly help solving the equation. However, this approach is not helpful here, since our aim is to *characterize the behavior* of the solutions we find.

2. Since both real and monetary shocks are multiplicative in the model, the lognormality assumption is very natural; it will hold, for instance, if θ and x can be considered as products of "numerous" independent, identically distributed "small" random shocks.

3. In Chiappori and Guesnerie 1990 we instead consider solutions of the form $\Sigma_{k=0}^{\infty} a_k(z) m^{\lambda k}$. These solutions have different boundary properties (especially when m tends to zero or infinity); moreover, they raise some difficulties linked with the revelation of information through prices.

4. More precisely, consider any solution φ belonging to S; let m_0 be the intial quantity of money. Suppose, now, that m_0 is changed into some $m_0' > 0$. It is easy to show that there exists a function φ' in S, such that

$$\varphi(m_0', z) = \varphi'(m_0, z)$$

for all z. That is to say, changing m_0 into m_0', and keeping φ constant, is always equivalent to changing φ into some (conveniently chosen) φ' in S, m_0 remaining unchanged.

5. The diagrams were obtained by numerical computation of the power series. However, their qualitative properties can be derived formally.

6. A heteroclinic orbit is a stable orbit linking two stationary points.

7. To see this, note that $\mathrm{Log}\, m_{t+1} = \mathrm{Log}\, m_t + \mathrm{Log}\, x_t$. Taking the stationary distribution for m_t and m_{t+1} gives

$$\mathrm{E}[\mathrm{Log}\, m_{t+1}] = \mathrm{E}(\mathrm{Log}\, m_t) + \mathrm{E}[\mathrm{Log}\, x_t],$$

hence $\mathrm{E}(\mathrm{Log}\, x_t) = 0$—a contradiction with $\mathrm{E}(x_t) = 1$ unless x_t is not random.

8. The mere fact that the power series actually converge was not totally expected a priori. It must be remembered that in numerous cases—particularly in the physical sciences (including the well-known "three-body" problem)—*all* power series derived from the resolution of a functional equation diverge, though it is clear that the equation does admit solutions (see Poincaré 1890). In this sense, the functional equations derived from the rational-expectations framework—at least for the Lucas–Azariadis model—are "well behaved"!

5   Rational Random Walks

Pierre-André Chiappori and
Roger Guesnerie

I   Introduction

Many economic models consider exogenous variables that follow stochastic processes of a random walk type. The present paper considers a category of rational expectation equilibria in which the path of endogenous variables exhibits a similar qualitative feature: the state of the system "walks" randomly. Furthermore, this random walk takes place between two steady states of the system. We call such equilibria *random walk* (because of the temporal stochastic process followed by the equilibrium state), *heteroclinic* (because the support of the process connects two steady states in the state space) equilibria.

This chapter defines and discusses such equilibria, and proposes a general methodology for assessing their existence. It shows on a simple example that they do exist: they may be either of sunspot type (in the case where fluctuations are driven by beliefs only, or "extrinsic" in Cass and Shell (1983) terminology) or non-sunspot (when some underlying fundamentals actually follow a random walk).

Although the study has an exploratory dimension, it strongly suggests that the random walk (rational expectation) equilibria under scrutiny exist within a large class of models. In particular, an explicit example of sunspot random walk equilibria is exhibited in a subclass of overlapping-generations models that do not have "traditional" sunspot equilibria (i.e., sunspot equilibria triggered by *stationary* Markov processes).[1] Finally, when the exogenous uncertainty becomes intrinsic, we show that random walk heteroclinic equilibria also become truly intrinsic.

We proceed as follows. In Section 2, we present the basic n-dimensional one-step forward-looking model, for which many results on sunspot equilibria are available. In this framework we define random walk equilibria and show how their study can be associated—when the random walk has a countable support—with the study of an *associated dynamical system*. In this case, in a random walk equilibrium, the state variables wander upon a countable set of points. In *heteroclinic equilibria* this countable support has two accumulation points that are steady states of the system. A necessary condition for the existence of heteroclinic equilibria— bearing on the characteristics of the random walk and on the properties of the initial model around the two steady states under consideration—is provided and discussed.

In Section 3, we restrict the general framework of Section 2 to a specific overlapping-generations (OLG) model. In this simplified framework we are able to exhibit a large class of random walks that sustain heteroclinic equilibria wandering between the golden rule and the autarky equilibrium.

Finally, Section 4 extends the analysis of Section 3 to the case where money has some *intrinsic* influence on the economy.

II   Model, Concepts and the Existence Problem

(a)   The Model and Equilibrium Concepts

We are considering a n-dimensional one-step forward-looking dynamical model, whose deterministic dynamics is governed by

$$Z(x_t, x_{t+1}^e) = 0, \tag{1}$$

where $x_t (x_t \in X \subset R^n)$ denotes the vector of state variables at time t and where x_{t+1}^e denotes the (common) point deterministic expectations of x_{t+1} (at time t) $(x_{t+1}^e \subset X)$.

When expectations are no longer point expectations, but are given by some probability distribution over x_{t+1} (let us denote it $\mu_{t+1} \in \mathcal{P}(X)$, $\mathcal{P}(V)$ denoting the set of probability distributions over V), the dynamics of the system is governed by

$$\tilde{Z}(x_t, \mu_{t+1}) = 0. \tag{2}$$

Naturally, (2) is a more general formalization and we should have

$$\tilde{Z}(x_t, \delta(x_{t+1})) = Z(x_t, x_{t+1}) \tag{3}$$

when $\delta(x_{t+1})$ is the Dirac measure at x_{t+1}. More general consistency requirements called consistency of derivatives (CD) will also be introduced later.

Throughout the paper, we shall be interested in a particular type of stochastic processes, namely random walks. Specifically, we consider a Markovian stochastic process $(M_t, t \in N)$, characterized by the two properties defined below:

DEFINITION 1   The Markovian process (M_t).

· The support $\mathcal{M}$ of the process is discrete: $\mathcal{M} = \{M^s, s \in Z\}$.

· From any state M^s, the process can only reach at the next period the $2k + 1$ "neighbour states" M^{s+l}, $|l| \leq k$, with positive probability. The probability of reaching state M^{s+l} at time $t + 1$, conditional on the process being in state s at date t, is denoted α_l; by assumption, it does not depend either upon s or upon t.

Denoting $\{y^1 \ldots y^n, \beta_1, \beta_2, \ldots \beta_n\}$ the probability distribution with finite support $y^1 \ldots y^n$ and probabilities β_l for y^l, $(\Sigma_1^n \beta_l = 1)$ we are in a position to define a (sunspot) random walk equilibrium.

DEFINITION 2   Random walk equilibrium.

A (sunspot) random walk equilibrium, based on the stochastic process of Definition 1, consists of a countable sequence $(\bar{x}^s)$, $\bar{x}^s \in X$, $s \in (-\infty, \ldots 0 \ldots, +\infty)$ such that, for all s:

$$\tilde{Z}(\bar{x}^s, \{\bar{x}^{s-k}, \ldots \bar{x}^s, \ldots \bar{x}^{s+k}, \alpha_{-k}, \ldots, \alpha_0, \ldots \alpha_k\}) = 0. \tag{4}$$

A (sunspot) random walk equilibrium is described by its support and the stochastic laws of motion of the state variables that it generates.

· The support consists of a countable number of states $\bar{x}^s$, in the state space X. We denote it $\bar{X} = U_s \bar{x}^s$.

· Over this countable support, the stochastic motion of equilibrium states reproduces the motion of the random walk (M_t) in the sense that there exists, at each period t, a one to one correspondence between the state of the exogenous variable M_t and the equilibrium state of the system: when $M_t = M^s$ then the equilibrium state is x_t such that $x_t = \bar{x}^s$.

An interpretation is that agents believe in a "theory," which says that the state variables follow a random walk triggered by M_t over $\bar{X}$. Then equation (4) expresses the fact that this theory is self-fulfilling. The random walk (M_t) is thus a "sunspot" generator of beliefs.

The stochastic properties of the random walk, and hence of the corresponding heteroclinic equilibria, will obviously differ according to the values of the coefficients α. The states M^s may be transient (in the sense that once in M^s the probability of coming back to it is strictly smaller than one) or, on the contrary, recurrent. For example, the states are recurrent for a random walk with $\alpha_1 = \alpha_{-1} = \frac{1}{2}$. The same obtains more generally whenever $\Sigma_j j \alpha_j = 0$ (which includes in particular all symmetric random walks). However, even random walks with transient states are generally such that the probability of reaching any given state, starting from any other one, is strictly positive.

In this paper, we are interested in one special category of random walk equilibria. In order to define this category, let us assume:

MS (Multiplicity of steady states)   The deterministic system (1) has (at least) two steady states E^i such that

$$Z(E^i, E^i) = 0, \quad i = U, L, \dots. \tag{5}$$

Then

DEFINITION 3   Heteroclinic Equilibria.

An heteroclinic (random walk) equilibrium is a random walk equilibrium $(\bar{x}^s)$, $\bar{x}^s \in X$, $s \in (-\infty, \dots 0 \dots, +\infty)$ such that there exist two distinct deterministic steady states E^U, E^L with

$$\lim_{s \to +\infty} \bar{x}^s = E^U, \qquad \lim_{s \to -\infty} \bar{x}^s = E^L.$$

Hence a heteroclinic equilibrium is a random walk equilibrium whose support has two accumulation points that are steady states of the deterministic system. In an heteroclinic equilibrium, the state of the system will indefinitely wander between the steady states. Naturally the precise stochastic behaviour of the system will depend on the precise characteristics of the random walk.

(b)   The Strategy of an Existence Proof

The Associated Dynamical System
We first indicate how, under adequate circumstances, the existence problem for random walk equilibria can be viewed as the search for solutions (or trajectories) of some *associated* dynamical system. This system is defined on a space of dimension higher than the state space of our initial problem.

Let us consider some given random walk (M_t) and the basic equation:

$$\tilde{Z}(x^s, \{x^{s-k}, \ldots x^s, \ldots x^{s+k}, \alpha_{-k}, \ldots, \alpha_0, \ldots \alpha_k\}) = 0. \tag{6}$$

Suppose the latter can be "solved" in x^{s+k} and in x^{s-k} i.e. that there exist two functions $\overline{\Lambda}, \underline{\Lambda}$ such that (6) is equivalent to

$$x^{s+k} = \overline{\Lambda}(x^{s-k}, \ldots x^s, \ldots x^{s+k-1}, \alpha_{-k}, \ldots \alpha_0, \ldots \alpha_k), \tag{7}$$

$$x^{s-k} = \underline{\Lambda}(x^{s-k+1}, \ldots x^s, \ldots x^{s+k}, \alpha_{-k}, \ldots \alpha_0, \ldots \alpha_k). \tag{8}$$

From $\overline{\Lambda}$, we can define an associated *"forward" dynamical* system in the space R^{2nk}.

$$
\begin{aligned}
x^{s+k} &= \overline{\Lambda}(x^{s-k}, \ldots x^{s+k-1}, \alpha_{-k}, \ldots \alpha_k) \\
x^{s+k-1} &= x^{s+k-1} \\
&\vdots \\
x^{s-k+1} &= x^{s-k+1}.
\end{aligned}
\tag{9}
$$

Putting $y^s = (x^{s+k}, \ldots, x^{s-k+1})$, (9) can be written in a compact way:

$$y^{s+1} = \overline{\Phi}(y^s, \alpha). \tag{10}$$

Similarly we can define a *"backward" dynamical system*:

$$
\begin{aligned}
x^{s-k} &= \underline{\Lambda}(x^{s-k+1}, \ldots x^{s+k}, \alpha_{-k}, \ldots \alpha_k) \\
x^{s-k+1} &= x^{s-k+1} \\
&\vdots \\
x^{s+k-1} &= x^{s+k-1}
\end{aligned}
\tag{11}
$$

that is compactly written as

$$y^{s-1} = \underline{\Phi}(y^s, \alpha). \tag{12}$$

Then, starting from some y^0 *and* considering both the itineraries of the forward and the backward dynamical systems, one generates a solution to (6).

   The precise meaning of equations (9) and (11)—or (10) and (12)—must be emphasized. Here, the index $s \in Z$ is *not* a time index; rather, it indexes the various states of a (countable) set $X = \{x^s, s \in Z\}$. This set, in turn, is the *support* of the process (x_t) followed throughout time by the state variable; specifically, (x_t) will follow a random walk on X, with the same transition probabilities as the (M_t) process.

Naturally, the just sketched procedure might fail because along the itinerary (either backward or forward) the relevant function might cease to be defined. This occurs whenever either (6) has no solution or when it is not invertible in this point. In the former case, we would have to conclude that there is no random walk equilibrium whose support contains the y^0 under consideration but the attempt can be repeated from any admissible y^0.

The above discussion stresses the close theoretical connections of the search of sunspot random walk equilibria with the determination of solutions of some associated dynamical system in higher dimensional spaces. This suggests that there will be different categories of random walk equilibria corresponding to different types of solutions of dynamical systems (i.e., among other "homoclinic" solutions, "strange attractors" . . .) This idea is developed in Chiappori and Guesnerie (1988) to whom we refer the interested reader.

Also, the terminology "heteroclinic" equilibrium can now be justified not only by the fact that this type of random walk equilibrium establishes a "connection" between two steady states, but also by the fact that it is associated with a *heteroclinic* orbit of the associated dynamical systems. More precisely:

CLAIM Every heteroclinic orbit of the forward (resp. backward) dynamical system determines a heteroclinic equilibrium in the sense of Definition 2.

Proof Take the forward dynamical system (6). An heteroclinic orbit of this dynamical system is an orbit (y^s) linking two fixed points, let us say, $\bar{y}^U$ and $\bar{y}^L$. It is straightforward to check that necessarily both $\bar{y}^U$ and $\bar{y}^L$ are of the form $(E, \ldots, E)$; and from (3) E must be a steady state of the deterministic system; we may take that $\bar{y}^U = (E^U, \ldots, E^U)$ and $\bar{y}^L$ and $(E^L, \ldots, E^L)$. Then from (y^s), one can construct a random walk equilibrium which is heteroclinic in the sense of Definition 2. ‖

Solving the Dynamical System
Viewing the existence problem as the search for heteroclinic orbits of the associated dynamical system provides an encouraging perspective for the existence study. However, there is no standard recipe for finding an heteroclinic orbit of a dynamical system. We propose here a strategy of proof which will indeed be succesful in the particular case we consider in the next section. This strategy is presented within the general framework adopted in the present section; such a setting does not significantly complicate the presentation while allowing to derive useful general information on the stochastic processes that are good candidates for supporting a heteroclinic equilibrium.

First Step   Local existence analysis around the fixed points of the dynamical system.

If a heteroclinic equilibrium does exist, then *necessarily* the basic equation (4) must be solvable in a small enough neighbourhood of each of the steady states $\bar{y}^U$ and $\bar{y}^L$. For the forward dynamical system $\overline{\Lambda}$, for instance, this condition means that *one of the corresponding fixed points necessarily has (at least) an attracting direction when the other one has (at least) a repulsing direction*. In Figure 5.1, where we visualize this fact, the state variable of the initial model is one-dimensional ($n = 1$), the random walk has $k = 1$, and consequently the associated dynamical system is two-dimensional (as it will be in next section as well). If our initial system has the steady states E^U and E^L, the corresponding fixed points of the dynamical system are (E^U, E^U) and (E^L, E^L); the figure indicates the local properties of a trajectory that may generate a heteroclinic equilibrium. (Incidentally, note that in the just sketched discussion the role of the

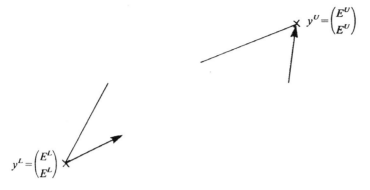

Figure 5.1

upper and of the lower equilibrium can be exchanged). Of course, the insights provided by the diagram are relevant for higher-dimensional problems as well.

The next question is of course whether the above condition is fulfilled by equation (6). For answering this question, one must know how the mapping $\tilde{Z}$ behaves in a neighbourhood of the steady state. In such neighbourhoods, uncertainty is small and in most models of economic origin, where agent are utility maximizers, there will be a close connection between the derivatives of $\tilde{Z}$ and those of Z. Such a connection, that the economic nature of the problem does justify, is expressed in an axiomatic way as condition (CD) (consistency of derivatives).

More precisely, the consistency condition linking the deterministic and stochastic dynamics is the following:

(CD) Consistency of Derivatives Whatever $\beta = (\beta_1, \ldots, \beta_k)$ belonging to the $(k-1)$-dimensional simplex, and whatever x_1 belonging to X, let $x = (x_1, \ldots, x_1)$, then

$$\partial_{x0} \tilde{Z}(x_0, (x, \beta)) = \partial_0 Z(x_0, x_1)$$
$$\forall i, \partial_{x_i} \tilde{Z}(x_0, (x, \beta)) = \beta_i \cdot \partial_1 Z(x_0, x_1)$$

where $\partial_x F(\cdot)$ is the Jacobian matrix associated with a function F, with respect to the variables x and taken in $(\cdot)$, and where for simplicity we use $\partial_i Z$ for $\partial_{x_i} Z$.

This axiom is the adaptation to our context of an axiom called (A2) in Guesnerie (1986) or Chiappori and Guesnerie (1989). The reader will first notice that the first condition is redundant; it says that when future "prices" are certain (x_1) the derivatives of Z and $\tilde{Z}$ w.r.t. present "prices" x_0 must coincide, hence is a consequence of our definition of Z and $\tilde{Z}$ above. We however made it part of (CD) for the reader's convenience. The second part, which considers at the margin of the same certainty situation an infinitesimal change dx_i in x_i, is truly an axiom. It states that, given that it only introduce infinitesimal uncertainty, the random change tomorrow (it occurs with probability β_i) is equivalent to a *sure* change of *magnitude* $\beta_i \cdot dx_i$ (i.e., the expected value of the initial change). To the best of our knowledge (CD) holds in all economic models fitting the above formalization (where it appears as a consequence of expected utility maximization).

The necessary condition visualized above will then depend on the two factors which, according to (CD), determine the derivatives of $\tilde{Z}$, namely the derivatives of the deterministic mapping Z at the steady state and the characteristics of the random process that triggers shocks and/or beliefs. This is indeed what Proposition 1 below asserts. Before stating it, let us introduce some pieces of notation. We call B the matrix $-(\partial_0 Z)^{-1}(\partial_1 Z)$, and we consider both $\bar{B}$ (the matrix at E^U) and $\underline{B}$ (the matrix at E^L). Then $\bar{B}$ (resp. $\underline{B}$) governs the local perfect-foresight dynamics around the corresponding steady state E^U (resp. E^L); i.e., the dynamics is locally "of the form" $x_t = B \cdot x_{t+1}$.

The necessary condition of Proposition 1 relates the characteristics of (the eigenvalues and the eigenspaces of) the matrices B and those of the random process α.

PROPOSITION 1   Necessary conditions for the existence of heteroclinic equilibria.

Let the economic system (1) (2) satisfy conditions (CD) and (MS)
and suppose that it has exactly two steady states E^U, E^L. Then

(i) A necessary condition for the existence of a heteroclinic random-
walk equilibrium (the random walk being associated with the
process of Definition 1 in which $\alpha_j > 0$, $j = -k, \ldots +k$) is the follow-
ing: There exists $\bar{\mu}$ and $\underline{\mu}$ respectively eigenvalues of $\bar{B}$ and $\underline{B}$ such
that the equation

$$\sum_{j=-k}^{+k} \alpha_j \gamma^j = 1/\mu \tag{13}$$

has a solution $\bar{\gamma}$ of modulus smaller than one when $\mu = \bar{\mu}$ and a
solution γ of modulus greater than one when $\mu = \underline{\mu}$.

(ii) Furthermore, if the previous condition is fulfilled, then $\bar{\gamma}$
(resp. γ) is an eigenvalue of the Jacobian of the forward dynamical
system (7) at E^U (resp. at E^L); the associated eigenvector is of the
form $(\gamma^k v, \ldots, \gamma^{-k+1} v)$, where v is an eigenvector of $\bar{B}$ (resp. $\underline{B}$) corresponding to the eigenvalue $\bar{\mu}$ (resp. $\underline{\mu}$).

Proposition 1, the proof of which is in Appendix 1, provides the
algebraic conditions that guarantee in a general framework the
geometric features vizualized in the two-dimensional Figure 5.1.
Part one of the proposition stresses the connection between on the
one hand, the relevant eigenvalues—those associated with the
attracting and repulsing directions of Figure 5.1—of the associated
dynamical system and on the other hand, the eigenvalues governing the perfect-foresight dynamics of the initial system around
its steady states and the characteristics of the random process
triggering beliefs. Such a connection, as made explicit through
equation (13), is rather complex and not immediately amenable to
intuition.[2] Part two of the proposition emphasizes a much simpler
relationship between the corresponding eigenvectors of the (linearized) associated dynamical system and the (linearized) initial

deterministic system. Though it may not be of straightforward interpretation, Proposition 1 makes clear that the existence of a heteroclinic orbit between two steady states is possible only when the characteristics of the random walk (i.e., the α_j) under consideration fit the characteristics of the perfect foresight dynamics around the two candidate steady states (as summarized through the spectrum of $\bar{B}$ and $\underline{B}$) in a way that is in principle easy to check. Given some dynamical system Z with multiple steady states and some random walk, checking condition (13) involves finding the spectrum of $\bar{B}$ and $\underline{B}$ and computing the zeroes of (at most) $2n$ polynomials of degree $2k$.

The complete study of Proposition 1 is outside the scope of this paper; from now on, we shall mainly see how it can be applied to the simple model of the next section. Let us however mention a few remarks.

(i) Given some a priori random walk α, the necessary conditions for having a heteroclinic equilibrium with E^U as the "lower" steady state and E^L as the "upper" steady state are symmetric to the ones above—i.e., $\bar{\gamma}$ must have modulus greater than one and $\underline{\gamma}$ must have modulus smaller than one. Hence, given E^U, E^L, one can conclude, from the inspection of local conditions, that a heteroclinic equilibrium between these points is impossible only when (the k replicate of) these two equilibria are *both* sources or *both* sinks for the associated dynamical system i.e., when the $2nk$ solutions of equation (13) have either all modulus smaller than one or all modulus greater than one.

(ii) Proposition 1 focuses attention on random-walk equilibria based on an a priori given exogenous random process. It can also read as a statement on those processes which are good candidates for triggering a random-walk equilibrium in an a priori given economic system. In this perspective, one easily sees that for a given spectrum of $\bar{B}$ and $\underline{B}$, equation (13) generally leaves many degrees of freedom in the choice of random walks which meet the necessary condition.[3] In particular, whatever the spectrum of $\bar{B}$ and $\underline{B}$ there are random walks that *always* meet the necessary condition. This is the case for symmetric random walks ($\alpha_j = \alpha_{-j}$), for which the equation reduces to:

$$\alpha_0 + \sum_{j=1}^{k} \alpha_j \left(\gamma^j + \frac{1}{\gamma^j} \right) = 1/\mu. \tag{14}$$

If γ is a solution of such an equation, then $1/\gamma$ is also automatically satisfied (though, of course, the solution might have a modulus exactly equal to one).

Second Step   Extension of the local solution to a global one.

At this stage, we have explored the problem of existence of an heteroclinic equilibrium from a local viewpoint—i.e., in the neighbourhood of the steady states under consideration.[4] In some sense, Proposition 1 allows one to exhibit local solutions, or "germs," of a heteroclinic orbit. How can these local germs be connected in order to generate a full heteroclinic solution? We have no general method for answering the question and we conjecture that the appropriate method is likely to depend on the nature of the problem. We present in the next section a somewhat ad hoc method—showing that the stable manifold of the associated dynamical system at the upper equilibrium points must remain in a fixed subset and is then necessarily "captured" by the "lower" equilibrium point—that applies to a simple one-dimensional OLG model.

III   Heteroclinic Sunspot Equilibria: An Example

The present section studies a specific example, in which a set of heteroclinic sunspot equilibria can be exhibited, along the lines of the strategy defined above. The example takes place in a simple OLG framework with representative consumer and separable utility. In addition, the random walk process is taken to be as simple as possible; specifically, we assume that, from any state M^s, only the immediate neighbours M^{s-1} and M^{s+1} can be reached with positive probability (this is equivalent to assuming that $k = 1$ in the notation of the previous section). We first introduce the model (3.1), then characterize the basic set of heteroclinic sunspot equilibria (3.2); lastly, a particular case is considered with some care (3.3).

3.1   The Model

We consider an OLG model with a representative consumer, whose utility is given by

$$W(c_{t+1}, x_t) = U(c_{t+1}) - V(x_t) \tag{15}$$

where c_{t+1} is consumption at period $t + 1$ and x_t labour supply at period t. Both U and V are increasing and twice differentiable; U is concave, while V is convex. Returns are constant (one unit of labour produces one unit of good); hence, nominal wage at period t is simply the price p_t of the consumption good. Money supply follows the stochastic process $M_{t+1} = \rho_{t+1} M_t$ where the ρ_t are i.i.d. random variables, so that the budget constraint of the representative agent is

$$p_{t+1}c_{t+1} = \rho_{t+1}p_t x_t. \tag{16}$$

Maximizing expected utility under budget constraint gives the first-order conditions:

$$E\left[\frac{\rho_{t+1}p_t}{p_{t+1}} U'\left(\frac{\rho_{t+1}p_t}{p_{t+1}} x_t \right) \right] = V'(x_t). \tag{17}$$

Since equilibrium is characterized by:

$$p_{t+1}x_{t+1} = M_{t+1} = \rho_{t+1}M_t = \rho_{t+1}p_t x_t, \tag{18}$$

the following equation, that describes the dynamics of the economy under rational expectations, holds:

$$E[x_{t+1}U'(x_{t+1})] = x_t V'(x_t) = 0. \tag{19}$$

This form fits the general framework developed in the previous section. In particular, we have:

$$Z(x_t, x_{t+1}) = x_{t+1}U'(x_{t+1}) - x_t V'(x_t). \tag{20}$$

Then $Z(x_t, x_{t+1}) = 0$ governs the *deterministic* dynamics of the economy[5] when the stochastic dynamics is governed by $\tilde{Z}$ (that satisfies CD)

$$\tilde{Z}(x_t, \mu_{t+1}) = E_{\mu_{t+1}}(x_{t+1}U'(x_{t+1})) - x_t V'(x_t). \tag{21}$$

In what follows, we assume that $U'(0) > V'(0)$ ("Samuelson case"); then the economy has two steady states, $\underline{e} = 0$ and $\bar{e} > 0$ defined by

$$U'(\bar{e}) = V'(\bar{e}). \tag{22}$$

Also, we mentioned above the fact that heteroclinic sunspot equilibria may exist for models in which traditional, stationary sunspot equilibria cannot occur. We shall illustrate this claim in the example we are considering. Specifically, in the OLG model without government expenditures, a well-known condition for existence of stationary sunspot equilibria is that the offer curve is backwards bending at the upper steady state. Here, we explicitly exclude this case, by assuming that U is "not too concave" on $[0, \bar{e}]$, in the following sense:

$$\forall x \in [0, \bar{e}], \quad \frac{d}{dx}[xU'(x)] = U'(x) + xU''(x) > 0. \tag{23}$$

In particular, the offer curve is upward-sloping, and the function $x \to xU'(x)$ is one-to-one, on $[0, \bar{e}]$.

The local deterministic dynamics around the steady states is governed respectively by the matrices

$$\underline{B} = -(\partial_0 Z)^{-1} \partial_1 Z(0) = \frac{U'(0)}{V'(0)} = \underline{\mu} \tag{24}$$

and

$$\overline{B} = -(\partial_0 Z)^{-1}\partial_1 Z(\overline{e}) = \frac{U'(\overline{e}) + \overline{e}U''(\overline{e})}{V'(\overline{e}) + \overline{e}V''(\overline{e})} = \overline{\mu}. \tag{25}$$

Trivially, $\underline{B}$ (resp. $\overline{B}$) has a single eigenvalue $\underline{\mu} > 1$ (resp. $\overline{\mu} < 1$).

Now, money supply is supposed to follow a random process. With our multiplicativity assumption ($M_{t+1} = \rho_{t+1}M_t$), the law of motion of M_{t+1} can be described from the law of motion of ρ_{t+1}. To keep the analysis tractable, we take the dimension of the problem to be as small as possible, by assuming that, for any t, ρ_t can only take three values: $1/\lambda$, 1 or λ (for some $\lambda > 1$). It results that, from state $M^s = (\lambda)^s \cdot M^0$, the process can only reach (in one period) one of the states M^s, $M^{s-1} = (\lambda)^{s-1}M^0$ or $M^{s+1} = (\lambda)^{s+1}M^0$ with positive probability. Then let:

$$P(M_{t+1} = M^{s+1}/M_t = M^s) = P(\rho_{t+1} = \lambda) = \alpha_1 \overset{def}{=} \alpha\beta, \tag{26}$$

$$P(M_{t+1} = M^{s-1}/M_t = M^s) = P(\rho_{t+1} = 1/\lambda) = 1 - \alpha_1 - \alpha_0 \overset{def}{=} (1-\alpha)\beta, \tag{27}$$

$$p(M_{t+1} = M^s/M_t = M^s) = P(\rho_{t+1} = 1) = \alpha_0 \overset{def}{=} 1 - \beta, \tag{28}$$

where, for the sake of clarification, we introduce additional notation: here, β denotes the probability of leaving the current state, and α is the conditional probability of moving "upwards."

As said above, since the quantity of money is not an "effective" fundamental of the economy, it can only influence consumption of labour supply through sunspot effects. Specifically, a sunspot theory may state that labour supply will be in state x^s if and only if money supply is in state M^s. The theory will be self-fulfilling iff the set $(x^s, s \in Z)$ satisfies the following self-fulfillment condition:

$$\forall s \in Z, \quad x^s V'(x^s) = (1-\alpha)\beta x^{s-1}U'(x^{s-1}) + (1-\beta)x^s U'(x^s) \\ + \alpha\beta x^{s+1}U'(x^{s+1}). \tag{29}$$

This condition is the form taken, in our particular framework, by the general relation (4) of the previous section; a doubly-infinite sequence of positive x^s meeting condition (29) is what we termed a *random walk equilibrium*. Whether x^{s+1} (resp. x^{s-1}) can be expressed, from (29), as a function of x^s and x^{s-1} (resp. x^{s+1}) depends on the form of the function U. However, a consequence of hypothesis (23) above is that this is always possible when x^s belongs to $[0, \bar{e}]$. In that case, (29) can be transformed into the following, well-defined dynamical system (the *forward* dynamical system of Section 2):

$$\begin{pmatrix} x^{s+1} \\ x^s \end{pmatrix} = \overline{\Phi} \begin{pmatrix} x^s \\ x^{s-1} \end{pmatrix} = \begin{pmatrix} \overline{\Lambda}(x^s, x^{s-1}) \\ x^s \end{pmatrix}, \quad s \in Z \tag{30}$$

where $x^{s+1} = \overline{\Lambda}(x^s, x^{s-1})$ is equivalent to (29). Again, it should be remembered that s is *not* a time index, but indices the states of the countable support of the process.

We first look at random walk equilibria that have their support within $[0, \bar{e}]$. It is intuitively plausible (and could be made rigorous) that such equilibria necessarily have two accumulations points at the steady states i.e. that they are *heteroclinic equilibria* in the sense of Section 2.

3.2   Existence of Heteroclinic Equilibria

Our problem in this subsection, is to find an heteroclinic equilibrium i.e., a sequence $\{x^s\}$, with $x^s \in [0, \bar{e}]$ such that it satisfies (30) and $x_s \to 0, s \to -\infty, x_s \to \bar{e}, s \to +\infty$.

Our methodology has been discussed in Section 2. One has however to take into account one difficulty that does not appear in the general discussion—i.e., the fact that the lower steady state lies at the boundary of the domain of definition of the state space. We proceed as follows. First, forgetting temporarily about the non-negativity constraints, we focus attention on the local analysis of the dynamical system (30) around the steady states $(0, 0)$ and $(\bar{e}, \bar{e})$. We will thus identify values of the random-walk parameters for which two "germs" of heteroclinic equilibria can be identified: the first one starts from the lower equilibrium in the direction of an eigenvector (of the Jacobian of $\overline{\Lambda}$) that belongs to the positive orthant; the second one starts from the upper equilibria in the direction of an appropriate eigenvector. Second, we show that these two upper and lower germs can indeed be connected.

We now study the dynamics defined by (30), in a neighbourhood of the two steady states. From Proposition 1 above, the eigenvalues are the solutions of the equation:

$$\alpha\beta\gamma^2 + \left(1 - \beta - \frac{1}{\mu}\right)\gamma + (1 - \alpha)\beta = 0 \tag{31}$$

where $\mu = \underline{\mu}$ at zero and $\bar{\mu}$ at $\bar{e}$; note that $\mu > 0$ in both cases. The qualitative properties of the roots essentially depend on whether μ is greater or smaller than one. Lemma 1 in Appendix 2 provides a comprehensive description of the solutions of (31) as a function of α and β in both cases. As a consequence of this Lemma, the following can be asserted:

PROPOSITION   Take the parameters α and β (that determine money supply) as given. Then the necessary conditions of Proposition 1 are satisfied for $e = 0$ in the following cases:

(i) $\beta < \dfrac{1 - 1/\underline{\mu}}{2}$

(ii) $\beta > \dfrac{1 - 1/\underline{\mu}}{2}$ and $\alpha \leq \dfrac{1}{2}$.

They are not whenever

(iii) $\beta > \dfrac{1 - 1/\underline{\mu}}{2}$ and $\alpha > \dfrac{1}{2}$.

The necessary conditions of Proposition 1 are always satisfied for $\bar{e}$ (whatever the random walk under consideration). The fixed point $(0, 0)$ of the associated dynamical systems (30) is respectively a saddle point, a source or a sink whenever respectively (i), (ii), (iii) hold. Moreover, in the case where it is a source and whenever

$$\beta \geqq \beta* = \frac{1 - 1/\mu}{1 - \sqrt{4\alpha(1-\alpha)}}$$

the two eigenvalues are real and greater than one. Lastly, the fixed point $(\bar{e}, \bar{e})$ is always a saddle point for the dynamical system (30).[6]

Now we will focus on random walks for which $\beta \geqq \beta*$, $\alpha < \frac{1}{2}$. In this case $(0, 0)$ is a source for the dynamical system (30) and the corresponding eigenvectors $(\vec{V})$ are both in the positive orthant (see Appendix 2 for a formal proof). One may expect that this "germ" of solution be linked with another "germ" at the upper steady state that reaches $B = (\bar{e}, \bar{e})$ along the "attracting" eigenvector $\vec{W}$ (which is shown, again in Appendix 2, to be located as in Figure 5.2). This intuition turns out to be correct; indeed, as shown in Appendix 2, the backwards motion of the system (30), starting from B in the direction W remains in the triangle OBH of Figure 2 (this is the delicate part of the proof). Then, there exists a heteroclinic orbit for (30) and hence a heteroclinic equilibrium.

The conclusion is summarized in the next statement:[7]

PROPOSITION 2   Assume that $\alpha < \frac{1}{2}$, $\beta \geqq \beta*$. Then there exist a family of trajectories $(x^s, s \in Z)$ of the system (30) with the following properties:

(i) $\forall s \in Z, 0 < x^s < x^{s+1} < \bar{e}$.

(ii) $\lim_{s \to +\infty} x^s = \bar{e}$.

(iii) $\lim_{s \to -\infty} x^s = 0$.

A specific equilibrium can be chosen by fixing arbitrarily (below $\bar{e}$) labour supply for $M = M^0$. To each choice is associated an heteroclinic equilibrium in the sense of Section 2 (hence there is a one-dimensional family of such heteroclinic equilibria).

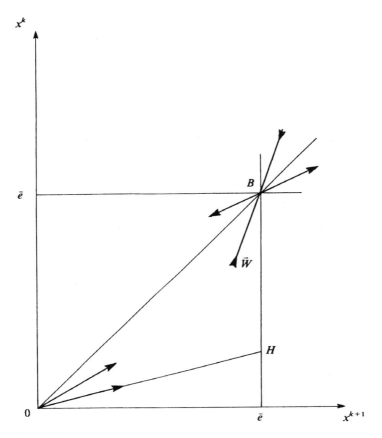

Figure 5.2

Also, it is interesting, for reasons that will become clear in the next section, to explicitly introduce the money supply process in the system; i.e., let us now take the vector

$$\begin{pmatrix} x^s \\ x^{s-1} \\ M^s \end{pmatrix}$$

as the state variable. The dynamical system becomes, with previous notation:

$$
\begin{pmatrix} x^{s+1} \\ x^s \\ M^s \end{pmatrix} = \overline{\Phi} \begin{pmatrix} x^s \\ x^{s-1} \\ M^{s-1} \end{pmatrix} = \begin{pmatrix} \overline{\Lambda}(x^s, x^{s-1}) \\ x^s \\ \lambda M^{s-1} \end{pmatrix}. \tag{32}
$$

As already remarked, $\overline{\Lambda}$ does *not* depend explicitly on M^s. A consequence is that this dimensional system is degenerate, in the sense that its projection upon the first two axes constitutes an autonomous dynamical system, which can be studied separately.

Along the third axis, the system is also autonomous, and orbits increase from zero to infinity. Since the exposition will be easier with a bounded support, we shall make the following change in variable:

$$
M'^s = \frac{M^s}{1 + M^s}
$$

and the system becomes:

$$
\begin{pmatrix} x^{s+1} \\ x^s \\ M'^s \end{pmatrix} = \overline{\Phi}' \begin{pmatrix} x^s \\ x^{s-1} \\ M'^{s-1} \end{pmatrix} = \begin{pmatrix} \overline{\Lambda}(x^s, x^{s-1}) \\ x^s \\ \lambda M'^{s-1}/1 + (\lambda - 1)M'^{s-1} \end{pmatrix}. \tag{33}
$$

Note that when $M^s \in \,]0, +\infty[$, $M'^s \in \,]0, 1[$; however, the above system is also defined on $[0, 1]$.

Lastly, the system does not have stationary points for M'^s in $]0, 1[$; but it may admit "quasi-stationary" orbits—i.e., trajectories whose projection upon the first two axes is a point. Clearly, these correspond to stationary points of the two-dimensional autonomous system followed by (x^{s+1}, x^s). Also, they can be associated to stationary points of the general system, either for $M'^s = 0$ or for $M'^s = 1$. The Proposition 2 can be immediately transposed to the system (33):

COROLLARY Assume $\alpha < \frac{1}{2}$ and $\beta \leq \beta^*$. Then the system (33) admits a two-dimensional heteroclinic manifold between $0 = (0, 0, 0)$ and $B = (\bar{e}, \bar{e}, 1)$. For each (x^s, x^{s-1}, M^{s-1}) on the manifold, $0 < x^{s-1} < x^s < \bar{e}$.

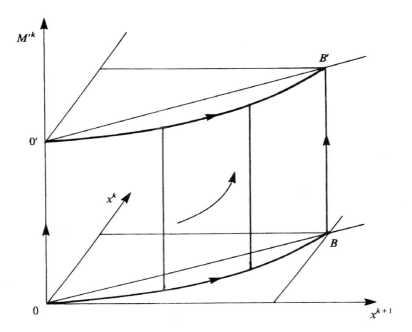

Figure 5.3

The phase diagram of the general system (33) represented on Figure 5.3 for $\beta \geqq \beta^*$. The two quasi-stationary orbits OO' and BB' correspond to the stationary points of the sub-system. In addition, the two-dimensional heteroclinic manifold between O and B is represented; specifically, the manifold is a cylinder whose projection over the (x^s, x^{s+1}) plane coincides with the (one-dimensional) heteroclinic manifold of the sub-system (30).

A last remark is that the previous solution is *not* the only heteroclinic sunspot equilibrium that can be generated by the money supply process we consider. Assume, for instance, that indices are reversed in people's expectations; i.e., agents believe that labour supply is x^s whenever money supply is M^{-s}. The difference is that, now, the transition probability from x^s to x^{s+1} is $(1 - \alpha)\beta$ (rather than $\alpha\beta$), and conversely from x^s to x^{s-1}. The fulfillment condition then becomes:

$$\forall s \in Z, \quad x^s V'(x^s) = (1-\alpha)\beta x^{s+1} U'(x^{s+1}) + (1-\beta)x^s U'(x^s)$$
$$+ \alpha\beta x^{s-1} U'(x^{s-1}). \tag{34}$$

Of course, the previous results apply to this new setting simply by "running the dynamical system in the opposite direction," i.e., replacing s by $-s$. Hence the following result:

PROPOSITION 3   Assume that $\alpha > 1/2$, $\beta \geq \beta^*$. Then there exist a continuum of trajectories of the system (3.12) with the following properties:

(i) $\forall s \in Z, 0 < x^s < x^{s-1} < \bar{e}$.

(ii) $\lim_{s \to +\infty} x^s = 0$.

(iii) $\lim_{s \to -\infty} x^s = \bar{e}$.

Proof Immediate. ‖

In this case, the "general" system including M^s can also be reformulated: the task is left to the reader.

It can be stressed that Proposition 3 leads to qualify a property of the heteroclinic solutions exhibited in Proposition 2, i.e., the fact that they have "Keynesian" features (in the sense that the level of activity increases with money supply). Proposition 3 indeed shows that "anti-Keynesian" solutions exist as well (see however Section 4).

3.3   A Particular Case

To conclude this section, we specialize the model described above by setting $U(x) = x$.

First, note that the basic equation (29) now becomes:

$$x^s V'(x^s) = (1-\alpha)\beta x^{s-1} + (1-\beta)x^s + \alpha\beta x^{s+1}, s \in Z. \tag{35}$$

In particular, the equation is globally invertible; it becomes

$$x^{s+1} = \frac{1}{\alpha\beta}[1 - \beta - V'(x^s)]x^s + \frac{1-\alpha}{\alpha}x^{s-1}. \tag{36}$$

Since (36) is a particular case of (29), Proposition 2 obviously applies. But the set of solutions may be much larger. Indeed, assume that the domain of y is unbounded, i.e., that $V'(y) < +\infty$ for all $y \geq 0$. Then we have the following result:

PROPOSITION 4

(a) Consider the functional equation, and assume that $\alpha < \frac{1}{2}$. There exist at least three families of heteroclinic sunspot equilibria. More precisely:

- for the first family, labour supply is always greater than $\bar{e}$ and decreases with money supply asymptotically towards $\bar{e}$.
- for the second family, labour supply is always greater than $\bar{e}$, starts asymptotically from $\bar{e}$ when money supply tends to zero and increases with money supply:

A specific heteroclinic equilibrium can be chosen in each family by fixing arbitrarily (but above $\bar{e}$) labour supply for M^0; in particular, both families are one-dimensional.

- for the third family, labour supply remains above $\bar{e}$, first decreases with money supply and then increases.

The third family is a two-dimensional family, the vector of labour supplies for M^0 and M^1 can be chosen arbitrarily in a two-dimensional area of the plane.

(b) Assume, in addition, that

$$\beta \geq \beta^* = \frac{1 - 1/\mu}{1 - \sqrt{4\alpha(1-\alpha)}}.$$

Then, besides the family of Proposition 2, there exists an additional family in which labour supply tends to zero when money supply tends to zero, increases with money supply, and tends to $+\infty$ with money supply.

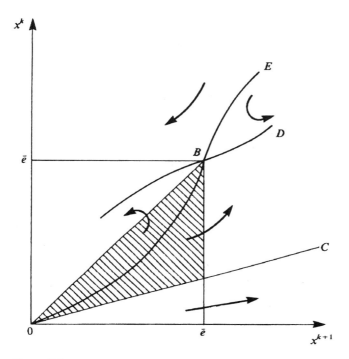

Figure 5.4

The latter family is a two-dimensional family; vector of labour supplies for M^0 and M^1 can be chosen arbitrarily in a two-dimensional area of the plane.

Proof See Appendix 2. ‖

The phase diagram for the case $\beta > \beta^*$ is given in Figure 5.4. The reader can easily check the following correspondence between families and orbits in the phase diagram:

· first family: part *EB* of the stable manifold in *B*;
· second family: part *BD* of the unstable manifold in *B*;
· third family: any orbit in the area *BED*

and, under the additional assumption $\beta \geqq \beta^*$:

• fourth family: any orbit, starting from O, between OC and OBD; to which one should add a fifth family, given by Proposition 2, and represented by the heteroclinic orbit OB (unstable manifold in O, stable manifold in B).

The fact that labour supply may be unbounded is somewhat unrealistic. It however allows us to provide a new illustration of the nature of random-walk equilibria. Indeed, viewing the point at infinity as a (degenerate) steady state, all equilibria of Proposition 4 can be considered as heteroclinic equilibria.

At this point, one should note that the analytical solutions of the Lucas equation (Lucas (1972)) found in Chiappori and Guesnerie (1991a) have the same qualitative features as those of the second family of Proposition 4. Indeed, similar analytical solutions can be computed in the present model (for a log-normal rate of increase of money supply).[8] They correspond to the limits of the Chiappori and Guesnerie (1991a) solutions of the Lucas equation when the real shock tends to zero.

Lastly, the solutions described above are not the only possible heteroclinic equilibria. Indeed, we may use the same trick as in Proposition 3 above—i.e., run the system in the opposite direction. On Figure 5.3, this will generate new families of solutions; e.g., the fourth family above will be transformed into an orbit starting from infinity when money supply is zero, and converging to autarky when money supply tends to infinity. The precise list of such solutions is left to the reader.

IV   Heteroclinic Equilibria with Intrinsic Money Supply

In the previous example, the economy we considered was homogeneous, in the sense that the equilibrium relationship only depended on money *balances*. The quantity of money was not a true fundamental of the economy. It could only influence real output through sunspot effect; in fact, the fundamentals of the economy were all constant, and the only source of randomness was extrinsic. In particular, the "sunspot" solutions (in which real output was following a random process) were obviously different, and could easily be distinguished from, the two "non-sunspot" stationary equilibria, in which real output was constant.

In this section, we modify the model in a way that does not preserve homogeneity. Now, money supply becomes a fundamental of the economy, the fluctuations of which do have an impact upon real output even in the absence of "sunspot-like" effects. Clearly, the basic intuition does not fundamentally depend on money being the source of fluctuation; any other fundamental of the economy (e.g., initial endowments) may (presumably) lead to similar insights. An interesting conclusion which emerges from the example we consider is that whenever the model at stake is (slightly) more complex than the basic one, it may become very difficult to distinguish, *even conceptually*, between the fluctuations caused by the "fundamental" role of the variable (here, money supply) and those due to "sunspot type" effects. Specifically, we show that *all bounded rational expectations equilibria* (but autarky) of the new setting are of the heteroclinic kind. They can be classified in two families (at least); one is "sunspot connected," in the sense that it converges to a pure sunspot solution when the non-homogeneity component of the model tends to disappear, whereas the other is "non-sunspot connected," in the sense that it tends to stationary solutions. But in the non-homogeneous framework, both families have similar properties, and no clear-cut criterion can separate the sunspot and the non-sunspot solutions.

4.1   The Model

In order to introduce a non-homogeneity component into the model, we assume that government intervention, besides the random shock x_t on money balances, also includes a level G_t of public expenditures; the latter are financed through a lump-sum tax on old agents. Non-homogeneity arises because government expenditures are not constant in real terms; rather, we shall suppose that they are fixed in *nominal* terms, except for very low money supply, where they are made proportional to money supply (this last feature being necessary to avoid unbounded expenditures in real terms). Formally:

$$G_t = \text{Min}(\overline{G}, \sigma M_t). \tag{37}$$

Then the first-order conditions characterizing agent's behaviour become:

$$V'(x_t) = \frac{p_t}{M_t} E\left[\frac{M_{t+1}}{p_{t+1}} U'\left(\frac{M_{t+1}}{M_t} \frac{p_t x_t}{p_{t+1}} - \text{Min}\left(\frac{\overline{G}}{p_{t+1}}, \sigma \frac{M_{t+1}}{p_{t+1}}\right)\right)\right]. \tag{38}$$

Here, money is no longer neutral in general because any change in money supply, by altering the price level, also modifies the real level of government expenditures (except for low levels of money supply). In particular, using the equilibrium conditions (which are still $M_t = p_t x_t$ and $M_{t+1} = p_{t+1} x_{t+1}$), we get

$$x_t V'(x_t) = E\left[x_{t+1} U'\left(x_{t+1} - \text{Min}\left(\frac{\overline{G} x_{t+1}}{M_{t+1}}, \sigma x_{t+1}\right)\right)\right]. \tag{39}$$

Here, as expected, the basic equation explicitly depends on M_{t+1}, unless either $\overline{G} = 0$, or $\sigma = 0$, or U' is constant.

We introduce now the random process followed by (M_t), which is still defined by (26)–(28). The support $X = (x^s, s \in Z)$ of the random process (x_t) is defined recursively by the self-fulfilment condition: $\forall s \in Z$,

$$
\begin{aligned}
x^s V'(x^s) = {}&(1-\alpha)\beta x^{s-1} U'\left[x^{s-1} - \text{Min}\left(\frac{\overline{G} x^{s-1}}{M^{s-1}}, \sigma x^{s-1}\right)\right] \\
&+ (1-\beta) x^s U'\left[x^s - \text{Min}\left(\frac{\overline{G} x^s}{\lambda M^{s-1}}, \sigma x^s\right)\right] \\
&+ \alpha\beta x^{s+1} U'\left[x^{s+1} - \text{Min}\left(\frac{\overline{G} x^{s+1}}{\lambda^2 M^{s-1}}, \sigma x^{s+1}\right)\right]
\end{aligned} \tag{40}
$$

(where we have used the fact that $M^{s+1} = \lambda M^s = \lambda^2 M^{s-1}$).

We shall give below conditions on U which guarantee that (40) can be inverted in x^{s+1}. Then we can deduce, from this equation, a well defined dynamical system:

$$\begin{pmatrix} x^{s+1} \\ x^s \\ M^s \end{pmatrix} = \Phi \begin{pmatrix} x^s \\ x^{s-1} \\ M^{s-1} \end{pmatrix} = \begin{pmatrix} \Lambda'(x^s, x^{s-1}, M^{s-1}) \\ x^s \\ \lambda M^{s-1} \end{pmatrix} \tag{41}$$

where the function Λ' is implicitly given by (40). This system is reminiscent of system (32) in the previous section. A major difference, however, is that now the three-dimensional system is no longer degenerate, since x^{s+1} explicitly depends on M^{s-1}.

Just as before, we make a change in variable aimed at studying trajectories with bounded support. Hence, we define $M'^s = M^s / (1 + M^s)$, which leads to the system

$$\begin{pmatrix} x^{s+1} \\ x^s \\ M'^s \end{pmatrix} = \Phi' \begin{pmatrix} x^s \\ x^{s-1} \\ M'^{s-1} \end{pmatrix} \tag{42}$$

where x^{s+1}, as a runction of x^s, x^{s-1} and M'^{s-1}, is derived from Λ' or (40) in a straightforward way, and

$$M'^s = \frac{\lambda M'^{s-1}}{1 + (\lambda - 1) M'^{s-1}}. \tag{43}$$

Again, we consider (42) as a dynamical system upon $R_+^2 \times [0, 1]$. As it can easily be seen, the system admits four stationary points:

$$O = (0, 0, 0) \tag{44}$$

$$O' = (0, 0, 1) \tag{45}$$

$$B = (e, e, 0) \tag{46}$$

$$B' = (\bar{e}, \bar{e}, 1) \tag{47}$$

where, as before, $V'(\bar{e}) = U'(\bar{e})$, and e satisfies $V'(e) = U'[(1 - \sigma)e]$.

Note that $e > \bar{e}$. In what follows, we shall be interested in hetero-clinic orbits between those points. For this reason, we shall consider (42) as a system on $[0, e]^2 \times [0, 1]$. If hypothesis (23) is strengthened as follows:

$$\forall x \in [0, e], \quad \frac{d}{dx}[xU'(x)] = U'(x) + xU''(x) > 0, \tag{48}$$

then (40) can be solved in x^{s+1} whenever $x^{s+1} \in [0, e]$.

4.2   Non-Homogeneous Heteroclinic Equilibria

We now study the system (42). Specifically, we are interested in demonstrating the existence of trajectories $(x^s, s \in Z)$ which (i) satisfy (40), (ii) remain within $[0, e]$. This problem is solved by the following result:

PROPOSITION 5   Assume that $\alpha < \frac{1}{2}$ and

$$\beta > \beta^* = \frac{1 - V'(0)/U'(0)}{1 - \sqrt{4\alpha(1-\alpha)}}.$$

Then

(i) there exist four one-dimensional families of heteroclinic trajec-tories, respectively from O to O', from O to B, from O' to B' and from B to B';

(ii) there exists a two-dimensional family of heteroclinic trajectories from O to B'.

Proof   See Appendix 3.   ‖

The precise meaning of this result can be better understood from Figure 5.5, which represents the phase diagram of the system (42). The heteroclinic trajectories OO', OB and $O'B'$ are of little interest; they correspond respectively to autarky and the limit cases in which the quantity of money is either zero or infinite. The two remaining

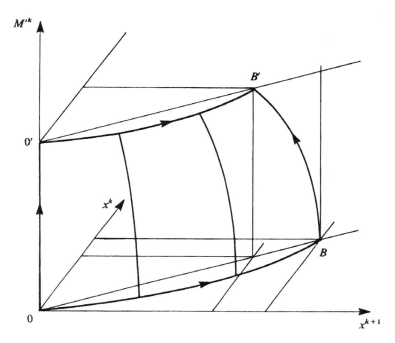

Figure 5.5

families are much more interesting. First, the *BB'* orbits correspond to heteroclinic equilibria which are "non-sunspot connected";
indeed it can be shown (see Chiappori and Guesnerie (1988)) that
when non-heterogeneity vanishes in the model (e.g., by letting $\overline{G}$
and/or σ go to zero), then the trajectory converges to a "quasi-
stationary" orbit in which real output is constant, while money
supply fluctuates randomly. More simply, a quick comparison
between Figures 5.3 and 5.5 suggests the basic intuition, namely that
the *BB'* orbit in Figure 5.5 is a "deformation" of the vertical orbit in
Figure 5.3. In the same way, the two-dimensional heteroclinic manifold between O and B' is very similar to the one in Section 3.

   In addition, the dimensions are important. The *BB'* orbit is one-
dimensional *within the three-dimensional set in which the system* (42)
is considered. This means that, for the reference quantity of money

M^0, there exists a *unique level* of labour supply x^0 compatible with a non-sunspot connected equilibrium. In contrast, the level of labour supply corresponding to M^0 can be freely chosen in the sunspot-connected set.

The following proposition translates the previous results in terms of heteroclinic equilibria:

PROPOSITION 6

(i) Assume that $\alpha < \frac{1}{2}$. There exists an heteroclinic rational expectations equilibrium with the following characteristics; when money supply tends to zero, labour supply tends to e; when money supply tends to infinity, labour supply tends to $\bar{e}$. For intermediate values of money supply, labour supply remains between $\bar{e}$ and e.

(ii) Assume that the stochastic process on money supply is such that $\beta > \beta^*$. Then, there exists a one-dimensional family of heteroclinic rational expectations equilibria with the following characteristics: when money supply tends to zero, labour supply tends to zero; when money supply tends to infinity, labour supply tends to $\bar{e}$.

The one-dimensional family can be parametrized by taking $M^0 = 1$ and choosing accordingly the couple (x^0, x^1) in an appropriate one-dimensional subset.

Remark   As in the previous section, it should be stressed that other solutions can be derived by "reversing the dynamics," i.e., replacing s by $-s$. This task is left to the reader.

The above statement shows the persistence under non-homogeneity of the types of solutions detected in the homogenous case. There are however a number of differences between the homogenous and the non-homogenous cases:

(i) Although a number of "sunspot-connected" solutions still have the Keynesian features of the sunspot equilibria of the homogenous case (i.e., the level of activity varies monotonically with money supply), others do not exhibit such features (the level of activity may decrease for high values of money supply but decrease for low values).

(ii) Again, the evolution of the dynamical system should not be confused with the probabilistic process followed by the relevant variables of the system. Also, except for the trivial equilibrium corresponding to the orbit OO' (labour supply always equal to zero), no solution is quasi-stationary, (i.e. such that labour supply is constant). Along any other equilibrium trajectory, labour supply depends on the quantity of money in a rather complex way; furthermore, the random process followed by labour supply is non-stationary.

This last point is worth emphasizing. In the homogenous case, it could be argued that the "stationary" solution $\bar{e}$ was the "most natural" one. On the one hand, unbounded equilibria could be dismissed as "unrealistic" (though this point deserves a more precise argument in this kind of over-simplified model). On the other hand, when compared to "sunspot" equilibria, "stationary" ones had two obvious advantages, namely simplicity (it could be expressed under a very simple and universally valid form, namely "real output tomorrow" will be $\bar{e}$ whatever M''_{t+1}) and stationarity. On the contrary, in the non-homogenous case, none of these criteria can be used to decide in favour of the "stationary equilibrium-connected" solutions (as opposed to the sunspot-connected ones). In other words, the analysis of this section in contrast to the intuition from the homogenous case—makes the "sunspot connected" and the "non-sunspot-connected" solutions candidates with *a priori* comparable credentials.

V Conclusion

This chapter explored the existence of a particular category of rational expectations equilibria, that we term random walk heteroclinic equilibria. The results reported suggest two provisional conclusions.

First, in systems with multiple steady states, random walk heteroclinic equilibria are likely to exist, possibly for many candidate "extrinsic" random walks. In particular, the necessary condition of Proposition 1 (especially when applied to both directions) can be viewed as rather weak in two different senses:

· considering a given economic system that has (at least) two steady states, the set of random walks (of the kind under consideration) that are good candidates for supporting a heteroclinic equilibrium (in the sense that they meet the necessary conditions of Proposition 1) is usually large.

· in general, for a given random walk, the necessary condition of Proposition 1 will be satisfied but for special (though robust) configurations of the dynamics of the associated system. The analysis in Section 2 indeed suggests that, in a very loose sense, these special configurations become less likely as the dimension of the state space increases.

Although Proposition 1 introduces restrictions that are surprisingly weak, existence proofs may still face serious analytical difficulties. In particular, our method of extension of the local solutions to the global solutions in Section 3 cannot be easily generalized.

A second conclusion is that these equilibra will have (non-sunspot) counterparts in systems where fundamentals follow random walks—a case that seems difficult to rule out for economic modelling.

Clearly, these conclusions require confirmation from further studies. Furthermore, their relevance for a positive theory of economic systems remains to be ascertained (something that is true for many studies in the theory of rational expectations). However, it seems clear that the exploration started here is a necessary step in any comprehensive and thorough understanding of the rational expectations construct.

Appendix 1

Proof of Proposition 1

We may first easily check that the eigenvectors of the forward dynamics associated with the eigenvalue γ, at any steady state, must be of the form $(\gamma^k v, \ldots, \gamma^{-k+1} v)$. Then linearizing the equilibrium equation (5) around a steady state and using (CD) repeatedly, we obtain the following relationship between γ and v:

$$\sum_{j=-k}^{j=k} \alpha_j (\partial_1 Z) \gamma^j v + (\partial_0 Z) v = 0.$$

Multiplying by $(\partial_0 Z)^{-1}$, we get:

$$-\sum_{j=-k}^{k-1} \alpha_j \gamma^j B v + v = 0. \tag{A.1}$$

Around the steady state $\bar{E}^U$, $B = \bar{B}$ and (A.1) shows that the function $\bar{\Lambda}$ of (7) and then the "forward" dynamical system (9) can be defined around $\bar{E}^U$. Also, it is clear from (A.1) that v must be an eigenvector of $\bar{B}$ for some eigenvalue $\bar{\mu}$ (since Bv and v are co-linear); and the γ must then satisfy:

$$\sum_{j=-k}^{+k} \alpha_j \gamma^j = 1/\bar{\mu}. \tag{A.2}$$

Now, a necessary condition for having a heteroclinic equilibrium (with $\bar{E}^U$ as the "upper" limit steady state) is that $\bar{E}^U$ is not a source for the system (9)—or, equivalently, that the system has at least one attracting direction in $\bar{E}^U$.

The first conclusion of Proposition 1 states precisely that there exists some $\bar{\mu}$ and a solution $\bar{\gamma}$ of (4) of modulus smaller than one. Also, the case of the other steady state can be deduced immediately, by noticing that:

- The forward (or the backwards) dynamical system is well-defined around $\bar{E}^L$.

- A necessary condition for the existence of a heteroclinic solution is that $\bar{E}^L$ is not a source for the backwards dynamical system (or a sink for the forward dynamical system).

The conditions obtained are stated symmetrically in Proposition 1. ‖

Appendix 2

Proof of the Proposition in Section III and Propositions 2 and 4

(a) The first step is to characterize the solutions of equation (31). This is done in the following lemma:

LEMMA 1   If $0 < \mu < 1$, then equation (31) has two real, positive roots; one is larger than one, one is smaller than one. If $\mu \geq 1$, the roots of (31) depend on α and β as stated in Figure A1.

Proof   By straightforward computation of the roots of (31).   ‖

Hence, the upper steady state is always a saddle point (and satisfies the corresponding requirement in Proposition 1). The lower steady state also satisfies the requirements when either it is a saddle point (case $\beta < \frac{1}{2}(1 - 1/ \underline{\mu})$) or it is a source (case $\alpha \leq \frac{1}{2}$, $\beta \geq \frac{1}{2}(1 - 1/\underline{\mu})$); it does not in the remaining case ($\alpha \geq \frac{1}{2}$, $\beta \geq \frac{1}{2}(1 - 1/\underline{\mu})$). (Note, however, that in the last case a permutation of the steady states ensures that the requirements are fulfilled).

An important remark is that in the particular model we are considering, non-negativity constraints should be added for the lower steady state; indeed, the latter corresponds to a zero labour supply, and negative labour supplies would be meaningless. This means that we shall be primarily interested here with the case in which at least one root is *positive*—and, of course, the steady state

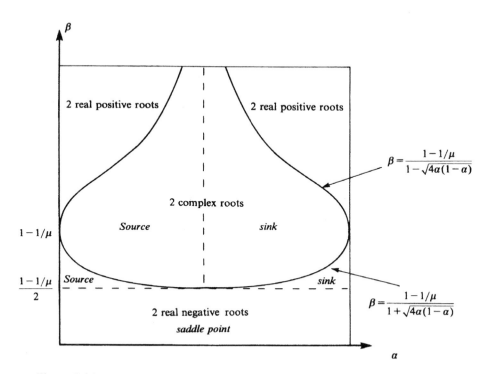

Figure 5.A1

is not a sink. The only possibility, then, is that $\alpha \leq \frac{1}{2}$ and

$$\beta \geq \beta^* = \frac{1 - 1/\mu}{1 - \sqrt{4\alpha(1 - \alpha)}}.$$

In the remainder of the proof, we shall consider this case only.

The corresponding eigenvectors are depicted in Figure 2 in the text (the proof is left to the reader).

(b) Global results for backwards dynamics. We now establish the existence of an heteroclinic trajectory of the system (30) between the two steady states. The crucial result is the following:

LEMMA 2   Suppose that $\beta \geq \beta^*$, and that there exists some $K \in N$, such that:

(H_K) $0 < \dfrac{x^{K+1}}{\gamma} < x^K < x^{K+1} \leqq \bar{e},$

where γ is one arbitrary eigenvalue at the lower steady state.

Then, for all $k \leqq K$:

(H_k) $0 < \dfrac{x^{k+1}}{\gamma I} < x^k < x^{k+1} \leqq \bar{e}.$

Proof   It is sufficient to prove that $(H_k) \Rightarrow (H_{k-1})$. Assuming that (H_k) is true, (34) gives:

$$\forall k \in Z,\ x^{k-1}U'(x^{k-1}) = \frac{1}{\beta(1-\alpha)}x^k[V'(x^k) - (1-\beta)U'(x^k)]$$
$$- \frac{\alpha}{1-\alpha}x^{k+1}U'(x^{k+1}). \tag{A.3}$$

Now, since $x^k \leqq \bar{e}$, we know that $V'(x^k) < U'(x^k)$; and $x^{k+1} > x^k$ implies that $x^{k+1}U'(x^{k+1}) > x^kU'(x^k)$. Hence:

$$x^{k-1}U'(x^{k-1}) < \frac{1}{\beta(1-\alpha)}x^k\beta U'(x^k) - \frac{\alpha}{1-\alpha}x^kU'(x^k) = x^kU'(x^k)$$

which implies that $x^{k-1} < x^k$.

Also, $U'(x^{k-1}) > U'(x^k)$; hence

$$x^{k-1} = \frac{1}{\beta(1-\alpha)}x^k\left(\frac{V'(x^k)}{U'(x^{k-1})} - (1-\beta)\frac{U'(x^k)}{U'(x^{k-1})}\right) - \frac{\alpha}{1-\alpha}x^{k+1}\frac{U'(x^{k+1})}{U'(x^{k-1})}$$
$$> \frac{1}{\beta(1-\alpha)}x^k\left(\frac{V'(x^k)}{U'(x^k)} - (1-\beta)\right) - \frac{\alpha}{1-\alpha}x^{k+1}$$

Lastly, $x^k > 0$ implies $U'(x^k) < U'(0)$, and $V'(x^k) > V'(0)$; moreover from (H_k), we have that $x^{k+1} < \gamma x^k$. Hence,

$$x^{k-1} > \frac{1}{(1-\alpha)\beta}x^k\left(\frac{V'(0)}{U'(0)} - (1-\beta)\right) - \frac{\alpha}{1-\alpha}\gamma x^k = \frac{x^k}{\gamma},$$

by the definition of γ. $\|$

This Lemma immediately implies the existence of a heteroclinic orbit, as described in Proposition 2. Indeed, take any point X on the south-west part of the stable manifold in the upper steady state, "close enough" to the upper steady state. By forward dynamics, the orbit starting from X converges to the upper steady state. But if X is "close to" the upper steady state, then it satisfies condition (H_K) of Lemma 5; this, in turn, implies that the orbit, by backwards dynamics, converges to 0.

Proof of Proposition 4

Since the model studied here is a particular case of the one studied above, the second part of Proposition 4 is an immediate consequence of Proposition 2. In order to prove the first part, we now characterize the backward dynamics of the north-east part of the stable manifold in the upper steady state.

LEMMA 3   Assume that, for some $K \in \mathbb{N}$, the following relation is satisfied;

(H_K') $x^K > x^{K+1} > \bar{e}$.

Then, for all $k \leq K$:

(H_k') $x^k > x^{k+1} > \bar{e}$.

Proof   We show that $(H_k') \Rightarrow (H_{k-1}')$. Since $x^k > \bar{e}$, $V'(x^k) > 1$. Moreover, $-x^{k+1} > -x^k$; hence:

$$x^{k-1} > \frac{1}{(1-\alpha)\beta}(\beta x^k) - \frac{\alpha}{1-\alpha}x^k = x^k. \quad \|$$

Lemma 3 immediately implies the following conclusion:

By backward dynamics, the north-east part of the stable manifold in B tends to infinity.

In the same way, we characterize the forward dynamics.

LEMMA 4   Suppose there exists $K \in N$ such that:

(H_K'') $(\bar{e} \leq x^K$ and $x^{K-1} < x^K)$.

Then, for all $k \geq K$,

(H_k'') $(\bar{e} \leq x^k$ and $x^{k-1} < x^k)$.

Proof   We show that $(H_k'') \Rightarrow (H_{k+1}'')$. Again, $V'(x^k) \geq 1$ and $-x^{k-1} > -x^k$. Then the basic equation implies

$$x^{k+1} > \frac{1}{\alpha\beta}(\beta x^k) - \frac{1-\alpha}{\alpha} x^k = \geq \bar{e}. \quad \|$$

COROLLARY

(a) The north-east part of the instable manifold tends to $+\infty$ by forward dynamics, and remains within the translation at the upper steady state of the positive orthant.

(b) For any $x \in [\bar{e}/\gamma_2, \bar{e}]$, where γ_2 is the larger eigenvalue at the lower steady state, the orbit defined by $x^0 = x$, $x^1 = \bar{e}$ tends to $+\infty$ by forward dynamics, and converges to 0 by backward dynamics; it remains within the positive orthant.

(c) For any $x > \bar{e}$, the orbit defined by $x^0 = x^1 = x$ tends to $+\infty$ by both forward and backward dynamics, and remains within the translation at the upper steady state of the positive orthant.

Proof   (a), (b), (c): immediate from the above Lemmas (left to the reader). $\|$

Appendix 3

Proof of Proposition 5

The existence of heteroclinic orbits from O to O' is trivial, and that of orbits from O to B and from O' to B' is immediate from Proposition 3. The difficult part, of course, is to show the existence of orbits from O to B', on the one hand, and from B to B' on the other hand.

(1) Local behaviour (in a neighbourhood of a stationary point). Let us compute the matrix of derivatives of Φ' at each stationary point. For $M' = 0$, the system (40) becomes:

$$\alpha\beta x^{s+1}U'((1-\sigma)x^{s+1}) = x^s V'(x^s) - (1-\beta)x^s U'((1-\sigma)x^s)$$
$$- (1-\alpha)\beta x^{s-1}U'((1-\sigma)x^{s-1}), \tag{A.4}$$

and for $M' = 1$:

$$\alpha\beta x^{s+1}U'(x^{s+1}) = x^s V'(x^s) - (1-\beta)x^s U'(x^s) - (1-\alpha)\beta x^{s-1}U'(x^{s-1}). \tag{A.5}$$

(a) *In $O = (0, 0, 0)$*: the matrix is

$$B_0 = \begin{bmatrix} \dfrac{1}{\alpha\beta}\left(\dfrac{V'(0)}{U'(0)} - 1 + \beta\right) & -\dfrac{1-\alpha}{\alpha} & 0 \\ 1 & 0 & 0 \\ 0 & 0 & \lambda \end{bmatrix}.$$

This matrix has three eigenvectors; two of them are in the plane $M'^k = 0$, the third is orthogonal. All eigenvalues are real and greater than one; hence the point is a source. The three eigenvectors are depicted in Figure 5.A2(a).

(b) *In $B = (e, e, 0)$*: where $V'(e) = U'((1 - \sigma)e)$, the matrix is

$$\overline{B} = \begin{bmatrix} \dfrac{1}{\alpha\beta}\left(\dfrac{V'(e)+eV''(e)}{U'(e)+(1-\sigma)\bar{e}U''(e)} - 1 + \beta\right) & -\dfrac{1-\alpha}{\alpha} & 0 \\ 1 & 0 & 0 \\ 0 & 0 & \lambda \end{bmatrix}.$$

Two eigenvectors are in the plane $M'^k = 0$; the eigenvalues are real and positive, one is greater than 1, one is smaller than 1. The last eigenvector is orthogonal to the plane, and is associated with the eigenvalue λ. Hence, there is a two-dimensional unstable manifold, and a one-dimensional stable manifold (Figure 5.A2(d)).

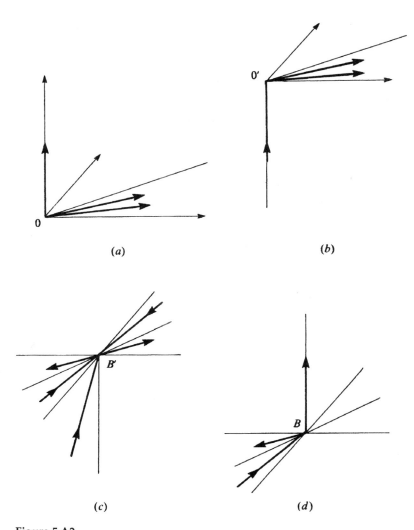

(a)   (b)

(c)   (d)

Figure 5.A2

(c) *In $O' = (0, 0, 1)$*: with the exception of the last diagonal element, the matrix is identical to

$$B' = \begin{bmatrix} \dfrac{1}{\alpha\beta}\left(\dfrac{V'(0)}{U'(0)} - 1 + \beta\right) & -\dfrac{1-\alpha}{\alpha} & 0 \\ 1 & 0 & 0 \\ 0 & 0 & 1/\lambda \end{bmatrix}.$$

Hence this steady state has a stable manifold of dimension 1, and an unstable manifold of dimension 2, as shown in Figure 5.A2(b).

(d) *In $B' = (\bar{e}, \bar{e}, 1)$*: the matrix is

$$\bar{B}' = \begin{bmatrix} \dfrac{1}{\alpha\beta}\left(\dfrac{V'(\bar{e}) + \bar{e}V''(\bar{e})}{U'(\bar{e}) + (1-\sigma)\bar{e}U''(\bar{e}) - 1 + \beta}\right) & -\dfrac{1-\alpha}{\alpha} & 0 \\ 1 & 0 & 0 \\ 0 & 0 & 1/\lambda \end{bmatrix}.$$

Again, two eigenvectors are in the plane $M'^k = 0$. The respective eigenvalues are real, respectively greater and smaller than 1. The last eigenvector is associated with the eigenvalue $1/\lambda > 1$; it is of the form (x, y, z) with $0 < x = 1/\lambda y < y$ (and $z > 0$ or < 0, depending on the parameters).

Thus B' has a two-dimensional stable manifold and a one dimensional unstable manifold (see Figure 5.A2(c)).

(2) Global behaviour: A recursive result. We now show a result on global behaviour of a subset of orbits. Precisely:

LEMMA 5 Let γ be such that $\alpha\beta\gamma^2 - ([V'(0)/U'(0)] - 1 + \beta)\gamma + \beta(1 - \alpha) = 0$. Suppose that, for some $K \in N$,

$$(H_K) \quad 0 < \frac{x^K}{\gamma} < x^{K-1} < x^K < e.$$

Then, for every $k \leq K$, the following relation is satisfied:

$$(H_k) \quad 0 < \frac{x^k}{\gamma} < x^{k-1} < x^k > e.$$

In words: consider any point in $]0, e[^2 \times [0, 1]$, whose projection upon $]0, e[^2$ is beneath the diagonal but above the line $x_{k-1} = x_k/\gamma$. Then, by backwards dynamics, the projection will always remain in this area.

Proof   Define:

$$F^s(x, y, z) = xV'(x) - (1-\beta)xU'\left\{x\left(1 - \text{Min}\left(\frac{\overline{G}}{\lambda^s}, \sigma\right)\right)\right\}$$

$$- \alpha\beta yU'\left\{y\left(1 - \text{Min}\left(\frac{\overline{G}}{\lambda^{s-1}}, \sigma\right)\right)\right\}$$

$$- (1-\alpha)\beta zU'\left\{z\left(1 - \text{Min}\left(\frac{\overline{G}}{\lambda^{s-1}}, \sigma\right)\right)\right\}.$$

Then (40) is equivalent to $F^s(x^s, x^{s+1}, x^{s-1}) \equiv 0$.

We now show that $(H_k) \Rightarrow (H_{k-1})$. Assume that some real numbers x, y satisfy $0 < y/\gamma < x < y < e$. Then the number z, defined by $F^k(x, y, z) = 0$, belongs to $(x/\gamma, x)$.

Indeed, on the one hand, since U' is decreasing:

$$F^k\left(x, y, \frac{x}{\gamma}\right) > xV'(x) - U'(0)\left[(1-\beta)x + \alpha\beta y + (1-\alpha)\beta\frac{x}{\gamma}\right].$$

Also, $y < e$, and $V'(x) > V'(0)$; hence:

$$F^k\left(x, y, \frac{x}{\gamma}\right) > xU'(0)\left[\frac{V'(0)}{U'(0)} - (1-\beta) - \alpha\beta\gamma - (1-\alpha)\frac{\beta}{\gamma}\right] = 0,$$

by the definition of γ; hence $F^k(x, y, x/\gamma) > 0$ for all k.

On the other hand:

$$F^k(x, y, x) < xV'(x) - (1-\beta)xU'(x) - \alpha\beta yU'(y) - (1-\alpha)\beta xU'(x).$$

But, $yU'(y)$ is increasing in y, and $y > x$ then gives

$$F^k(x, y, x) < xV'(x) - xU'(x) < 0.$$

Since $F^k(x, y, x/\gamma)$ and $F^k(x, y, x)$ have opposite sign, the solution z of $F^k(x, y, z) = 0$ must belong to $(x/\gamma, x)$.   ∥

(3) Existence of a heteroclinic manifold between O and B'. From the preceding argument, it is easy to deduce the existence of a heteroclinic manifold of dimension 2 between O and B'. Indeed, consider any point X on the "south-west" part of the stable manifold in B', "close to" B', and which third coordinate is strictly less than 1. Then, from the study of the eigenvectors of the stable manifold in B', it is clear that the first two coordinates of X satisfy (H_K) for some ("high") K. Consider the backwards dynamics starting from X. First, the projection of the orbit onto the plane defined by the first two coordinates remains within the shaded area of Figure 1, and is decreasing (since $x^{k-1} < x^k$ for all $k \leq K$). So it must converge to (O, O). Also, the third coordinate obviously converges to zero. Hence the orbit in $]0, e[^2 \times]0, 1]$ converges to O. And, by definition of the stable manifold, the forwards dynamics converges to B'; hence, there exists an heteroclinic manifold between O and B'. Lastly, the dimension of this manifold is exactly the dimension of the stable manifold in B', namely 2.

In particular: for any (*given*) value of M^0, there exists a one-dimensional continuum of points in the plane $M^k = M^0$, belonging to the heteroclinic manifold.

(4) Existence of a heteroclinic manifold between B and B'. The technique, here, is quite different from above, and relies upon a fixed-point theorem in an adequate space. Define, first, the mapping G^s, s belonging to N, by:

$$G^s(t, x, y, z) = tV'(t) - (1 - \beta)xU'\left\{x\left(1 - \text{Min}\left(\frac{\overline{G}}{\lambda^s}, \sigma\right)\right)\right\}$$
$$- \alpha\beta yU'\left\{y\left(1 - \text{Min}\left(\frac{\overline{G}}{\lambda^{s+1}}, \sigma\right)\right)\right\}$$
$$- (1 - \alpha)\beta zU'\left\{z\left(1 - \text{Min}\left(\frac{\overline{G}}{\lambda^{s-1}}, \sigma\right)\right)\right\}.$$

Consider the set $E = \Pi_{-\infty}^{+\infty}[\bar{e}, e]$, and define a mapping ∇, from E to E, by:

$$\nabla : \{x^k\} \to \{z^k\}$$

s.t. $\forall k \in$, $G^k(x^k, x^{k-1}, x^k, x^{k+1}) = 0$.

We must first check that G^s actually maps E into E. But, since U' is decreasing, we know that, for all $x > 0$:

$$xU'(x) \leq xU'\left\{x\left(1 - \text{Min}\left(\frac{\overline{G}}{\lambda^s}, \sigma\right)\right)\right\} \leq xU'\{x(1-\sigma)\}.$$

For $\bar{e} \leq x \leq e$, this equation implies that:

$$-\bar{e}U'(\bar{e}) \geq -xU'(x) \geq -xU'\left\{x\left(1 - \text{Min}\left(\frac{\overline{G}}{\lambda^s}, \sigma\right)\right)\right\}$$

$$\geq -xU'\{x(1-\sigma)\} \geq -eU'\{e(1-\sigma)\}.$$

Hence:

$$G^k(e, x^{k-1}, x^k, x^{k+1}) \geq eV'(e) - eU'\{e(1-\alpha)\} = 0,$$
$$G^k(\bar{e}, x^{k-1}, x^k, x^{K+1}) \leq \bar{e}V'(\bar{e}) - \bar{e}U'(\bar{e}) = 0$$

Then z^k, defined as above, exists (and is uniquely defined) in E.

Now, ∇ is continuous. From Tychonoff's theorem, E is convex and compact. The Ky-Fan's extension of Brouwer's theorem to locally convex spaces allows us to conclude that ∇ has indeed a fixed point.

It remains to check that this fixed point is associated with a heteroclinic orbit of the dynamical system. First, the fixed point will satisfy (40) by construction. And it can easily be checked that a sequence in E, solution of (40) has necessarily $\bar{e}$ and e as accumulation points.

Acknowledgements

This chapter is a greatly revised version of Sections 4 and 5 of "Self-fulfilling Theories: the Sunspot Connection," that was circulated in

1988. We thank the Editors for helpful comments, and the referees for excellent suggestions. Thanks are also due to R. A. Dana and M. Florenzano for helpful discussions on the techniques used in Appendix 4, and to participants to seminars in Cambridge, London and Paris.

Notes

1. A sample of contributions dealing with sunspot equilibria in OLG models includes Azariadis (1981b), Azariadis and Guesnerie (1982a,b 1986), Farmer and Woodford (1984), Woodford (1986), Grandmont (1986), Peck (1987), Chiappori and Guesnerie (1989), Woodford (1990). The reader may also consult the surveys by Chiappori and Guesnerie (1991b), Guesnerie and Woodford (1992).

2. The intuition of this result is the following. Consider a sequence of states of the initial model that are of the form $\gamma^k v, \ldots, v, \ldots, \gamma^k v$, where v is an eigenvector of the deterministic dynamics defined by B. Then (13) basically says that v is (locally) an equilibrium of the system (6) when the latter can jump to $\gamma^k v, \ldots, \eta^k v$ with respective probabilities α_{-k}. Also, it should be noted that there is a close connection between the existence of germs of heteroclinic equilibria, that we stress here, and the divergence (or convergence) of learning processes that "extrapolate growth rates" in the sense that was recently emphasized by Grandmont and Laroque (1990) (see also note 6).

3. If the upper steady state has an eigenvalue of modulus smaller than one and the lower steady state has an eigenvalue of modulus greater than one then the random walk $\alpha_j = 1$, for some $\bar{j} < 0$ satisfies the necessary conditions under consideration. In this limiting case, the heteroclinic random walk equilibrium would only be a deterministic perfect-foresight equilibrium going from the upper steady state to the lower steady state (such equilibria are trivially known to exist in the one-dimensional model of next section). However the set of random walks meeting the condition of Proposition 1 does not reduce to those trivial limit cases: in particular, it is open and contains all symmetric random walks (see next footnote).

4. The necessary conditions given in Proposition 1 might have been strengthened so as to include structural stability requirements (for the heteroclinic orbit of the associated dynamical system). These would typically entail considerations on the respective dimensions of the stable and unstable manifold at each steady state. Though these requirements are too technical for our present purpose, it can be mentioned that many random walks of interest—including the symmetric ones—will still pass the strengthened test. Hence the general qualitative conclusion of this section—i.e. that the existence of "germs" of heteroclinic equilibria for a reasonably large subset of random walks, is the rule rather than the exception (or at least is not a pathological phenomenon)—would be preserved.

5. Note however that the equation is only defined for $x_t \geqq 0$, $x_{t+1} \geqq O$. Also, a deterministic dynamics in real consumption is possible even though money supply is random. The reason, of course, is that, because of "super neutrality", money is not a true fundamental of the economy.

6. As the reader will notice, this last part of the statement can be re-interpreted as an alternative proof that, at the "high" steady state, learning processes that extrapolate growth rates in the sense of Grandmont and Laroque (1990) are diverging. We were not aware of this interpretation when writing the first version of the chapter.

7. This result does not hold true for

$$\beta < \frac{1 - 1/\underline{\mu}}{1 - \sqrt{4\alpha(1-\alpha)}} .$$

Specifically, for

$$\frac{1 - 1/\underline{\mu}}{2} \leq \beta < \frac{1 - 1/\underline{\mu}}{1 - \sqrt{4\alpha(1-\alpha)}} ,$$

the heteroclinic orbit between O and B does *not* remain within the positive orthant (and, it does not define any longer a self-fulfilling theory). This, incidentally, suggests that in a model with government expenditures (as in Farmer-Woodford (1984)) where the second steady state lies in the interior of the state space, it is likely that these solutions would generate heteroclinic equilibria as well. For

$$\beta = \frac{1 - 1/\underline{\mu}}{2} ,$$

there is a local bifurcation in $0{:}0$ becomes a saddle point rather than a source.

Also, it should be stressed that the difficulty for generating a solution that would be associated with a symmetric random walk of the form ($\beta = 1$, $\alpha = \frac{1}{2}$) is due to the low value of k in the Markov process. With $\alpha_0 = 1 - \beta = 0$ and $\alpha_1 = \alpha = \alpha_{-1}$, equation (13) above has necessarily two solutions of modulus one (a tricky situation for studying a dynamical process); but this fact crucially depends on k being equal to one.

8. The computation identifies, along the lines of the previous contribution, the (infinite number of) terms of a power series.

III

Endogenous Fluctuations in N-Dimensional Systems

6

Stationary Sunspot Equilibria in an N Commodity World

Roger Guesnerie

I Introduction

Consider a natural phenomenon such as the appearance of sunspots. It is a natural and widely accepted idea that such a phenomenon might be an explanatory variable of observed economic facts only if it could be proved that there are some channels through which it affects the basic data of the economy. This view reflects a form of determinism in the explanation of economic activity which has been common to most past schools of thought of the profession. Modern theory opposes intrinsic uncertainty, which affects preferences, endowments, and technologies, to extrinsic uncertainty which has not such an effect, and the conventional wisdom stresses that only intrinsic uncertainty should influence economic activity.

The so-called sunspot equilibria do not fit this conventional wisdom. They are equilibria in which real activity depends on exogeneous events (the sunspots of our previous example) which do not have any "objective" influence on the economy (they influence neither crops nor preferences). In other words, beliefs which are "arbitrary" in the conventional wisdom of educated economists appear to be self-fulfilling and are as exactly validated by facts as are "non-arbitrary" beliefs. Such a possibility mentioned first by Shell (1977) and Cass and Shell (1980) was further demonstrated through an example of Azariadis (1981b). It is now well established and has been the subject of a number of studies, among which the previous papers of the author with Azariadis (1982ab, 1986) are of particular relevance for the present contribution. The reader is referred to Woodford's survey (1984) for a more detailed assessment of the subject.[1]

Although the sunspot phenomenon is now better understood, we are not close to having a satisfactory and general enough theory. Also, several implications of the phenomenon for the understanding of the more general question of rational expectations equilibria are not fully comprehended.[2] The subject is still in an exploration phase, and this article intends to be a contribution to the exploration. Its starting point is the previous Azariadis and Guesnerie paper (1986) (from now on, AG), which considers the existence of stationary sunspot equilibria in the framework of the simplest version of the overlapping generations model (from now on, the OLG model). There, extrinsic uncertainty follows a stationary process which can take two values at each date.[3] Also attention is focused only on stationary equilibria. The article provides sufficient conditions for the existence of sunspot equilibria,[4] and also a strong characterization result: in the simple OLG model under consideration, stationary 2 sunspot equilibria exist if and only if deterministic cycles of order 2 exist.

Clearly, AG's analysis has a number of restrictive features which can be briefly listed when, at the same time, the options of the present chapter will be presented and compared.

• AG only consider stationary sunspot equilibria. There are a number of (mutually non-exclusive) reasons to be interested in stationary sunspot equilibria. Let us stress two. First, stationary sunspot beliefs are more likely to emerge from learning processes. Second, the understanding of stationary sunspot equilibria may be a decisive step for the understanding of the phenomenon in its full generality. In the present paper, attention is again strictly focused on *stationary sunspot equilibria* (SSE). Also, only *binary extrinsic uncertainty*, determining what is called 2-SSE, is considered. If one has to acknowledge that this is a restriction to the analysis, one has also to stress that sunspot of order 2 are not as special as they look at first sight. In fact, in the system we are considering, it is most generally the case that the existence of SSE of order 2 imply the existence of SSE of any order. (See Sect. II.) Although the reciprocal is not true (SSE of order 2 do not necessarily exist when SSE of order k do), the statements obtained here have direct relevance for the understanding of k-sunspot equilibria. In particular, the sufficient conditions given through Theorems 1 and 3 for the existence of 2 sunspot equilibria are in general sufficient for the existence of k-sunspot equilibria. Also, the methodology developed for proving Theorems 1, 2, and 3 can be closely followed for proving extensions of these theorems. Only computational difficulties, and not methodological novelties, explain that such a generalization is not exactly routine.

· The other restrictions of the AG analysis are inherent to the use of the simple version of the OLG model. There are mainly two:

Only one commodity per period (plus money) is allowed. This is clearly a simplifying assumption. For example, it guarantees a unique stationary monetary equilibrium. Also, the consumer's demand for savings associated with stochastic forecast obtains from the deterministic savings function through a simple deformation, a fact which is crucial for the strong equivalence between 2 sunspots and cycles of order 2 demonstrated by AG. It is the *main purpose of the present paper to remove these restrictions by considering an* n-*commodity world.*

The basic equations which govern the dynamics of the system relate price(s) today to expected price(s) tomorrow. Neither past prices nor expected prices for a period beyond tomorrow explicitly enter the basic laws of motion of the system. The present paper maintains the assumption that the motion of the system is governed by a relationship between present prices and expected future prices; it considers a *one step forward looking dynamical system without memory*. This is undoubtedly a restrictive assumption since the most general version of an *n* commodity OLG model does not enter this framework (however, the two period life, separable OLG model considered in Section 7 does). More complex cases should be considered later, but the present reflection is likely to be a useful step in view of further developments.

The conclusions which are obtained will provide a number of insights, sometimes complementary, sometimes contradictory to the AG findings.

• The connections between *sunspots and cycles* are still holding in this more general framework, but in their weaker form. The existence of cycles implies the existence of SSE, but the converse cannot be shown any longer. The positive part of the result will not surprise the reader who has some knowledge of the previous article by AG, since it follows from the same continuity argument. Also, *sufficient conditions for the existence of cycles and SSE* will be provided which actually generalize those previously given in AG.

• The relationship between the *multiplicity* of equilibria and *the existence of sunspot equilibria* will also be a theme of this paper. This theme was not really present in AG where the model was much too simplistic to make it meaningful. The interest of this problem lies in the following remark: consider a model with perfect foresight in which there is, at some date, multiple equilibria. The perfect foresight hypothesis assumes that agents' expectations (for tomorrow) are (today) coordinated. It is, however, unclear why it would be so. An alternative hypothesis consists in assuming that the selection of equilibria is made by nature (i.e., by something analogous to sunspots) and that the selection process is common knowledge. It is often believed that this is what sunspot equilibria are about. Clearly, such sunspot equilibria are not trivial extensions of the corresponding perfect foresight equilibria (the stochastic expectation changes demand), but one can argue that in such contexts, sunspot equilibria only describe a way of selecting between multiple equilibria and hardly imbed a conceptual novelty. Although one knows that the sunspot phenomenon is deeper (the original Azariadis example (1981b) cannot be viewed as a selection between multiple equilibria), it remains that it is important to understand the role played by multiplicity in the emergence of some (categories of) sunspot equilibria. Several results shedding light on this subject will be given here.

· Finally, particular attention will be focused on *sunspot equilibria close to the stationary deterministic equilibrium*. The fact that such sunspot equilibria can be studied in their own is explicitly suggested by Woodford (1986). However, in the one-good model such sunspot equilibria have few easily noticeable peculiarities (they correspond to the limit Markov matrices involving that the sufficient inequality of AG holds with equality). In the n-commodity world under consideration here, SSE close to deterministic stationary equilibria can be characterized in the sharpest way. *Their occurrence turns out to be closely related to the deterministic (perfect foresight) dynamics of the system around the stationary equilibrium.* In fact, they are necessarily associated, in a way which will be made precise later, to the real eigenvalues (and the corresponding eigen vectors) of the matrix governing the local (forward) dynamics of the system.

II The Formal Model and Definition

Let us describe first the exogenous stochastic sunspot process. Let us assume first that the process can only take *two values a, b*

at each date. It is a Markovian process the transition matrix of which is

$$\Pi = \begin{pmatrix} 1 - \pi_{ab} & \pi_{ab} \\ \pi_{ba} & 1 - \pi_{ba} \end{pmatrix} \quad \begin{array}{l} 0 < \pi_{ab} < 1 \\ 0 < \pi_{ba} < 1 \end{array}$$

where π_{ab} (resp. π_{ba}) is the probability of passing from a to b (resp. b to a). Note that the matrix can be identified with two numbers π_{ab}, π_{ba}, the probabilities of change of state. We also note $\Pi = (\pi_{ab}, \pi_{ba})$. Remark that the random variables become independent at each time if and only if $\pi_{ab} + \pi_{ba} = 1$.

Now, the basic dynamical system we consider is associated with two mappings Z and $\tilde{Z}$

$$Z: \mathbb{R}_+^n \times \mathbb{R}_+^n \to \mathbb{R}^n$$

and

$$\tilde{Z}: \mathbb{R}_+^n \times \mathbb{R}_+^n \times \mathbb{R}_+^n \times \mathbb{R}_+ \to \mathbb{R}^n.$$

The mapping Z describes the prefect foresight dynamics; the today price equilibrium vector, $p_t \in \mathbb{R}_+^n$, and the (perfectly foreseen) price equilibrium vector at period $t + 1$, $p_{t+1} \in \mathbb{R}_+^n$, are bound to satisfy

$$Z(p_t, p_{t+1}) = 0. \tag{1}$$

The difference between Z and $\tilde{Z}$ is the following: Z describes *excess demand* when *forecasts are point estimates*; $\tilde{Z}$ describes *excess demand when forecasts are stochastic*. More precisely we assume that there are only two possible price vectors tomorrow p_{t+1}^1, p_{t+1}^2, and that the probability of the second one p_{t+1}^2 is α ($0 < \alpha < 1$) when the probability of the first (p_{t+1}^1) is $(1 - \alpha)$. Excess demand today is a function of prices today, of (possible) prices tomorrow p_{t+1}^1, p_{t+1}^2, and of the (commonly agreed upon) probability (of p_{t+1}^2), α. Equilibrium at period t requires

$$\tilde{Z}(p_t, p_{t+1}^1, p_{t+1}^2, \alpha) = 0 \quad 0 \leq \alpha \leq 1. \tag{2}$$

$\tilde{Z}$ is the excess demand function associated with stochastic forecasts.

Note that both mappings Z and $\tilde{Z}$ do not depend upon time, allowing for stationary solutions of the system. Z and $\tilde{Z}$ are assumed to be C^p ($p > 2$) on the interior of their domain.

Now, a number of consistency requirements are in order. They will be stated as assumptions (or axioms). It is an instructive exercise in consumer or producer theory (left to the reader) to show that individual (consumer or producer) excess demand derived from utility maximizing or profit maximizing assumptions under the forecasting conditions described above obey the next 2 axioms. Intuitive explanations for the validity of the axioms are provided below.

(A1)   Quantity Consistency

$$\begin{aligned}
Z(p_t, p_{t+1}) &= \tilde{Z}(p_t, p_{t+1}, p_{t+1}, \alpha), \quad \forall p_t, p_{t+1}, \alpha \\
&= \tilde{Z}(p_t, p'_{t+1}, p_{t+1}, 1) \\
&= \tilde{Z}(p_t, p_{t+1}, p'_{t+1}, 0) \quad \forall p_t, p'_{t+1}, p_{t+1}
\end{aligned} \tag{3}$$

(A2)   Consistency of Derivatives

$$\left(\partial_3 \tilde{Z}\right)_{(p, \bar{p}, \bar{p}, \alpha)} = \alpha\left(\partial_2 Z\right)_{(p, \bar{p})} \qquad \forall p, \bar{p}, \alpha \tag{4a}$$

$$\left(\partial_2 \tilde{Z}\right)_{(p, \bar{p}, \bar{p}, \alpha)} = (1 - \alpha)\left(\partial_2 Z\right)_{(p, \bar{p})} \quad \forall p, \bar{p}, \alpha \tag{4b}$$

$$\left(\partial_1 \tilde{Z}\right)_{(p, \bar{p}, \bar{p}, \alpha)} = \left(\partial_1 Z\right)_{(p, \bar{p})} \qquad \forall p, \bar{p}, \alpha \tag{4c}$$

where $\partial_3 \tilde{Z}$, $\partial_2 \tilde{Z}$, $\partial_1 \tilde{Z}$ are respectively the Jacobian matrices of the derivatives of excess demand (with stochastic forecasts) with respect to the third block of prices (p_{t+1}^2), the second block (p_{t+1}^1) and the first block (p_t) and $\partial_1 Z$, $\partial_2 Z$, are the Jacobian matrices of the derivatives of excess demand (with deterministic forecasts) with respect to the first and second blocks of prices (p_t) (p_{t+1}).

Before stating the next assumption, let us introduce the following mappings:

$$Z^2: (p_1, p_2) \rightarrow (Z(p_1, p_2), Z(p_2, p_1))$$

$$\tilde{Z}_\pi^2: (p_a, p_b) \rightarrow (\tilde{Z}(p_a, p_a, p_b, \pi_{ab}), \tilde{Z}(p_b, p_b, p_a, \pi_{ba})).$$

Given that Z^2 and $\tilde{Z}_\pi^2$ can be viewed as vector fields on $\mathbb{R}_+^{2n}$, the next assumption is

(A3)   Boundary Assumptions

(A3α)   Take the rectangle in $\mathbb{R}_+^{2n}$ defined by $m_{\lambda,h} \leq p_{\lambda,h} \leq M_{\lambda h}$, $h = 1$ ... n, $\lambda = t, t + 1$. For $m_{\lambda,h}$ small enough and $M_{\lambda,h}$ large enough, the vector field Z^2 points inwards.

(A3β)   Take some rectangle in $\mathbb{R}_+^{2n}$ of the form defined above. $\forall \Pi = (\pi_{ab}, \pi_{ba})$, for $m_{\lambda,h}$ small enough, $M_{\lambda,h}$ large enough, (possibly dependent continuously upon Π) the vector field $\tilde{Z}_\pi^2$ points inwards.

Axiom (A1) (quantity consistency) is self-explanatory: The first part says if the two price forecasts p_{t+1}^1, p_{t+1}^2 are equal, the excess demand with stochastic forecast coincides with the perfect foresight excess demand. The second part is as much obvious.

Axiom (A2) (consistency of derivatives) is subtler: it says that, in the situation where initial forecasts are the same in events 1 and 2, the derivative of excess demand with respect to a price occurring tomorrow in event 2, i.e., with probability α, equals α times the derivative of excess demand with deterministic forecast with respect to the price of the same good. It is intuitively justified as follows. At the margin of a situation where the price vectors tomorrow are the same, a small price change only involves small uncertainty. The change of decision of an agent associated with a small uncertain price change is the same as the change of decision induced by a sure change whose magnitude is the expected value of the considered change (we are in a case in which parameters can be replaced by certain equivalents; see Malinvaud (1969)). Hence the formulas (4a) and (4b). (Note that (4c) derives from (A1) and is stated in (A2) only for convenience.)

Axiom (A3α) is a boundary assumption reminiscent of boundary assumptions validated by the utility or profit maximization hypothesis. Axiom (A3β) is an unsurprising extension to stochastic forecasts. Note, however, that in the frameworks of an OLG model, (A3) is valid for aggregate excess demand and not necessarily for individual excess demand of agents. (The fact that there is an old generation spending all its income in its last period of life plays a role.)

We are now in a position to give a number of definitions.

A *stationary price equilibrium* consists of a price vector p^* meeting

$$Z(p^*, p^*) = 0. \tag{5}$$

A *deterministic cycle of order* 2 is identified with a 2-uple of price vectors p_1^*, p_2^*, such that

$$Z\left(p_1^*, p_2^*\right) = 0 \tag{6α}$$

$$Z\left(p_2^*, p_1^*\right) = 0 \tag{6β}$$

$$p_1^* \neq p_2^*. \tag{6γ}$$

Equivalently p_1^*, p_2^* is a zero of the vector field Z^2 defined above.

A *stationary sunspot equilibrium* associated with the matrix $\Pi = (\pi_{ab}, \pi_{ba})$ (we will refer to it as a Π stationary sunspot equilibrium (Π-SSE) or as a (π_{ab}, π_{ba}) SSE or as a 2-SSE) is associated with price vectors p_a^*, p_b^*, such that

$$\tilde{Z}\left(p_a^*, p_a^*, p_b^*, \pi_{ab}\right) = 0 \tag{7α}$$

$$\tilde{Z}\left(p_b^*, p_b^*, p_a^*, \pi_{ba}\right) = 0 \tag{7β}$$

$$p_a^* \neq p_b^* \tag{7γ}$$

$$0 < \pi_{ab} < 1, \, 0 < \pi_{ba} < 1. \tag{7δ}$$

Equivalently p_a^*, p_b^*, is a zero of the vector field $\tilde{Z}_\pi^2$ defined above.

Definitions of *stationary equilibria and of* 2-*cycles* are classical and do not justify long comments. A SSE describes a situation in which all the agents believe that equilibrium prices are p_a^* (resp. p_b^*) when the natural event a (resp. b) occurs. When state a (resp. b) occurs, the probability of passing to b (resp. a) is π_{ab} (resp. π_{ba}); hence, Eq. (7α) (resp. (7β)) expresses the fact that the just described belief is self-fulfilling in state a (resp. b).

There are some obvious connections between stationary equilibria, 2-cycles and 2-SSE. Note, however, that the above definitions have an empty intersection: the 2-uple (p^*, p^*) built from a stationary equilibrium is neither a 2-SSE nor a 2-cycle (although it meets (6α), (6β) it does not meet (6γ)).

Also a 2-cycle is not a 2-SSE. Although, from (A1), (6α) and (6β) can be written:

$$\tilde{Z}\left(p_1^*, p_1^*, p_2^*, 1\right) = 0$$
$$\tilde{Z}\left(p_2^*, p_2^*, p_1^*, 1\right) = 0.$$

The corresponding Markov matrix $\Pi = \left(\begin{smallmatrix} 0 & 1 \\ 1 & 0 \end{smallmatrix}\right)$ is not acceptable because of (7δ). Note, however, that the fact of ruling out $\pi_{ab} = 1$, $\pi_{ba} = 1$ from the definition of 2-SSE is rather a matter of taste. With another semantic choice, cycles would only be SSE in which the natural events which govern price occurrences alternate with probability one. Here cycles rather appear as limits of 2-SSE.

This simple remark, made by AG (1986) is important to an understanding of SSE in the class of models under consideration here.[5] Particularly, here as in AG a continuity argument can be used to assert:

PROPOSITION 1   The following statement is "generically" true: If there exists a cycle of order 2 there exists an (infinity of) 2-SSE in the neighbourhood of the cycle.

It is left to the reader to give a more precise statement as well as a proof of the above proposition (an exercise in the application of Thom's transversality theorem, the basic object being the mapping $\tilde{Z}$). To avoid the burden of notation, I do not introduce a formal definition of k-sunspot equilibria (the detailed study of which is outside the scope of this paper). However, I state a second informal proposition, the proof and a rigorous statement of which are still left to the interested reader.

PROPOSITION 2   Assume that the system has (at least) one stationary equilibrium. Then, the following statement is "generically" true: To every $k - 1$ sunspot equilibrium which is not a bifurcation point of the mapping defining $k - 1$ sunspot equilibria (an extension to $k \geq 3$ of the above mapping $\tilde{Z}_n^2$), one can associate a (n infinity of) k-sunspot equilibrium (a).

The idea behind Proposition 2 is extremely simple. Take a $k - 1$ sunspot equilibrium. Add to the stochastic process a kth state with the following property: the probability of passing from the new state to itself is one, the probability of passing from one of the old states to the new one is zero. Associate with the new state, a stationary equilibrium price vector p^*. The k-uple constituted by p^* and the previous $(k - 1)$ equilibrium price vectors is a limit of a k-SSE (for a matrix which is forbidden because it contains 0 and 1). However, by continuity we can find true SSE (the fact that the initial $(k - 1)$ sunspot equilibrium is not a bifurcation point and the genericity consideration—for example GR1 below—intervene at this stage).

Proposition 2 makes clear that the results of the study we are just going to undertake have implications which go much beyond the class of 2-SSE to which we restrict attention.

III   Preparation Lemmas

The forthcoming analysis relies upon technical results, which are gathered here in three lemmas. Although these "preparation lemmas" are at the heart of the following theorems, their proofs may be skipped at first reading.

Consider the mapping $\tilde{Z}_\pi^2$ defined above (the zeros of which contain sunspot equilibria). It is associated with a given $\Pi = (\pi_{ab}, \pi_{ba})$ and defined on $\mathbb{R}_+^{2n}$. Consider now p^* a stationary equilibrium price vector (as defined by (5)). Let us consider the determinant of the Jacobian matrix of $\tilde{Z}_\pi^2$ in (p^*, p^*) and (dropping notation *) let us call it $\Delta(\Pi)$. Lemmas 1 and 2 provide explicit expressions for $\Delta(\Pi)$ when *Assumption A2 holds.*

LEMMA 1 $\Delta(\Pi) = (-1)^n \mid (\partial_1 Z)_{(*)} + (\partial_2 Z)_{(*)} \mid |(\pi_{ab} + \pi_{ba} - 1)(\partial_2 Z)_{(*)} - (\partial_1 Z)_{(*)}|$ where $| \,|$ designates a determinant and $(\partial_j Z)_{(*)}$ are the $n \times n$ square Jacobian matrices of the deterministic excess demand function evaluated at the stationary equilibrium (p^*, p^*).

Proof   We write $\Delta(\Pi)$ under the form

$$\Delta(\Pi) = \begin{vmatrix} \Delta_1 & \Delta_3 \\ \Delta_2 & \Delta_4 \end{vmatrix}$$

where Δ_i are $(n \times n)$ square matrices. For simplifying notation during the proof, we put $\pi_{ab} = \pi'$, $\pi_{ba} = \pi''$ and we drop the notation $(*)$. Since we are at the stationary equilibrium, (A2) (consistency of derivatives) implies

$$\Delta(\Pi) = \begin{vmatrix} (\partial_1 Z) + (1 - \pi')(\partial_2 Z), & \pi'(\partial_2 Z) \\ \pi''(\partial_2 Z) & , (\partial_1 Z) + (1 - \pi'')(\partial_2 Z) \end{vmatrix}.$$

The determinant does not change if we successively add the first column and the $(n + 1)$th column, then the second and the $(n + 2)$th, ..., then the pth and the $(n + p)$th, ...

Finally,

$$\Delta(\Pi) = \begin{vmatrix} (\partial_1 Z) + (\partial_2 Z), & \pi'(\partial_2 Z) \\ (\partial_1 Z) + (\partial_2 Z), & (\partial_1 Z) + (1 - \pi'')(\partial_2 Z) \end{vmatrix}. \tag{8}$$

Now let us perform a similar operation with lines: first, let us change the sign of lines $(n + 1)$ to $2n$ (the new determinant equals $(-1)^n$ the previous one). Let us add the first line and the $(n + 1)$th, ..., then, the pth line and the $(n + p)$th line, ... It becomes

$$\Delta(\Pi) = (-1)^n \begin{vmatrix} (\partial_1 Z) + (\partial_2 Z), & \pi'(\partial_2 Z) \\ 0 & , (\pi' + \pi'' - 1)(\partial_2 Z) - (\partial_1 Z) \end{vmatrix}. \tag{9}$$

Then we get (Laplace rule)

$$\Delta(\Pi) = (-1)^n |(\partial_1 Z) + (\partial_2 Z)| \, |-(\partial_1 Z) + (\pi' + \pi'' - 1)(\partial_2 Z)|. \tag{10}$$

Putting $\delta(\pi', \pi'') = |(\pi' + \pi'' - 1)(\partial_2 Z) - (\partial_1 Z)|$, we get

$$\Delta(\Pi) = (-1)^n |(\partial_1 Z) + (\partial_2 Z)| \delta(\pi', \pi''). \tag{10'}$$

Q.E.D.

LEMMA 2 $\Delta(\Pi)$ can be expressed as a polynomial of degree n in the variable $(\pi_{ab} + \pi_{ba})$

$$\Delta(\Pi) = a_0 + a_1(\pi_{ab} + \pi_{ba}) \ldots + a_p(\pi_{ab} + \pi_{ba})^p + \ldots a_n(\pi_{ab} + \pi_{ba})^n \tag{11}$$

where (with the same notation as in Lemma 1)

$$a_0 = |(\partial_1 Z)_{(*)} + (\partial_2 Z)_{(*)}|^2$$

$$\vdots$$

$$a_p = (-1)^{2n-p} |(\partial_1 Z)_{(*)} + (\partial_2 Z)_{(*)}|$$

$$\sum \left| \ldots, \left(\frac{\partial Z}{\partial p_k'} \right)_{(*)}, \ldots, \left(\frac{\partial Z}{\partial p_l'} \right)_{(*)} + \left(\frac{\partial Z}{\partial p_l} \right)_{(*)}, \ldots, \right|$$

where the last determinant is associated with a matrix formed of $n - p$ (different) columns of the matrix $(\partial_1 Z)_{(*)} + (\partial_2 Z)_{(*)}$ and p (different) columns of the matrix $(\partial_2 Z)_{(*)}$ and where the sum Σ is extended to all (C_p^n) such matrices:

$$a_n = (-1)^n |(\partial_1 Z)_{(*)} + (\partial_2 Z)_{(*)}| \, |(\partial_2 Z)_{(*)}|.$$

Proof Starting from (10'), we have to compute $\delta(\pi', \pi'')$. Let us write $\delta(\pi', \pi'')$ more explicitly as

$$\delta(\pi', \pi'') = \left| (\pi' + \pi'' - 1)\left(\frac{\partial Z}{\partial p_1'}\right) - \left(\frac{\partial Z}{\partial p_1}\right), \right.$$
$$\left. (\pi' + \pi'' - 1)\left(\frac{\partial Z}{\partial p_2'}\right) - \left(\frac{\partial Z}{\partial p_2}\right), \cdots, \right|$$

where $(\partial Z / \partial p_k)$, $(\partial Z / \partial p_k')$ are respectively the derivatives of Z (in p^*, p^*) with respect to the kth and the $(n + k)$th variables. A first decomposition gives

$$\delta(\pi', \pi'') = (\pi' + \pi'') \left| \frac{\partial Z}{\partial p_1'}, (\pi' + \pi'' - 1)\frac{\partial Z}{\partial p_2'} \right.$$
$$\left. -\frac{\partial Z}{\partial p_2}, \cdots, (\pi' + \pi'' - 1)\frac{\partial Z}{\partial p_k'} - \frac{\partial Z}{\partial p_k}, \cdots \right|$$
$$+ \left| -\frac{\partial Z}{\partial p_1'} - \frac{\partial Z}{\partial p_1}, (\pi' + \pi'' - 1)\frac{\partial Z}{\partial p_2'} \right.$$
$$\left. -\frac{\partial Z}{\partial p_2}, \cdots, (\pi' + \pi'' - 1)\frac{\partial Z}{\partial p_k'} - \frac{\partial Z}{\partial p_k}, \cdots \right|.$$

Each of the two determinants is itself decomposed from the second column according to the same principles, then each of the four determinants can again be decomposed according to the same principles (from the third column), and so on. After n steps, we get the expression of $\delta(\pi', \pi'')$. The lemma follows.

Lemma 3 establishes a connection between the zeros of Δ and the eigen-values of a matrix the interpretation of which will be given later.

LEMMA 3   Assume $|(\partial_1 Z)_{(*)} + (\partial_2 Z)_{(*)}| \neq 0$, $|(\partial_1 Z)_{(*)}| \neq 0$. Then $\Delta(\bar{\pi}_{ab}, \bar{\pi}_{ba}) = 0$ if and only if $1/(\bar{\pi}_{ab} + \bar{\pi}_{ba} - 1)$ is an eigenvalue of the matrix $(\partial_1 Z)^{-1}_{(*)}(\partial_2 Z)_{(*)}$

Proof   From Lemma 1 and the first assumption

$$\Delta(\bar{\pi}_{ab}, \bar{\pi}_{ba}) = 0 \Leftrightarrow |(\partial_1 Z)_{(*)} + (1 - (\bar{\pi}_{ba} + \bar{\pi}_{ab}))(\partial_2 Z)_{(*)}| = 0$$

$$\Leftrightarrow |I + (1 - (\bar{\pi}_{ba} + \bar{\pi}_{ab}))(\partial_1 Z)^{-1}_{(*)}(\partial_2 Z)_{(*)}| = 0$$

$$\text{since } |(\partial_1 Z)_{(*)}| \neq 0$$

$$\Leftrightarrow \left|(\partial_1 Z)^{-1}_{(*)}(\partial_2 Z)_{(*)} - \frac{1}{(\bar{\pi}_{ba} + \bar{\pi}_{ab} - 1)} I\right| = 0 \qquad \text{Q.E.D.}$$

IV   Sufficient Conditions for the Existence of Stationary Sunspot Equilibria: Sunspot Equilibria and Cycles

In this section and in the following, we always assume that the dynamical system under consideration satisfies A1, A2, and A3 above. In addition, we will restrict attention to functions Z and $\tilde{Z}$ which satisfy certain regularity assumptions.

(GR)   Generic Regularity

(GR1)   In any stationary equilibrium p^*, we have

$$|\partial_1 Z + \partial_2 Z|_{(p^*, p^*)} \neq 0, |\partial_1 Z - \partial_2 Z|_{(p^*, p^*)} \neq 0.$$

(GR2)   For all (π_{ab}, π_{ba}), but possibly on a set of measure zero of $]0, 1[\cdot]0, 1[$, for any (p_a, p_b) which is a zero of the mapping $\tilde{Z}^2_\pi(p_a, p_b)$ the determinant of the $(2n \times 2n)$ Jacobian matrix $D\tilde{Z}^2_\pi$ is different from zero, i.e., $|D\tilde{Z}^2_\pi| \neq 0$.

Assumption (GR1) calls for some regularity of the stationary equilibria when (GR2) asserts that for almost all Π, SSE are, in a standard sense, "regular." One guesses that if the set from which Z and $\tilde{Z}$ are extracted is "rich" enough (GR) is generic. Hence the terminology. More precise meaning of the genericity assumption could be given in the specific models considered in Section VII.

We are now in a position to state and prove the following theorem.

THEOREM 1   Sufficient Conditions for the Existence of 2-Cycles and of 2-SSE. Assume that the dynamical system meets (GR1) and (GR2) (generic regularity). Suppose that there exists a unique stationary equilibrium p^* in which the following condition holds:

(C) $\mathrm{Sign}\, |\partial_1 Z + \partial_2 Z|_{p^*} \neq \mathrm{Sign}\, |\partial_1 Z - \partial_2 Z|_{p^*}$

Then

(1) $\exists q_0 < 2$ such that for any $\Pi = (\pi_{ab}, \pi_{ba})$ such that $q_0 < \pi_{ab} + \pi_{ba} < 2$, there exists a Π-SSE.

(2) q_0 is a zero of the polynomial of (maximal) degree n, given by (11) in Lemma 2 (the coefficients of which only depend on the first derivatives of (deterministic) demand at the stationary equilibrium).

(3) The system has a cycle of order 2.

Proof   The core of the argument is the one used in a different context by Azariadis and Guesnerie (1982a). Consider the stationary equilibrium p^*; for any given Π, the 2-uple (p^*, p^*) solves Eqs. (7α), (7β). Consider then the Jacobian of $\tilde{Z}_\pi^2$ in (p^*, p^*). Note that for almost all Π (from (GR2)), the Poincaré–Hopf theorem applies to the mapping $\tilde{Z}_\pi^2$ restricted to a rectangle conveniently chosen from (A3) (boundary condition). This means that the sum of the indices of the zeros of the mapping $\tilde{Z}_\pi^2$ (the index is +1 (resp. −1) if the determinant of the mapping is positive (resp. negative)) equals $(-1)^{2n}$. Now, if the determinant in (p^*, p^*) of the Jacobian of $\tilde{Z}_\pi^2$ has a sign *opposite* to the sign of $(-1)^{2n}$, i.e., has a negative sign, the system (7α),

(7β) has necessarily zeros other than (p^*, p^*). As these zeros cannot be stationary equilibria, they are necessarily SSE.

The determinant of the Jacobian of $\tilde{Z}^2_\pi$ has been computed in Lemmas 1 and 2. From Lemma 1, $\Delta(1, 1) = |(\partial_1 Z) + (\partial_2 Z)|_{(*)} \; |(\partial_1 Z) - (\partial_2 Z)|_{(*)}$ and from (C) it is strictly negative. Also, still from Lemma 1 (or 2) and with (GR1), $\Delta(0, 0) > 0$. Then there is at least one $q(= \pi_{ab} + \pi_{ba})$ between 0 and 2 such that $\Delta(\pi_{ab}, \pi_{ba}) = 0$. Let q_0 be the highest such q.

For every $\Pi = (\pi_{ab}, \pi_{ba})$ such that $\pi_{ab} + \pi_{ba} > q_0$, $\Delta(\pi_{ab}, \pi_{ba}) < 0$. For almost all such Π, the Poincaré–Hopf theorem applies and assures the existence of a Π-SSE. But a specific continuity argument allows us to show that Π-SSE also exist on the complementary set. Hence, (1) and (2) of the theorem. Part (3) follows immediately if one remembers that the exclusion of 2-cycles from the definition of 2-SSE is purely semantic.   Q.E.D.

When condition (C), which assures the existence of cycles of order 2, holds, Theorem 1 establishes the existence of a continuum of matrices Π for which there exists at least one Π-SSE. Note that the existence of such a set of matrices in the neighbourhood of the matrix associated with cycles (i.e., $\left(\begin{smallmatrix} 0 & 1 \\ 1 & 0 \end{smallmatrix}\right)$) could have been proved more cheaply as follows: (1) prove that (C) implies the existence of 2-cycles (the argument is the same as the above argument but with Z^2 instead of $\tilde{Z}^2_\pi$); (2) use a continuity argument (inspired from Proposition 1 above) to get zeros of $\tilde{Z}^2_\pi$ for neighbour Π. However, Theorem 1 shows more than what would have been obtained with the sketched argument. It identifies a set of matrices necessarily associated with SSE as a subset of the square which has the shape visualized as the shaded area of Fig. 6.1 (strictly speaking, the interior of the shaded area). Also, an inspection of the proof allows us to say more on the set of matrices for which SSE exists. Consider the polynomial of Lemma 2, $P(\lambda) = \Sigma^n_0 a_p \lambda^p$, and let Λ be the set of λ such that $P(\lambda) < 0$. Then, it follows from the proof of Theorem 1 that

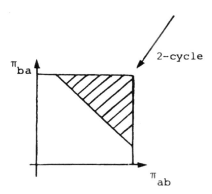

Figure 6.1

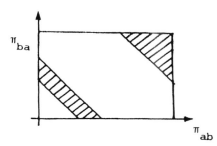

Figure 6.2

for every Π such that $(\pi_{ab} + \pi_{ba}) \in \Lambda$, there exists a Π-SSE. For example, if $P(\lambda)$ has three simple roots the set of matrices associated with SSE necessarily includes the disconnected shaded area of Fig. 6.2. After noting what the theorem says, let us stress what it does not say: First, although the area of the square which is identified by our statements is limited by lines of the equation $\pi_{ab} + \pi_{ba} = K$, it is *not true* that SSE only depend upon $\pi_{ab} + \pi_{ba}$. It will be seen from inspection of Theorem 3 that SSE tend to be similar in the neighbourhood of the lines of the frontier of the shaded area; however, they depend in general on π_{ab} and π_{ba} and not only on their sum. Second, it is not claimed that the entire set of matrices associated with SSE has necessarily the shape suggested by the diagrams. This is sometimes true, but not always. What is asserted here is that subsets having this shape are necessarily parts, under the condition of the theorem, of the entire set of matrices associated with SSE.

Finally, the methodology used for proving Theorem 1 can be duplicated for exhibiting sufficient conditions for the existence of k-sunspots equilibria. However, the expression giving the value of the determinant equivalent to $\Delta\left(\Pi\right)$ above is no longer as simple as the one given by the polynomial (11). In particular, the conditions would identify a set of matrices (in $\mathbb{R}^{k(k-1)}$) which is limited by surfaces and not hyperplanes (as happens with $k = 2$).[6]

V Sufficient Conditions for the Existence of Stationary Sunspot Equilibria: Sunspot Equilibrium as a Selection Between Multiple Equilibria

Let us come back now to the fulfillment mechanism described in Eqs. (7α), (7β). There are two possible readings of Eqs. (7) according to whether the mapping $\tilde{Z}(\cdot, \pi_{ab})$ and the mapping $\tilde{Z}(\cdot, \pi_{ba})$ are identical or not.

· If the mappings $\tilde{Z}(\cdot, p_a^*, p_b^*, \pi_{ab})$, $\tilde{Z}(\cdot, p_b^*, p_a^*, \pi_{ba})$ are not identical, the occurrence of a or b changes present behaviour. This is generally the case when $\pi_{ab} + \pi_{ba} \neq 1$, i.e., when the probability distributions of a and b tomorrow conditionally on a or b today differ. In that case, for believers in sunspot theory, the occurrence of a or b brings information on tomorrow. Such information, which again is information because sunspot theory is believed, changes behaviour in such a way that the belief $a \to p_a$, $b \to p_b$ is fulfilled.

· If the mappings $\tilde{Z}(\cdot, *, \pi_{ab})$, $\tilde{Z}(\cdot, *, \pi_{ba})$ are identical, then the reasoning breaks down. As argued above, such an identity of mappings should only occur systematically when $\pi_{ab} + \pi_{ba} = 1$. In that case, Eqs. (7) can still have several solutions (here, two at least) which then correspond to multiple zeros of the mapping $\tilde{Z}(\cdot, *, \pi)$. The SSE so obtained can be viewed as a random selection of multiple equilibria through the random process picking up a or b at each date.

It follows that SSE associated with a stochastic sunspot process of independent random variables should be given a specific status; they correspond to the polar case of SSE which are pure selections between multiple spot equilibria. Hence the following definition.

• A SSE, as defined through Eqs. (7), is called *non-informative* (*or semi-trivial, or of pure multiplicity*) if it is associated with a matrix Π such that $\pi_{ab} + \pi_{ba} = 1$.

Let us comment on the (optional) terminology. Non-information refers to the first explanation of SSE (sketched above). This explanation emphasizes the information brought by the occurrence of sunspots when the random variables are not independent; on the contrary, when they are independent, the occurrence of sunspots brings no information on tomorrow prices.[7] We already emphasized in the Introduction that such sunspot equilibria may not involve high conceptual novelty. However, it should be understood that such SSE are not trivial selections of multiple deterministic equilibria; here, the uncertainty of tomorrow prices does modify the behaviour today when compared to deterministic behaviour. Hence, the term semi-trivial. Finally, such SSE could be said SSE of pure multiplicity, since the natural events have the function to select between multiple equilibria. Let us be aware that there are no clear-cut lines between SSE which do not relate with multiplicity and SSE which do. For example, when the matrix Π is close to a non-informative one, both arguments, informativeness and multiplicity, can be invoked. However, SSE of pure multiplicity are unambiguous *polar cases*.

Before going further, let us introduce the following definition.

Given the deterministic system Z, we say that p_t is a *backward looking price equilibrium*, associated with fixed (tomorrow) prices $\bar{p}_{t+1}$ if

$$Z(p_t, \bar{p}_{t+1}) = 0.$$

Introduce now the (generic) regularity assumption (GR3).

(GR3) For any stationary equilibrium (p^*, p^*) and any backward looking equilibrium associated with p^*, $(\tilde{p}, p^*)$ then $|\partial_1 Z|_{(\tilde{p}, p^*)} \neq 0$.

The next theorem shows close connections between the existence of non-informative (or semi trivial) SSE and the occurrence of multiple equilibria in the deterministic system.

THEOREM 2 Sufficient Conditions for the Existence of Non-Informative SSE. Assume that (GR1), (GR2), (GR3) (Generic Regularity) hold. Then, each of the two following (mutually exclusive) conditions guarantees the existence of semi-trivial SSE.

1. There exist several stationary equilibria, but each of them has a unique backward looking equilibrium associated with it.

2. There exists a unique stationary equilibrium (p^*, p^*) but it meets the following sufficient condition for the existence of several backward looking equilibria associated with it: i.e., Sign $|\partial_1 Z|_{(p^*, p^*)} = $ Sign $(-1)^{n+1}$.

Proof The proof has 6 steps.

Step 1: This step consists in noticing that (A3α) implies that the vector fields on $\mathbb{R}^n_+$: $p_t \to Z(p_t, \bar{p}_{t+1})$, $p \to Z(p, p)$ have the property of pointing inwards on "well chosen" rectangles (of the form $m_h \leqslant p_h \leqslant M_h$).

Step 2: The following is shown: Under (A3α) and (GR1), the number of stationary equilibria is odd. If this number is one then Sign $|\partial_1 Z + \partial_2 Z|_{p^*, p^*} = $ Sign$(-1)^n$. If this number is strictly greater than one, then there is at least one in which Sign $|\partial_1 Z + \partial_2 Z|_{p*,p*} =$ Sign$(-1)^{n+1}$. This statement follows again from the Poincaré–Hopf theorem; it is applied to the vector field $p \to Z(p, p)$ (because of Step 1 above and (GR1)). The sum of the indices is $(-1)^n$,

Step 3: Assume there are several stationary equilibria; from Step 2 take one (call it $(p*, p*)$) such that Sign $|(\partial_1 Z) + (\partial_2 Z)| =$ Sign$(-1)^{n+1}$. As in the proof of Theorem 1 evaluate the Jacobian of $\tilde{Z}_\pi^2$ in $(p*, p*)$. From Lemma 1, taking Π such that $\pi_{ab} + \pi_{ba} = 1$ (assumption of non-informativeness) we get

$$\Delta(\Pi) = (-1)^{2n}|(\partial_1 Z) + (\partial_2 Z)| \, |(\partial_1 Z)| \tag{12}$$

where all derivatives are taken in $(p*, p*)$.

Step 4: The following is shown: Under (A3α) and (GR3), if a stationary equilibrium is such that Sign $|(\partial_1 Z)|_{(p*,p*)} =$ Sign$(-1)^{n+1}$, then there are multiple backward looking equilibria associated with $p*$. Conversely, if a stationary equilibrium is such that there exists a unique backward looking equilibrium associated with it, then Sign $|(\partial_1 Z)| =$ Sign$(-1)^n$. The proof of this assertion follows from the Poincaré–Hopf theorem which applies, thanks to Step 1 and (GR3), to the vector field $p \to Z(p, p*)$. Again the sum of indices is $(-1)^n$.

Step 5: Take the stationary equilibrium of Step 3, and assume that it has a unique backward looking equilibrium associated with it. From Step 4, Sign $|(\partial_1 Z)| =$ Sign$(-1)^n$. Given Step 3 and (12), it follows that Δ is strictly negative. The conclusion of the first part of Theorem 2 either follows from the Poincaré–Hopf theorem if Π belongs to the set identified in Assumption (GR2) or if not from the Poincaré–Hopf theorem for neighbour Π plus a continuity argument.

Step 6: The proof of the second part of Theorem 2 considers the unique stationary equilibrium and proceeds as in the proof of the first part.

But here Sign $|(\partial_1 Z) + (\partial_2 Z)| = \text{Sign}(-1)^n$ (Step 2),

and Sign $|(\partial_1 Z)| = \text{Sign}(-1)^{n+1}$ (Assumption)

Then $\Delta < 0$.

The proof terminates as in Step 5.   O.E.D.

VI Stationary Sunspot Equilibria in the Neighbourhood of Stationary Equilibria: Sunspot Equilibria and the Local Dynamics of the Deterministic System

Let us consider a stationary equilibrium (p^*, p^*). Let us linearize the deterministic system around (p^*, p^*). We get

$$(\partial_1 Z)_{(*)} x_t + (\partial_2 Z)_{(*)} x_{t+1} = 0$$

or with (GR3),

$$x_t = -(\partial_1 Z)_{(*)}^{-1} (\partial_2 Z)_{(*)} x_{t+1} = B x_{t+1} \qquad (13)$$

where $-(\partial_1 Z)_{(*)}^{-1}(\partial_2 Z)_{(*)} = {}^{\text{def}} B$ is the matrix governing the local dynamics of the linearized system. It is known from the general theory of dynamical systems that the local dynamics of the original system can be studied from the local dynamics of the linearized system as soon as B has no eigenvalue on the unit circle (see Irwin (11)).

We will assume

(GR4) The matrix (B) has no eigenvalue on the unit circle.

Now let us consider Eqs. (7) governing the occurrence of sunspot equilibria:

$$\tilde{Z}(p_a, p_a, p_b, \pi_{ab}) = 0$$
$$\tilde{Z}(p_b, p_b, p_a, \pi_{ba}) = 0. \qquad (7')$$

Assume that $(p_a, p_b, \pi_{ab}, \pi_{ba})$ is a SSE close to the stationary equilibrium. From A1, we know

$$\tilde{Z}(p^*, p^*, p^*, \pi) = 0 \quad \text{for} \quad \pi = \pi_{ab} \text{ and } \pi = \pi_{ba}.$$

Calling $\Delta p_a = p_a - p^*$, $\Delta p_b = p_b - p^*$, we have

$$(\partial_1 \tilde{Z})_{(\alpha)} \Delta p_a + (\partial_2 \tilde{Z})_{(\alpha)} \Delta p_a + (\partial_3 \tilde{Z})_{(\alpha)} \Delta p_b = \Delta p_a \cdot O_1(\Delta p)$$
$$(\partial_1 \tilde{Z})_{(\beta)} \Delta p_b + (\partial_2 \tilde{Z})_{(\beta)} \Delta p_b + (\partial_3 \tilde{Z})_{(\beta)} \Delta p_a = \Delta p_b \cdot O_2(\Delta p) \tag{14}$$

where $\Delta p = (\Delta p_a, \Delta p_b)$ and O_1, O_2 are functions tending to zero with $\|\Delta p\|$ and where $\alpha = (*, \pi_{ab})$ $\beta = (*, \pi_{ba})$.

From the consistency conditions (A2), we know

$$(\partial_1 \tilde{Z})_{(\alpha)} = (\partial_1 Z)_{(*)}, \quad (\partial_2 \tilde{Z})_{(\alpha)} = (1 - \pi_{ab})(\partial_2 Z)_{(*)}, \text{ etc.} \ldots$$

Then, dividing both equations by $\|\Delta p\|$ and calling $\Delta p_a / \|\Delta p\| = \dot{p}_a$, $\Delta p_b / \|\Delta p\| = \dot{p}_b$, we get

$$[(\partial_1 Z)_{(*)} + (\partial_2 Z)_{(*)} - \pi_{ab}(\partial_2 Z)_{(*)}]\dot{p}_a + \pi_{ab}(\partial_2 Z)_{(*)}\dot{p}_b = \varepsilon_1 \tag{15a}$$

$$\pi_{ba}(\partial_2 Z)_{(*)}\dot{p}_a + [(\partial_1 Z)_{(*)} + (\partial_2 Z)_{(*)} - \pi_{ba}(\partial_2 Z)_{(*)}]\dot{p}_b = \varepsilon_2 \tag{15b}$$

when ε_1, $\varepsilon_2 \to 0$ with $\|\Delta p\|$.

This analysis leads to the following formal lemma.

LEMMA 4 Take a sequence of (π_{ab}^n, π_{ba}^n) stationary sunspot equilibria associated with the price system (p_a^n, p_b^n) where $(\pi_{ab}^n, \pi_{ba}^n) \to (\bar{\pi}_{ab}, \bar{\pi}_{ba})$ and $(p_a^n, p_b^n) \to (p^*, p^*)$.

1. Then necessarily

$$\Delta(\bar{\pi}_{ab}, \bar{\pi}_{ba}) = |D\tilde{Z}_{\bar{\pi}}^2(*)| = 0. \tag{16}$$

2. Let $\Delta^n(p) = (p_a^n - p^*, p_b^n - p^*)$ and let a subsequence be such that $\Delta^n(p)/\|\Delta^n(p)\| \to \bar{p} = (\bar{p}_a, \bar{p}_b)$; then $(\bar{p}_a, \bar{p}_b)$ belongs to the kernel of $D\tilde{Z}_{\bar{\pi}}^2(*)$.

Proof The proof immediately follows from the considerations preliminary to the lemma. Taking the limit of Eqs. (15a), (15b), one gets

$$[(\partial_1 Z)_{(*)} + (\partial_2 Z)_{(*)} - \bar{\pi}_{ab}(\partial_2 Z)_{(*)}]\bar{p}_a + \bar{\pi}_{ab}(\partial_2 Z)_{(*)}\bar{p}_b = 0 \tag{17a}$$

$$\bar{\pi}_{ba}(\partial_2 Z)_{(*)}\bar{p}_a + [(\partial_1 Z)_{(*)} + (\partial_2 Z)_{(*)} - \bar{\pi}_{ba}(\partial_2 Z)_{(*)}]\bar{p}_b = 0 \tag{17b}$$

(with necessarily $\bar{p} \neq 0$). Hence the conclusion.[8]

We are now in a position to characterize SSE "close" to the stationary equilibrium.

THEOREM 3 Necessary Conditions for the Existence of Stationary Sunspot Equilibria Close to the Stationary Equilibrium. Take a stationary equilibrium of the deterministic system meeting (GR1) and assume that the matrix B (which governs the local dynamics of the deterministic system around the stationary equilibrium) satisfies (GR4). Take a sequence of (π_{ab}^n, π_{ba}^n) stationary sunspot equilibria associated with the price systems (p_a^n, p_b^n), and such that $(\pi_{ab}^n, \pi_{ba}^n) \rightarrow (\bar{\pi}_{ab}, \bar{\pi}_{ba})$. The price vectors sequence tends to the stationary equilibrium (p^*, p^*) only if the following holds

(1) $-(1/(\bar{\pi}_{ab} + \bar{\pi}_{ba} - 1)) = \bar{\mu}$ is a real eigenvalue (strictly greater than one in absolute value) of the matrix B (which governs the local dynamics of the deterministic system).

(2) For any subsequence such that $\lim_n (p_a^n - p^*, p_b^n - p^*)/\|(p_a^n - p^*, p_b^n - p^*)\|$ exists and equals $(\dot{p}_a, \dot{p}_b)$, then $\dot{p}_a$ and $\dot{p}_b$ belong to the tangent hyperplane to the stable manifold of the deterministic system in (p^*, p^*) and are colinear to an eigen vector $\bar{\lambda}$ associated with the real eigenvalue $\bar{\mu}$ of B, with the proportionality factors $\bar{\pi}_{ab}$ and $-\bar{\pi}_{ba}$.

Proof

(1) Immediately obtains from previous Lemma 4 and Lemma 3, Section III.

(2) To prove (2) let us subtract (17b) from (17a). We then have (arranging notation in a straightforward way)

$$[(\partial_1 Z) + (1 - \bar{\pi}_{ab} - \bar{\pi}_{ba})(\partial_2 Z)](\dot{p}_a - \dot{p}_b) = 0. \tag{18}$$

Multiplying (17a) and (17b) by $(\partial_1 Z)^{-1}$, we have

$$[I + (\partial_1 Z)^{-1}(\partial_2 Z)]\dot{p}_a = \bar{\pi}_{ab}(\partial_1 Z)^{-1}(\partial_2 Z)(\dot{p}_a - \dot{p}_b) \tag{19a}$$

$$\left[I+(\partial_1 Z)^{-1}(\partial_2 Z)\right]\dot{p}_b = \bar{\pi}_{ba}(\partial_1 Z)^{-1}(\partial_2 Z)(\dot{p}_b - \dot{p}_a). \tag{19b}$$

The following lemma is in order.

LEMMA 5   Consider A, C (($n \times n$) matrices) and μ, $v \in \mathbb{R}$. Suppose that the matrix $A + (1 - \mu) C$ is singular, A is invertible, and $I + A^{-1}C$ is invertible. Consider the equations $[I + A^{-1}C]x = vA^{-1}C\lambda$ where λ is a vector belonging to the kernel of $(I + (1 - \mu)C)$; then the only solution to these equations is $x = (v/\mu)\lambda$.

Proof λ being in the kernel of $A + (1 - \mu)C$, we have $[A + (1 - \mu)C]\lambda = 0$, and multiplying by A^{-1}, $[I + (1 - \mu)A^{-1}C]\lambda = 0$. So λ is an eigenvector of $A^{-1}C$ with eigenvalue $-1/(1 - \mu)$; then $vA^{-1}C\lambda = -(v/(1 - \mu))\lambda$ and the equation is written $(I + A^{-1}C)x = -(v/(1 - \mu))\lambda$. Looking for a solution $x = \alpha\lambda$ we get

$$\alpha - \frac{\alpha}{1-\mu} = -\frac{v}{1-\mu}, \quad \text{i.e.,} \alpha = \frac{v}{\mu}.$$

As $I + A^{-1}C$ is invertible $\alpha\lambda$ is the only solution.   Q.E.D.

Now considering (18) and (19a) (resp. 19b), the lemma applies with $A = \partial_1 Z$, $C = \partial_2 Z$, $\mu = \bar{\pi}_{ab} + \bar{\pi}_{ba}$, $\lambda = \dot{p}_a - \dot{p}_b$ (resp. $(\dot{p}_b - \dot{p}_a)$), $x = \dot{p}_a$ (resp. $\dot{p}_b$), $v = \bar{\pi}_{ab}$ (resp. $\bar{\pi}_{ba}$). Hence the conclusion.

Forgetting about the complications required for a rigorous statement, Theorem 3 provides a very simple characterization of SSE close to the stationary equilibrium. For such SSE, price p_a and p_b slightly depart from p^*, the difference $p_a^* - p^*$, $-(p_b - p^*)$ being in the direction of an eigenvector of B associated with a real eigenvalue μ of modulus greater than one. Furthermore, the matrices Π for which this occurs are such that $\pi_{ab} + \pi_{ba}$ is close to $1 - 1/\mu$, and the length of $p_a - p^*$, $-(p_b - p^*)$ is respectively (almost) proportional to $\bar{\pi}_{ab}$, $\bar{\pi}_{ba}$.

The question arises whether some reciprocal holds, i.e., whether one can build, from any real eigenvalue of modulus greater than one and from the corresponding eigenvector of B, SSE close to the stationary equilibria. To prove the converse, let us consider a one dimensional family of matrices $\Pi(\alpha)$ defined on $[\alpha_1, \alpha_2]$. Consider a real eigenvalue μ of B.

One can state

Assume the following:

(D1) (differentiability) $\Pi(\alpha)$ is C^1.

(S1) μ is a simple eigenvalue of B.

(RC) (regular crossing) $\Pi(\cdot)$ has a regular crossing with μ, i.e.,

(RC1) $-[\pi_{ab}(\alpha^*) + \pi_{ba}(\alpha^*) - 1]^{-1} = \mu$ for some $\alpha^* \in [\alpha_1, \alpha_2]$

(RC2) $\dfrac{\partial}{\partial \alpha}[\pi_{ab}(\alpha) + \pi_{ba}(\alpha)]_{(2*)} \neq 0$ for the same α^*.

One can state

THEOREM 4 Sufficient Conditions for the Existence of Stationary Sunspot Equilibria Close to the Stationary Equilibrium. Let p^* be an (isolated) stationary equilibrium of the dynamical system, and B be the associated matrix governing the local dynamics of the system around p^*. Consider a one dimensional differentiable (D1) family of matrices which has a regular crossing (RC) with a simple eigenvalue of B (S1), the modulus of which is strictly greater than one. Then, $\forall N$ a neighbourhood of (p^*, p^*)—in $\mathbb{R}^{2n}$—there exists $\alpha \in [\alpha_1, \alpha_2]$ such that N contains (at least) one $\Pi(\alpha)$-SSE.

Proof Call $\Delta(\alpha) = |D\tilde{Z}^2_{\pi(\alpha)}|$. From Lemma 3, $\Delta(\alpha^*) = 0$. From (RC2) one can choose α_1, α_2 such that Sign $\Delta(\alpha_1) \neq$ Sign $\Delta(\alpha_2)$ and Sign $\Delta(\alpha) \neq$ Sign $\Delta(\alpha')$ for $\alpha \in [\alpha_1, \alpha^*[$ and $\alpha' \in] \alpha^*, \alpha_2]$. Assume that there is a neighbourhood N of (p^*, p^*) such that $\tilde{Z}^2_{\pi(\alpha)}(p_a, p_b) \neq 0$, $\forall (p_a, p_b) \neq (p^*, p^*)$, $\forall \alpha$ in (α_1, α_2). Then there is an open bowl B of N such that on $B \cup \partial B/(p^*, p^*)$ (where ∂B is the boundary of B) $\tilde{Z}^2_{\pi(\alpha)} \neq 0$, $\forall \alpha$. Then, note the following:

First, as $\tilde{Z}^2_{\pi(\alpha)}(\cdot)$ is a smooth homotopy, the degree of $\tilde{Z}^2_{\pi(\cdot)}$ over ∂B is a homotopy invariant (cf. Milnor [1965, p. 28, Theorem B]).

Second, remember the definition of the degree of a vector field in one of its isolated zeros (Milnor, p. 32) and note that this definition

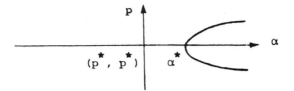

Figure 6.3

does not depend upon the small sphere chosen around the zero as soon as this sphere does not contain another zero. This latter point can be shown by contradiction using the findings of Milnor [1965, p. 28 Lemma 1] (the argument parallels the one leading to the Poincaré–Hopf theorem). Then the degree of $\tilde{Z}^2_{\pi(\cdot)}$ over ∂B is nothing else than the degree of the vector field $\tilde{Z}^2_{\pi(\cdot)}$ in (p^*, p^*). Consequently it changes when α crosses α^*. A contradiction to the first remark obtains and the theorem is proved.   Q.E.D.

From the theorem, one deduces that there exists a whole branch of equilibria in the neighbourhood of (p^*, p^*). However, the theorem is a priori compatible with different configurations of these branches, i.e., with different types of *bifurcations*.

For a one-dimensional system, it can be shown that the configuration of Fig. 6.3 actually occurs, i.e., that we have a *pitchfork* or *transcritical* bifurcation. I conjecture that a similar property is true in the more general case we are considering here.

VII   Application to the Overlapping Generations Model

Consider an overlapping generations (OLG) model in which at each date identical consumers of the old generation and consumers of the young generation coexist. Assume that there are n goods per period, instead of one in the standard version of this model. Consumers of the old generation only get $\overline{M}$ units of money and p_t is the price vector of commodities (in terms of money).

Assume also that the utility of consumers of each generation t is separable between period t and period $t + 1$. Then it is left to the reader to show that the perfect foresight equilibria are associated with the reduced[9] equation

$$d(p_t, \overline{M}) = s(p_t, p_{t+1})$$

where p_t, p_{t+1} are vectors of $\mathbb{R}^n_+$, where d is the demand function of an old consumer having income $\overline{M}$ and faced with the price system p_t, and where s is the (net) supply of a young consumer faced with p_t and expecting p_{t+1}.[10] Then

$$Z(p_t, p_{t+1}) = d(p_t, \overline{M}) - s(p_t, p_{t+1}) \qquad (20)$$

Note that it follows from the separability assumption that the matrix $(\partial_2 Z)$ is of rank one. This comes from the fact that $s(p_t, p_{t+1})$ can be written as a demand function $d'(p_t, R(p_t, p_{t+1}))$ (where $R(\ )$ is the net income spent at period t), so that $\partial_2 Z$ has columns all proportional to $\partial d' / \partial R$.

The matrix B governing the local dynamics is then of rank one. It is easy to check form (11) that

$$\Delta(\Pi) = |\partial_1 Z + \partial_2 Z|^2 - |\partial_1 Z + \partial_2 Z| \sigma_1 (\pi' + \pi'') \qquad (21)$$

with

$$\sigma_1 = \sum \left| \frac{\partial Z}{\partial p_k}, \ldots, \frac{\partial Z}{\partial p_i'}, \ldots, \frac{\partial Z}{\partial p_j}, \ldots \right| \qquad (22)$$

where the sum is over all matrices having one column $\partial Z / \partial p_i'$ (in the notation of Section III).

All these findings can be summarized in the following proposition.

PROPOSITION 3   In the n-commodity OLG model, the dynamics of which is governed by Eqs. (20), all results of Theorem 1, 2, 3 apply. However, the following specific facts can be noted.

(1) q_0 of Theorem 1 can be computed explicitly and equals $|(\partial_1 Z) + (\partial_2 Z)|/\sigma_1$ when σ_1 is defined in (22).

(2) The real eigenvalue appearing in Theorem 3 is unique and equals $-(1/(q_0 - 1))$. Hence there exists a unique direction of prices associated with 2-SSE in the neighbourhood of the stationary equilibrium.

Note that this latter result is closely related to Kehoe and Levine's (1984) result according to which separable OLG economies only have one dimension of indeterminacy. The "direction" of indeterminacy coincides with the dimension in which SSE are obtained.

Now in the one commodity OLG model, the general function Z identifies to $Z(\ ) = 1/p_t - s(p_t/p_{t+1})$. A simple computation shows that $|(\partial_1 Z) + (\partial_2 Z)| = -1/p^2$, $\sigma_1 = +s'/p$.

COROLLARY   If $n = 1$, $q_0 = 1/\varepsilon^*$ where $\varepsilon^* = -p^*(s')_{(*)}$ is the elasticity of supply of the young generations at the stationary equilibrium. The standard results on sufficient conditions for the existence of 2-cycles (Grandmont [1985]) or of 2-SSE (AG (1982]), AG [1986]) immediately obtain from this corollary and Theorem 1.

Conclusion

This chapter focuses on nonlinear n-dimensional one-step-forward-looking dynamical systems. It exhibits a number of results concerning the relationship between stationary sunspot equilibria and perfect foresight equilibria. Connections are hence established among deterministic cycles, deterministic stationary equilibria, and sunspot equilibria; also, the role of the multiplicity of deterministic perfect foresight equilibria for the existence of sunspot equilibria is analyzed.

Rational expectations solutions of n-dimensional linear dynamical systems are now reasonably well understood (see Broze and

Szafarz [1985]). The present paper hopefully goes one step further towards an understanding of the (more complex) nature of rational expectations solutions of *nonlinear n*-dimensional systems.

Acknowledgment

While writing the chapter, I benefited from conversations with J. Green, J. J. Laffont, and M. Magill. Comments from M. Woodford and F. Hahn at the Paris Conference, and more recently from S. Burnell, J.-M. Grandmont, C. Oddou, and the participants of seminars in Cambridge, Geneva, London (L.S.E.), Marseille, and Louvain, are gratefully acknowledged. I am particularly indebted to the referee. His thorough understanding of the issues and de-tailed comment helped me improve the content and presentation of the paper Remaining errors are mine.

Notes

1. For recent contributions on the subject, see Cass and Shell (1983), Farmer and Woodford [1984], Spear (1984).

2. A paper by Chiappori and Guesnerie (1991a) shows that the phenomenon of infi-nite multiplicity of stationary solutions in a model à la Lucas (1972) has a nature very similar to that of the sunspot phenomenon, although sunspots are explicitly absent from the analysis. A related point, relying on multiple equilibrium responses to government policy shocks, has been made by Farmer and Woodford (1984). Also, stochastic speculative bubbles relate to sunspot equilibria.

3. In the recent literature on sunspots, sunspot equilibria seem sometimes to be associated with a binary extrinsic uncertainty (sunspot, no sunspot). The term, however, is used in a broader sense; it will be convenient to use the term 2-sunspot equilibria to make clear that we consider processes having only two values and the term k-sunspot for processes with k values. The referee pointed out to me that in the old literature, the term sunspot did not suggest a binary random variable. "The original sunspot numbers were counts of the number of spots observed and the number took many more than two values. It was apparently the cyclical variations in these numbers that led Jevons to postulate that variations in solar activity caused business cycles. If it had been a binary variable, no one would have thought it looked like a deterministic cycle, and the connection would never have been suggested!"

4. They were already, for the essential, in Azariadis and Guesnerie (1982a,b); for related results, see also the article of Spear (1984).

5. The referee rightly mentioned to me that the connection between cycles and sunspot equilibria found here had no immediate counterpart in systems with memory (where for example excess demand depends upon p_{t-1}, p_t, p_{t+1}).

6. However, it would not be too difficult to check, that the projection on $\mathbb{R}^2$ of the set of matrices identified by the theorem in $R^{k(k-1)}$ would actually contain the subsets identified here by Theorem 1, a point which is in line with Proposition 2 above.

7. Concerning the informativeness issue, the referee rightly mentioned that what matters is not that a sunspot realization gives information about future sunspots, but that it gives information about future prices. It is true that one could have informative sunspot equilibria in the case of i.i.d. sunspot, if atttention were concentrated on equilibria in which prices depend on sunspot histories. However, if in that case, sunspots were of order n at each period, they could still be interpreted within the present framework as *nonindependent* sunspots of order n^2.

8. Note a (slightly different) more elegant proof of (16). If $\Delta\ (\ ) \neq 0$, the implicit functions theorem applies in (*) and determines sunspot equilibria as a function of Π in a neighbourhood of (*). But since stationary equilibria are SSE for any Π, there cannot exist "true" SSE in the neighbourhood of (*).

9. This is a reduced form since it comes from the concentration of the equilibrium equations on the commodity market and on the money market.

10. Note that in the absence of separability, d should be made dependent upon p_{t-1}. This case is not covered by our formulation.

7

Sunspot Fluctuations around a Steady State: The Case of Multidimensional, One-Step Forward Looking Economic Models

Pierre-André Chiappori,
Pierre-Yves Geoffard, and
Roger Guesnerie

1   Introduction

This chapter is concerned with the sutdy of the fluctuations of an economic dynamical system.[1] The system is defined in an abstract way, and exhibits the following properties. The state variables at each period are n-dimensional; the system has no memory and is one-step forward looking (i.e., the equilibrium state at date t only depends on the expectations, common among agents, of the value of the future state variables). Also, the specification of the characteristics of the abstract system reflects, through axioms that relate stochastic and deterministic behavior, the fact that equilibrium conditions describe the interaction of optimizing agents. For a description of a number of economic models, the characteristics of which fit the framework we consider, the interested reader is referred to Chiappori and Guesnerie (1991b).[2]

Also, the kind of fluctuations that will be considered throughout the paper is characterized by three features. First, the fluctuations take place under the assumption that agents' expectations are *rational* in Muth's (1961) sense. Second, rather than by exogenous shocks, the fluctuations are generated by *endogenous beliefs* that are of *sunspot* type; i.e., they are based on stochastic variables which are extrinsic in Cass and Shell's (1983) terminology. Third, the paper is only concerned with *small* fluctuations generating a stochastic stationary process of state variables which has its support within a neighborhood of a steady state.

Our contribution thus belongs to the literature on stationary sunspot equilibria, and specifically focuses on what has been called local stationary sunspot equilibria (hereafter local SSE)—i.e., sunspot equilibria the support of which is within a neighborhood of the steady state. The existence of a connection between the existence of local SSE and the indeterminacy[3] of the steady state has been apparent since the early work of Azariadis (1981b) and Azariadis and Guesnerie (1982a) in the framework of an overlapping generation (hereafter OLG) model.[4] In fact, in one-dimensional systems, both properties are essentially equivalent, and depend on whether the (unique and real) eigenvalue governing the local perfect foresight dynamics is larger or smaller than one.[5]

However, the extension of the latter result to more general systems, where, as here, the local perfect foresight dynamics is associated with n eigenvalues can take several directions. For example, when *all* eigenvalues are located outside the unit disk, the one-dimensional argument of Farmer and Woodford (1989) and Grandmont (1986), in which one identifies an invariant compact, has a multidimensional counterpart (Theorem 2 in Chiappori and Guesnerie (1991b)), that allows establishment of the existence of local SSE. Also, as suggested by the latter proof as well as by other contributions dealing with systems including predetermined variables (for instance, Woodford (1986)), the invariant compact argument is potentially very general. For example, a version of this argument underlies the result of indeterminacy of equilibrium in an OLG exchange economy obtained by Spear, Srivastava, and Woodford (1990), who (indeed) suppose explicitly that all relevant eigenvalues of the local linear dynamics are located outside the unit disk.

It is however known that conditions of the kind just evoked, although sufficient for the existence of local SSE, are not necessary (for instance, in an n-dimensional system of the kind we consider here, Theorem 3 in Guesnerie (1986) exhibits local SSE when only one eigenvalue is outside the unit disk). In fact, an extrapolation of previous work on linear systems suggests that indeterminacy of the steady state—i.e., the existence of *at least one* eigenvalue outside the unit disk—should be a sufficient condition for the existence of local SSE; and Woodford has early conjectured (1984) that the connection between indeterminacy and local SSE should be very general.

The present chapter proposes a systematic exploration of Woodford's conjecture in the one-step forward looking framework under scrutiny. Our approach is based upon bifurcation theory; its main results can be summarized as follows:

Our first result is that, in line with the conjecture just recalled, *indeterminacy implies the existence of local SSE*; in other words, the existence of (at least) one eigenvalue outside the unit disk is shown to be sufficient—a confirmation of the conjecture in our framework. Technically, we prove the existence of local SSE that are based on the current state of a *Markovian* extrinsic process. Also, the *structure* of local SSE is shown to display qualitative differences (reflecting the qualitative differences of the bifurcation) according to whether the relevant eigenvalues are real or complex.

These local SSE can be found even if we impose that their support should be *finite* (in the complex case, additional conditions may be needed, that are related to the cardinality of the support). The scope of this conclusion depends, in part, on the effective interest of finite SSE. Though the latter are somewhat specific beings, there are at least two reasons why they should receive special attention. On the one hand, should sunspot theory be considered as a positive approach, then intuitive bounded rationality arguments suggest that finite SSE may be more likely to emerge. On the other hand, existing (convincing) arguments that conclude at the possibility of "learning to believe in sunspots"[6] have been formalized in a finite support framework.

Lastly, our results provide a direct *characterization* of the Markovian processes triggering local SSE. Hence, besides the "existence" problem, the "characterization" problem receives a complete solution.

Two remarks can be made at that point. First, this study aims at contributing to the understanding of the rational expectations construct. This construct plays a central role in modern economic theory. Our goal here, and this is true of the so-called sunspot literature in general, is to understand the nature of multiplicity of rational expectation equilibria. The present chapter does not exhaust the problem, and should be viewed as a step in what we believe to be a coherent research program. Second, the reader familiar with the literature will realize that this chapter shares some of its objectives with that of Woodford (1986), which adopts a different and more complex framework than the one we consider here. In the Conclusion, we proceed to a careful comparison of the two approaches; it shows that the two works are indeed more complementary than substitute.

The chapter proceeds as follows:

Section 2 presents the abstract dynamical system under consideration. It discusses the basic axioms which we adopt and derives the crucial technical lemmas on which the analysis is based.

Section 3 focuses attention on the linearized version of the model. Theorem 1 provides existence and characterization results of stationary sunspot equilibria of finite order in the linear model. Theorem 2 describes the connection between the existence of local SSE within a nonlinear framework and that of SSE in the "tangent" linear model.

Section 4 analyzes the bifurcations of the system from the steady states when the exogenous sunspot process is varied. Local stationary sunspot equilibria appear around the bifurcations beyond the point when a path of sunspot Markov matrices passes critical values. These critical values depend on the relative position of eigenvalues of the Markov matrix and of the linear operator which governs the evolution of the deterministic system around the steady state. The analysis has to be significantly differentiated according to whether the eigenvalues under scrutiny are real (we have then real crossing) or complex (this is the case of complex crossing).

Lastly, a general assessment of the scope of our results is given in the Conclusion.

2 Model, Assumptions, and Preliminary Results

As already announced in the Introduction, we are considering an n-dimensional, one-step forward looking dynamical system. The state variables denoted p belong to some compact subset P of $\mathbb{R}^n$. The system is one-step forward looking in the sense that the state at each period depends upon the expectation on the state variables at next period only. Expectations on next period which are assumed to be commonly held by all agents are described by a probability distribution on P denoted θ. Furthermore, the system entails no memory and it is time independent. These assumptions translate into a formal definition of the system through a mapping $\tilde{Z}$:

$$\tilde{Z}: P \times \mathcal{P}(P) \to \mathbb{R}^n,$$
$$P_0 \times \theta \to \tilde{Z}(p_0, \theta),$$

where $\mathcal{P}(P)$ is the set of probability measures on P.

An equilibrium of the dynamical system at time t is defined by the following equations:

$$\tilde{Z}(p_t, \theta) = 0,$$

where θ is the probability measure (on p_{t+1}) which describes expectations at time t. We will often refer, for the sake of convenience, to p_t as a price vector, and, correspondingly to $\tilde{Z}$ as an excess demand function. But naturally the model applies in contexts where the state variables are not prices (but, for example, capital stocks) and where $\tilde{Z}$ has not the interpretation of excess demand. Also, when $\tilde{Z}$ (p, θ) = 0, we shall sometimes say that the distribution θ *rationalizes* the value p of the state variable.

A specific case of interest is when expectations on future prices are point expectations: then θ is simply the Dirac measure at p denoted $\delta(p)$. The specification of $\tilde{Z}$ to this case yields the *deterministic excess* demand function Z (by opposition to $\tilde{Z}$, the "stochastic" one):

$$\tilde{Z}: P \times P \rightarrow \mathbb{R}^n,$$

$$Z(p_0, p) \stackrel{def}{=} \tilde{Z}(p_0, \delta(p)).$$

In the following, a large part of the analysis will be concerned with the case where θ is a measure with finite support $(p_1, \dots, p_k)$. We note then $\theta = \{p_1, \dots, p_k; \lambda_1, \dots, \lambda_k\}$ where λ_i is the probability of getting p_i. For the class of such measures with finite support of cardinal k, it is convenient to view $\tilde{Z}$ as a mapping (denoted then $\tilde{Z}^k$) from $P \times P^k \times S_{k-1}$ to $\mathbb{R}^n$, where S_{k-1} is the simplex of $\mathbb{R}^k$.

Technically, for $k \geq 2$,

$$\tilde{Z}^k(p_0, p_1, \dots, p_k, \lambda_1, \dots, \lambda_k) \stackrel{def}{=} \tilde{Z}(p_0, \{p_1, \dots, p_k; \lambda_1, \dots, \lambda_k\})$$

and by convention $\tilde{Z}^1 = Z$.

Throughout the paper, we shall assume that the function $\tilde{Z}^k$ are smooth of class C^2 for all k.

We are now in a position to define our equilibrium concepts.

First, a *stationary equilibrium* consists of a vector $\bar{p}$ such that

$$Z(\bar{p}, \bar{p}) = 0. \tag{2.1}$$

Second, a *stationary sunspot equilibrium* (SSE) is defined as follows.

DEFINITION   A (*time independant*) sunspot equilibrium (SE) is a Markov process on a subset $P_0 \subset P$, with a transition function $\tilde{\theta}: P_0 \times \mathcal{B}(P_0) \rightarrow [0, 1]$ (where $\mathcal{B}(P_0)$ is the Borel field of P_0), such that:

(i) for at least one p_0, $\theta_{p_0} = \tilde{\theta}(p_0, \cdot)$ is truly stochastic (i.e., it is not a Dirac measure);

(ii) for each $p_0 \in P_0$,

$$\tilde{Z}(p_0, \theta_{p_0}) = 0. \tag{2.2}$$

Lastly, the sunspot equilibrium is a *stationary sunspot equilibrium* (*SSE*) if the Markov process is stationary.

Thus, a sunspot equilibrium is defined as a Markov process over some P_0, with the transition probability function $\tilde{\theta}$. To each today value of the state variable p_0, $\tilde{\theta}$ associates a (conditional) probability measure θ_{p_0} over P_0 that "rationalizes" p_0. At least one of the distribution must be truly stochastic (i.e., it must "stochastically rationalize" p_0).

We shall focus attention in the following on SSE (which we call local SSE) which are close to the stationary equilibrium in the following sense.

DEFINITION   We say that *local SSE exist around the steady state* $\bar{p}$, when for every open set P' containing $\bar{p}$, there exists a subset $P_0 \subset P'$ and a SSE with support in P_0.

Some comments are in order.

First, the reader will easily check that a stationary equilibrium would be a particular case of a stationary sunspot equilibrium (for $P_0 = \{\bar{p}\}$ and $\theta = \delta(\bar{p})$) if Dirac measures were allowed in the definition of a SSE. Since they are not, SSE in our definition have to be truly stochastic.

Second, for readers unfamiliar with the concept of SSE, let us give some motivation and intuition. Assume that the economy is subject to some exogenous Markovian random signal ("sunspots"); the signal is moreover *extrinsic* à la Cass-Shell (1983), i.e., it does not affect the fundamentals of the economy. Assume, however, that agents believe the signal directly influences the global behavior of the economic system; specifically, they believe that there is a one-to-one correspondence between the signal and the (current) state. Under such a "theory", the *present* signal brings information, not only upon *present* prices, but also upon the probability distribution of *future* prices p. Indeed, the distribution of p, conditional on present price being p_0, can be immediately deduced from the transition probability of the Markovian, signal (i.e., the distribution of future signal, conditional on present signal). But, of course, this information upon future price may, and generally will, alter present behavior. Now, we have a SSE associated with the random process of the signal whenever the "theory" is self-fulfilling—that is, for any possible signal today, which induces expectations about tomorrow prices, the today prices corresponding to the signal clear all markets. In this interpretation, the probability distribution in the definition of a SSE is then associated with the stochastic behavior of an exogenous "sunspot" phenomenon.

Third, local sunspot equilibria are sunspot equilibria which generate stochastic equilibrium prices which remain very close to the deterministic steady state. They provide a possible formalization of the idea of a system with small fluctuations around the steady state. The present paper is indeed devoted to the study of such "local" SSE.

Now, we are going to come back to SSE with finite support. We shall specialize the general definition to this case, while introducing notation appropriate for our further study.

In the finite support case with k different states, the extrinsic process under consideration is fully characterized by a $(k \times k)$ Markov *matrix* M. Let M_i denote the ith line of M; i.e., $M_i = (m_{i1}, \ldots, m_{ik})$, where m_{ij} is the probability of being tomorrow in state j, given that today state is i (in particular, $\Sigma_j m_{ij} = 1$ for all i). The associated beliefs are simply that there exist k price vectors $p_1, \ldots, p_k$ such that, whenever today price vector is p_i, the probability of reaching vector p_j tomorrow is exactly m_{ij}.

Formally, a *SSE of order k* consists of a matrix M and of k *different* vectors $p_1, \ldots, p_k$ such that

$$\tilde{Z}^k(p_i, p_1, \ldots, p_k, m_{i1}, \ldots, m_{ik}) = 0 \quad \forall i = 1, \ldots, k, \tag{2.3}$$

or more compactly,

$$\tilde{Z}^k(p_i, p, M_i) = 0 \tag{2.3'}$$

where $M_i = (m_{i1}, \ldots, m_{ik})$ is the ith line of M, $\forall i = 1, \ldots, k$.

Calling $\mathcal{M}_k$, the set of $(k \times k)$ Markov matrices, it will be useful to define the mapping

$$\hat{Z}^k: P^k \times \mathcal{M}_k \to \mathbb{R}^{nk}$$

by

$$\hat{Z}^k(p, M) = (\tilde{Z}^k(p_1, p, M_1), \ldots, \tilde{Z}^k(p_k, p, M_k)).$$

A SSE of order k is then a pair (p, M) such that $p = (p_1, \ldots p_k)$ consists of different vectors and

$$\hat{Z}^k(p, M) = 0. \tag{2.4}$$

In other words, SSE of order k appear as zeroes of the above mapping $\hat{Z}^k$. We use constantly this fact in the following. Naturally, not all zeroes of (2.4) define SSE. For example we already noted that a stationary state was a degenerate SSE, which, here, means that $p = (\bar{p} \ldots \bar{p})$ associated with any M in $\mathcal{M}^k$ is a solution of (2.4). A zero of (2.4), where $p \neq (\bar{p}, \ldots \bar{p})$ for any (stationary) price (equilibrium) $\bar{p}$, is called a SSE *of cardinal k*. Such a zero actually defines a SSE (it has at least two different components) but not necessarily SSE of order k (some of the components may be identical).

Now we shall introduce some consistency requirements which concern the relationship of the derivatives of the function $\tilde{Z}$ and of its deterministic trace Z.

AXIOM (A)   Consistency of derivatives: Whatever $\lambda = (\lambda_1, \ldots, \lambda_k)$ belonging to the $(k - 1)$-dimensional simplex, and whatever p_1 belonging to P, let $p = (p_1, \ldots, p_1)$; then

$$\partial_{p_0} \hat{Z}^k(p_0, p, \lambda) = \partial_0 Z(p_0, p_1), \tag{2.5}$$

$$\partial_{p_i} \tilde{Z}^k(p_0, p, \lambda) = \lambda_i \partial_1 Z(p_0, p_1) \quad (i = 1, \ldots, k), \tag{2.6}$$

where $\partial_x X(\cdot)$ is the Jacobian matrix associated with a function X, with respect to the variables x and taken in $(\cdot)$, and where for simplicity we use $\partial_i Z$ for $\partial_{p_i} Z$.

This axiom is the adaptation to our context of an axiom called (A2) in Guesnerie (1986) or Chiappori and Guesnerie (1989).[7] The reader will first notice that (2.5) is redundant; it says that when future prices are certain (p_1), the derivatives of Z and $\tilde{Z}^k$ with respect to present prices p_0 must coincide; hence it is a consequence of our definition of Z and $\tilde{Z}$ above. We however made it part of Axiom (A) for the reader's convenience. Part (2.6), which considers at the margin of the same certainty situation an infinitesimal change dp_i in p_i, is truly an axiom. It states that, given that it only introduces infinitesimal uncertainty, the random change tomorrow (which occurs with probability λ_i) is equivalent to a *sure* change of *magnitude* $\lambda_i \cdot dp_i$ (i.e., the expected value of the initial change).

It must be stressed that consistency of derivatives holds in all the specific models which we know and which fall in our formalism. For example, in the n-commodity version of the OLG model with representative consumer with time separable utility, Axiom (A) is a consequence of expected utility maximization. Elsewhere it will be a consequence of profit maximization. The axiom reflects a general fact in maximizing contexts, i.e., the principle of certainty equivalence for small stochastic changes at the margin of a certainty situation (cf. Malinvaud (1969)).

Lastly, we shall need a regularity assumption, which concerns the derivatives of deterministic excess demand Z at a stationary equilibrium $\bar{p}$.

ASSUMPTION (R) Regularity at a Stationary Equilibrium $\bar{p}$: At $\bar{p}$ we have (i) $\partial_0 Z (\bar{p}, \bar{p})$ is of full rank; (ii) matrix $B = -(\partial_0 Z)^{-1} \partial_1 Z$ has no eigenvalue of modulus 1; the eigenvalues of B outside the unit disk (if any) are all different; lastly, B is diagonalizable.

Clearly Assumption (R) is "generically true" when we pick up $\tilde{Z}$ and Z in a "rich enough" set of functions. Also (R) holds, to the best of our knowledge, when Z is extracted from subsets of functions corresponding to the specific versions of the present model which have been studied in the economic literature (generically on the given subsets).

Given that we have the model and assumptions, we can pursue our preliminary investigation. Our study of "local" SSE will crucially rest on the study of bifurcations which themselves will be dependent on the property of the mapping $\hat{Z}^k$ (which defines SSE of cardinal k) in the neighborhood of a stationary state. Given Axiom (A) these derivatives of $\hat{Z}_k$ with respect to prices can be expressed as a function of the derivatives of deterministic excess demand Z. Lemma 1 provides indeed a simple expression of the Jacobian of $\hat{Z}_k$. This leads to considering matrices of certain types whose eigenvalues are analyzed in Lemma 2.

LEMMA 1 Consider the mapping $\hat{Z}_k$ defined above and call $D_p\hat{Z}_k(\bar{p}, M)$ its ($nk \times nk$) Jacobian matrix (with respect to $p = (p_1, \ldots, p_k)$), evaluated at $(\bar{p}, \ldots, \bar{p}, M)$. We have:

$$D_p\hat{Z}^k(\bar{p}, M) = \left(\begin{array}{ccc} \partial_0 Z + m_{11}\partial_1 Z & m_{12}\partial_1 Z \ldots & m_{1k}\partial_1 Z \\ \hline m_{k1}\partial_1 Z & m_{k2}\partial_1 Z \ldots & \partial_0 Z + m_{kk}\partial_1 Z \end{array} \right) \tag{2.7}$$

where m_{ij} is the (i, j) element of M and all derivatives are taken in $\bar{p} = (\bar{p} \ldots \bar{p})$.

If we denote $\otimes$ the tensorial product of matrices and I_l the identity matrix of $\mathbb{R}^l$,

$$D_p\hat{Z}^k(\bar{p}, M) = I_k \otimes \partial_0 Z + M \otimes \partial_1 Z$$
$$= (I_k \otimes \partial_0 Z)(I_{nk} - M \otimes B) \tag{2.8}$$

where B is as defined above in (R).

Proof Coming back to the definition of $\hat{Z}^k$, let us consider the matrix $D_p\hat{Z}^k(\bar{p}, M)$ as a set of k^2 blocks, each block being a ($n \times n$)

matrix. Let us call z_{ij} one of the generic block; it is the $(n \times n)$ Jacobian matrix of $\tilde{Z}^k (p_i, p, M_i)$ with respect to the vector p_j, taken in $\bar{p}, \ldots, \bar{p}$. Then

$$z_{ij} = \delta_i^j \left(\partial_{p_0} \tilde{Z}^k \right)_{(\cdot)} + \left(\partial_{p_j} \tilde{Z}^k \right)_{(\cdot)}$$

where $(\cdot) = (\bar{p}, \ldots, \bar{p}, M_i)$.

Applying now Axiom (A), we get the first part of the Lemma. Also, the rules of tensorial product imply that

$$(I_k \otimes \partial_0 Z^{-1})(I_k \otimes \partial_0 Z + M \otimes \partial_1 Z) = I_k \otimes I_n + M \otimes (\partial_0 Z)^{-1} (\partial_1 Z)$$
$$= I_{nk} - M \otimes B.$$

But $I_k \otimes \partial_0 Z^{-1} = (I_k \otimes \partial_0 Z)^{-1}$; hence the conclusion.   Q.E.D.

Since, by the regularity assumption, $I_k \otimes \partial_0 Z$ is invertible, the rank of $D_p \hat{Z}^k (\bar{p}, M)$ is that of $I_{nk} - M \otimes B$. The eigenvalues of the latter matrix are given by the following results:

LEMMA 2   Let A and C be arbitrary matrices of respective dimension $(k \times k)$ and $(n \times n)$, and let $S(A)$ and $S(C)$ denote their respective spectrum (i.e., set of eigenvalues). Then, if $D = I_{nk} - A \otimes C$, the spectrum $S(D)$ of D is

$$S(D) = \{1 - ac / a \in S(A), c \in S(C)\}.$$

Proof   Let x (resp. y) be an eigenvector of A (resp. C) associated with an eigenvalue a (resp. c). Define $z = x \otimes y$; then

$$D_z = x \otimes y - (A \otimes C)(x \otimes y) = x \otimes y - Ax \otimes Cy$$
$$= (1 - ac)(x \otimes y) = (1 - ac)z;$$

hence $(1 - ac)$ is an eigenvalue of D, associated with the eigenvector $x \otimes y$. Hence $\{1 - ac / a \in S(A), c \in S(C)\} \subset S(D)$. If A (resp. C) has k (resp. n) different eigenvalues, then $S(D) = \{1 - ac / a \in S(A), c \in S(C)\}$, since the above construction generates nk different eigenvectors. Since the set of matrices with different eigenvalues is dense, the conclusion follows by continuity.   Q.E.D.

We may note that, when combined, Lemmas 1 and 2 provide actual generalizations of Guesnerie's preparation lemmas (1986) (which apply only to sunspot problems of order 2) and Chiappori and Guesnerie's (1989) lemma (which applies to sunspots of order k but for one-dimensional systems).

3 The Linear Model

This section focuses attention on a linear system which can be viewed as "tangent," in a sense which will be made precise later, to the original nonlinear system. This system is defined as follows.

First we assume that the deterministic system is linear—i.e., that the function Z writes down

$$Z(p_0, p) = A(p_0 - \bar{p}) - A'(p_0 - \bar{p}) \tag{3.1}$$

where A, A' are $(n \times n)$ matrices and A is invertible.

Equilibrium conditions write down

$$p_0 - \bar{p} = (A^{-1}A')(p - \bar{p}).$$

We call $B \overset{def}{=} A^{-1}A'$; normalizing at $\bar{p} = 0$, the system writes down

$$p_0 = Bp. \tag{3.2}$$

Also we shall forget nonnegativity which the original system imposes on the new variable p (i.e., $(\bar{p} + p \in \mathbb{R}^n_+)$); the local analysis is only modified in a straightforward way by the incorporation of these conditions. Note also that, if 1 is not an eigenvalue of B, then $\bar{p}$ is the only stationary equilibrium.

Now, if p is a random vector which can take k values $p_1, \ldots, p_k$ with respective probabilites $\lambda = (\lambda_1, \ldots, \lambda_k)$ with $\Sigma\lambda_k = 1$, we define the stochastic linear excess demand function $\tilde{Z}$ (or rather its restriction to measures with finite support of cardinal k, $\tilde{Z}^k$) as

$$\tilde{Z}^k(p_0, p, \lambda) = Ap_0 - A'\sum_{i=1}^{k}\lambda_i p_i. \tag{3.3}$$

The reader will notice that such a stochastic extension of Z is the only linear extension compatible with the above Axiom (A). We shall refer to it as the *stochastic linear system* associated with B.

Still $\tilde{Z}^k = 0$ can be written

$$p_0 = E_\lambda(Bp). \tag{3.4}$$

Let us now specialize the above definitions to the present linear system.

A *SSE* consists of a subset $P_0 \subset \mathbb{R}^n$ and of a transition function $\tilde{\mu}$, with the same properties as above, such that

$$\int_{p_0} Bpd\mu(p) = p_0 \quad \text{for all } p_0 \text{ in } P_0. \tag{3.5}$$

A *SSE* of *order k* consists of k all *different* vectors $p_1, \ldots, p_k$ in $\mathbb{R}^n$ and a Markov matrix M such that

$$\sum_{j=1}^{k} m_{ij} Bp_j = p_i, \quad \forall i = 1, \ldots, k. \tag{3.6}$$

Remember that the SSE is of cardinal k if the vectors p_i are not necessarily all different (though two of them at least must differ).

Note that equation (3.5) (hence also 3.6) is homogenous: if $(p_1, \ldots, p_k)$ is a solution, then also $(vp_1, \ldots, vp_k)$ for any real number v. This is why the nonnegativity restrictions alluded to above can be dropped.

The technical result which is central to our conclusion is the following proposition.

PROPOSITION 1   Consider a nonzero solution $\hat{p} = (p_1, \ldots, p_k)$ of the linear system

$$\sum_{j=1}^{k} m_{ij} Bp_j = p_i \quad (i = 1, \ldots, k), \tag{3.6}$$

where B is a $n \times n$ matrix, p_i a vector in $\mathbb{R}^n$, and $M = (m_{il})$ a $k \times k$ Markov matrix. Then:

(i) Such a $\hat{p}$ exists if and only if there exists (at least) one nonzero eigenvalue μ of M, such that $1/\mu$ is an eigenvalue of B.

(ii) Then the vectors $p_1, \ldots, p_k$ belong to the stable subspace of $\mathbb{R}^n$ spanned by the eigenvectors of B associated with eigenvalues of modulus greater than one.

Proof

(i) The system (3.6) can be written

$$(I_{nk} - M \otimes B)p = 0$$

where $p = (p'_1, \ldots, p'_k)'$. This equation has a nonzero solution in p if and only if

$$\mathrm{Det}\,(I_{nk} - M \otimes B) = 0.$$

From Lemma 2, this determinant is the product of the $(1 - \mu b)$, where μ (resp. b) is an eigenvalue of M (resp. B). It is zero if and only if $\mu = 1/b$ for some μ and b.

(ii) Let $(p_1, \ldots, p_k)$ be a solution of (3.6). Consider a basis of n eigenvectors of B, such that the l first eigenvectors ($l \leq n$) correspond to eigenvalues of modulus greater than one, the $n - l$ others to eigenvalues less than one. Take $j > l$, and let p_i be the vector whose jth component, in this new basis, is of maximum modulus. The jth component of (3.6) gives

$$\sum_{s=1}^{k} m_{is} b_j p_s^j = p_i^j$$

where b_j is the jth eigenvalue of B and p_s^j is the jth component of p_s in the new base. But here, $|p_i^j| \geq |p_s^j|$ by definition of i, and $|b_j| < 1$; hence this relationship is not possible unless $p_i^j = 0$, which implies $p_s^j = 0$ for all s. This shows that the last $(n - l)$ components, in the new base, of every p_s are zero.

Remark 1   There is a close link, in the linear model, between the existence of sunspot equilibria, on the one hand, and the property of the deterministic dynamics generated by Z on the other hand. Specifically, consider the dynamical system defined by:

$$\forall t, \quad Z(p_t, p_{t+1}) = Ap_t - A'p_{t+1} = 0$$

or, equivalently,

$$p_t = A^{-1}A'p_{t+1} = Bp_{t+1}.$$

The stable (linear) manifold of this dynamical system is spanned by the eigenvectors of B of modulus more than one. Hence: (i) (finite) sunspot equilibria exist if and only if the system has a stable eigenspace; (ii) in that case, the sunspot prices are located on this stable eigenspace.

As we shall see, these properties have a counterpart in the non-linear case.

Remark 2 Another point that will be important later on is the following. Consider a "path" of Markov matrices $M(\alpha)$, indexed by some real parameter α. Assume that, for some value α_0, $\mathrm{Det}(I_{nk} - M(\alpha_0) \otimes B) = 0$. Then one of the eigenvalues of $M(\alpha_0)$, say $\mu(\alpha_0)$, is equal to $1/b$, where b is an eigenvalue of B. Assume, moreover, that $(d\mu(\alpha_0)/d\alpha) \neq 0$. If $\mu(\alpha_0)$ is a *real* eigenvalue, the determinant will change sign at α_0. However, if $\mu(\alpha_0)$ is complex, the sign will not change; indeed, the determinant includes the factor $(1 - \mu(\alpha_0)b)(1 - \bar{\mu}(\alpha_0)\bar{b})$ where $\bar{\mu}(\alpha_0)$, $\bar{b}$ are the complex conjugates of $\mu(\alpha_0)$, b. This point will be crucial for the analysis of the next sections.

The results on the existence of SSE of order k are gathered in Theorem 1, of which Proposition 1 is the technical substratum.

THEOREM 1   Under Assumption (R):

(i) If B has no eigenvalue of modulus greater than 1, there exists no SSE for the linear system. If B has a real eigenvalue of modulus greater than 1, then for every $k \geq 2$ there exists a SSE of order k. If B has a complex eigenvalue b of modulus greater than 1, then there exists a SSE of order k for any k such that $|b|\cos(\pi/k) > 1$.

(ii) The Markov matrices associated with SSE of order k necessarily have (at least) one eigenvalue that coincides with the inverse of an eigenvalue of B. Conversely, to any Markov matrix M with an eigenvalue that coincides with the inverse of an eigenvalue of B, one can associate a SSE of cardinal k.

(iii) For any SSE of cardinal k, the corresponding price vectors $p_1, \ldots, p_k$ belong to the "stable" subspace of the deterministic dynamics—i.e., the subspace generated by the eigenvectors of B with eigenvalues of modulus greater than one.

Proof (ii) and (iii) follow from Proposition 1; we only need to show that, if an eigenvalue of M coincides with the inverse of an eigenvalue of B, then the nonzero solution of system (3.6) is indeed a SSE—i.e., that it is not of the form $(p, \ldots, p)$. But this would imply $Bp = p$, and 1 will be an eigenvalue of B, a contradiction with Assumption (R).

Let us prove (i). First, it is well known that the modulus of eigenvalues of a Markov matrix cannot be greater than 1. From Proposition 1, if B has no eigenvalue of modulus greater than 1, (3.6) does not have nonzero solutions.

Assume, now, that $\bar{x}$ is an eigenvector of B associated with the real eigenvalue $b > 1$, hence $B\bar{x} = b\bar{x}$. Note that $\hat{p} = (\bar{x}, -\bar{x})$ is a SSE of order 2. (This immediately follows from the fact that $\bar{x}$ (resp. $-\bar{x}$) lies in the convex hull of $(B\bar{x}, -B\bar{x})$). Also $\hat{p} = (\bar{x}, \bar{x} \ldots \bar{x}, -\bar{x})$ is a SSE of cardinal k. It is enough to perturbate slightly $(\bar{x}(1 + \varepsilon_1), \bar{x}(1 + \varepsilon_2) \ldots \bar{x}(1 + \varepsilon_{k-1}), -\bar{x})$ with $\varepsilon_1, \ldots, \varepsilon_{k-1}$ small enough to obtain a SSE of order k.

Lastly, assume that B has two complex eigenvalues b and $\bar{b}$ outside the unit disk. Consider the (stable) two-dimensional eigenspace E associated with them. We shall show, from a purely geometric argument, that we can find a Markov matrix M associated with a SSE $(p_1, \ldots, p_k)$ where p_i belongs to E for each i.

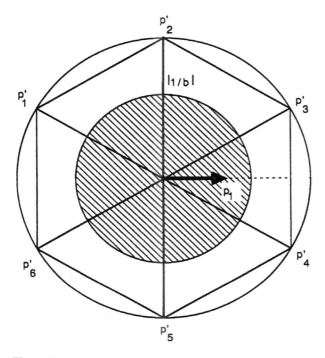

Figure 7.1

Indeed, pick up k different points $p'_1, \ldots, p'_i$ on the unit circle in
E, in such a way that their convex hull contains the circle C of center
O and radius $|1/b|$. An illustration, for $k = 6$, is given by Figure 7.1;
it is easy to show that such points exist whenever $\cos(\pi/k) > |1/b|$
(just take the vertices of a regular k-polygon). Now, the restriction
B_E of B to E is one-to-one; hence, we can define $A_E = (B_E)^{-1}$. The norm
of A_E is $|1/b|$; it follows that, for $i = 1, \ldots, k$,

$$|A_E p'_i| \leq |A_E| |p'_i| = |1/b|.$$

If we define $p_1, \ldots, p_k$ by $p_i = A_E p'_i$, the p_i thus belong to the circle
C—hence to the convex hull of $p'_1, \ldots, p'_k$. This means that, for each
$i = 1, \ldots, k$, there exist k real numbers $m_{i1}, \ldots, m_{ik}$ such that $m_{ij} \geq 0$,
$\Sigma_{j=1}^{k} m_{ij} = 1$ and $p_i = \Sigma_{j=1}^{k} m_{ij} p'_j$. But this relation can be written $\forall i\ 1, k$,
$p_i = \Sigma_{j=1}^{k} m_{ij} B_E p_j$, which is exactly the equation (3.6) defining SSE of

cardinal k; moreover, since the p_i are all different (remember that the p_i' are all different, and B_E is one-to-one), the order of the SSE is also k. The Markov matrix of the SSE is $M = (m_{ij})$.

Two points can be stressed to conclude. First, it follows from the analysis above that M has an eigenvalue equal to $|1/b|$. This shows that, for any complex number $\lambda = 1/b$ and any integer k such that $|\lambda| < \cos(\pi/k)$, there exists a $(k \times k)$ Markov matrix M with eigenvalues λ and $\bar{\lambda}$. Second, we can choose the coefficients of M to be all nonzero. To see why, note that any point in the hull is a convex combination of O, p_i', and p_{i+1}' for some i (see Figure 7.1); but O can always be written as $\Sigma_{j=1}^{k}(1/k)\, p_k'$, hence the conclusion. (This remark will be important in the proof of Lemma 3 below.)

Remark 3 We can actually say more upon the *order* of the SSE if we are ready to make an additional assumption, that will be used throughout the next sections. Assume that the matrix M is such that: (i) $m = 1/b$, where m (resp. b) is an eigenvalue of M (resp. B); (ii) m is a single eigenvalue; (iii) for any eigenvalue m' of M, m' being different from m (and m' being different from $\bar{m}$, the complex conjugate of m, if m is complex), and for any eigenvalue b' of B, $m' \neq b'$. In other words, the "crossing" between an eigenvalue of M and the inverse of an eigenvalue of B is one-dimensional (or, technically, the kernel of $I_{nk} - M \otimes B$ is one-dimensional) if the eigenvalue is real, and bi-dimensional if it is complex. Then we have the following result:

Fact 1 Under the previous assumptions, if matrix M is associated with a SSE of order k, then all SSE associated with M are of order k.

Proof In the real case, the vector $(p_1, \ldots, p_k)$ is unique up to a multiplicative constant; this is because p is a solution of $(I_{nk} - M \otimes B)p = 0$, and the kernel of $I_{nk} - M \otimes B$ is one-dimensional. A consequence is that, if there is a SSE of order k associated with M, then all SSE associated with M are of order k. This conclusion holds true in the complex case as well, though the proof is more tricky. The idea goes as follows. We know, from the proof of Lemma 2, that the kernel of $I_{nk} - M \otimes B$ is generated by the complex vectors $v \otimes w$ and $\bar{v} \otimes \bar{w}$, where v (resp. w) is the complex eigenvector of M (resp. B) associated with the eigenvalue μ (resp. b). Hence, any p in the kernel of $I_{nk} - M \otimes B$ is of the form $\gamma(v \otimes w) + \bar{\gamma}(\bar{v} \otimes \bar{w})$, where γ is an arbitrary complex number. Assume, now, that such a p generates a SSE of order less than k. Then it must be the case that, for some i and j, $\gamma v_i w + \bar{\gamma} \bar{v}_i \bar{w} = \gamma v_j w + \bar{\gamma} \bar{v}_j \bar{w}$. Since w is the eigenvector of a *real* matrix associated with a *complex* eigenvalue, it cannot be colinear to its complex conjugate. Hence we must have $v_i = v_j$; but then *all* SSE are of order less than k, a contradiction.

Theorem 1 stresses three key facts.

(i) The existence of SSE (of finite order) in a linear system is intimately related with the existence of eigenvalues of modulus larger than one for the linear operator—i.e., with the existence of a stable manifold for the associated, deterministic dynamical system. However, a complex eigenvalue only guarantees the existence of SSE of "high enough" order.

(ii) The characteristics of the extrinsic sunspot phenomena generating SSE must be intimately related with the characteristics of the linear operator; specifically, the product of some eigenvalue of M and some eigenvalue of B must be one.

(iii) The vectors corresponding to a SSE must belong to the stable subspace spanned by the eigenvectors of B with eigenvalues outside the unit disk; i.e., they are supported by the stable linear manifold of the deterministic system. Also, it is worth noting a subproduct of our analysis: the spectrum of $k \times k$ Markov matrices can contain any real number between -1 and 1 (a fact which is well known— see, for example, Chiappori and Guesnerie (1989)) and also *any complex number which lies within the disk of radius* $\cos(\pi/k)$ (a fact which, to our knowledge, may not have been known so far).[8]

Let us summarize what we have performed at the present stage. Starting from the abstract dynamical system of Section 2 and from the "tangent" linear deterministic system, we have defined a stochastic linear system. We have then studied SSE in this stochastic linear system.

Such a study, which is of independant interest, has also a close connection with our original problem—the characterization of "local" SSE in the nonlinear system. This connection is made clear in the next statement.

THEOREM 2   Necessary Conditions for the Existence of Stationary Sunspot Equilibria Close to the Steady State: *Let $\bar{p}$ be a steady state at which (R) holds true. Consider a sequence of SSE of order k $p^{(n)}$ = $(p_1^{(n)}, \ldots, p_k^{(n)})$, $M^{(n)}$ such that $p^{(n)}$ converges towards $(\bar{p}, \ldots, \bar{p}) = \bar{p}$ and $M^{(n)}$ converges to $\bar{M}$. Then,*

(i) *the matrix $\bar{M}$ has an eigenvalue which coincides with the inverse of an eigenvalue of the matrix B;*

(ii) *if*

$$\frac{p^{(n)} - \bar{p}}{\|p^{(n)} - \bar{p}\|} \to \dot{p} = (\dot{p}_1, \ldots, \dot{p}_k),$$

then $(\dot{p}, \bar{M})$ defines a SSE of cardinal k for the linear system associated with B.

Proof   We will only provide a heuristic proof. The technical limiting argument can be borrowed from Guesnerie (1986).

Starting from the definition (2.4) of a SSE,

$$\hat{Z}^k(p_1^{(n)}, \ldots, p_k^{(n)}, M^n) = 0,$$

we obtain after linearization around $\bar{p}$, M^n,

$$(D_p\hat{Z}^k)_{\bar{p}, M_n}\left(\frac{p^{(n)} - \bar{p}}{\|p^{(n)} - \bar{p}\|}\right) \simeq 0.$$

But from Lemma 1 $(D_p\hat{Z}^k)(\bar{p}, M_n) = (I_k \otimes \partial_0 Z)^{-1}(I_{nk} - M_n \otimes B)$.

Passing at the limit and taking into account R, we conclude that $\dot{p}$ belongs to the kernel of $(I_{nk} - \overline{M} \otimes B)$; such a $\dot{p} \neq 0$ when associated with M is indeed a SSE of cardinal k for the linear system associated with B.

Conclusion (i) of the theorem is then an immediate application of Lemma 2 above (or of Theorem 1).   Q.E.D.

The conclusion is clear. Local SSE for a nonlinear system can only exist when associated with Markov matrices close to the ones which "sustain" SSE in the linear stochastic system. Such matrices are indeed characterized in Theorem 1. Now the question to be addressed is the following: *Do Markov matrices close to the matrices characterized in Theorem 1 generate beliefs which sustain local SSE?*

In order to answer the question, the next section adopts a bifurcation aproach. We consider paths of matrices which "cross" the critical values associated with SSE in the linear tangent system and we show that along many such paths bifurcations occur around which local SSE indeed exist.

4   A Bifurcation Analysis of Local SSE of the General System

A   The General Strategy

Let us make more precise the strategy of the approach of the present section as well as the difficulties we are likely to face.

Our strategy consists in taking a path of matrices $M(\alpha)$ indexed by some parameter α. Whatever α, the steady state $\bar{p}$ is a degenerate SSE associated with $M(\alpha)$. Furthermore, if $(D_p\hat{Z}^k)_{(\bar{p}, M(\alpha))}$ is invertible, the implicit function theorem tells us that $\bar{p}$ is a locally unique solution of equation (2.4) associated with SSE of order k.

In other words, in such circumstances, there exist no local SSE of order k. The argument fails for critical values α_0 where the above matrix is no longer invertible. We will consider paths which pass through such critical values (of course, we shall have to show that there are indeed such paths). We show that under some weak assumption, a bifurcation indeed occurs at the critical value. Then on one side of the bifurcation local SSE must appear.

From the analysis of the previous section, the reader will realize that critical values of α_0 obtain for matrices $M(\alpha_0)$ an eigenvalue of which "crosses" the inverse of one eigenvalue of matrix B. As we already suggested in the previous section, a crucial point will turn out to be whether the crossing eigenvalues are real or complex. The reason is that, for real crossing, $|D_p\hat{Z}_k|$ changes its sign, while it does not for complex crossing. The first case is classical and leads to standard bifurcations (namely, transcritical or pitchfork) repeatedly analyzed in the mathematical literature. The second case is more tricky. The corresponding bifurcations are of codimension superior to one (this assertion will become clear later on). These bifurcations are rather unusual and require specific analysis.[9]

Specifically, this section is devoted to the proof of two theorems, dealing respectively with the cases of real and complex crossing. Our strategy, however, will be first to develop a common approach to both cases, then to specialize the last part of the proof to each theorem. The idea of the general approach is to reduce the nk-dimensional problem we start from to a one- or two-dimensional problem, which will be much earlier to solve (using such specific tools as the Morse Lemma). This, of course, is a general method in bifurcation theory. In the present situation, it has two obvious advantages.

First, by replacing both problems within an identical framework, it outlines the general nature of the argument. In particular, the first theorem (the real eigenvalue case) could easily be deduced from traditional results in bifurcation theory. However, the conclusion, in that case, would stem from the "black box" of a mathematical proposition, while the proof adopted here clarifies the basic ideas at stake. Also, the proof of the second theorem requires a specific argument, and the construction presented here is both (reasonably) simple and powerful.

The second advantage of the method is that it highlights a well known but essential fact, namely, that the form of the bifurcation only depends on its codimension, and not on the dimension of the initial set. In particular, our proof can be extended at little cost to infinite SSE. Though this task shall not be carried out in full details, the basic hints will be given in the next section.

B   The Two Basic Theorems

Let us state the two fundamental results.

THEOREM 3   ("Real Crossing") Consider a dynamical system $\tilde{Z}$, satisfying Axiom A, with a stationary equilibrium $\bar{p}$, meeting condition (R). Let us assume that the matrix $B = -(\partial_0 Z)^{-1}(\partial_1 Z)$ (which governs the local dynamics of the deterministic system around the stationary equilibrium) has at least one real eigenvalue b of modulus greater than one. Then the dynamical system has local SSE of any order k $(k \geq 2)$.

More precisely, given any open set $\mathcal{O}$ in $\mathbb{R}_+^{nk}$ containing $(\bar{p}, \ldots, \bar{p})$, one can find a $(k \times k)$ Markov matrix M, *and* a vector $\hat{p} = (p_1, \ldots p_k)$ in $\mathcal{O}$ such that $(\hat{p}, M)$ is a SSE of order k. When $\mathcal{O}$ is small, M has necessarily one eigenvalue close to the inverse of (one of) the real eigenvalue(s) of B.

THEOREM 4 ("Complex Crossing") Consider a dynamical system $\tilde{Z}$, satisfying Axiom A, with a stationary equilibrium $\bar{p}$, meeting condition (R). Let us assume that the matrix $B = -(\partial_0 Z)^{-1}(\partial_1 Z)$ (which governs the local dynamics of the deterministic system around the stationary equilibrium) has at least one complex eigenvalue b of modulus greater than one. Then, for any k such that $|b| \cos(\pi/k) > 1$, the dynamical system has local SSE of order k.

More precisely, given any open set $\mathcal{O}$ in $\mathbb{R}_+^{nk}$ containing $(\bar{p}, \ldots \bar{p})$, one can find a $(k \times k)$ Markov matrix M, and a vector $\hat{p} = (p_1, \ldots p_k)$ in $\mathcal{O}$ such that $(\hat{p}, M)$ is a SSE of order k. When $\mathcal{O}$ is small, M has necessarily one eigenvalue close to the inverse of (one of) the complex eigenvalue of B outside the unit disk.

C   The Proof

(i)   The basic argument: the Lyapunov-Schmidt procedure

In what follows, k is an integer. We shall consider a path of $k \times k$ Markov matrices, $M(\alpha)$, indexed by some real α belonging to$] - \varepsilon$, $\varepsilon[$for some $\varepsilon > 0$. At $\alpha = 0$, one of the eigenvalues of matrix $M(0)$ crosses the inverse of some eigenvalue b of B. (Note that, since the eigenvalues of a Markov matrix belong to the unit disk, the modulus of b must then be more than one.) In addition, the path must have some specific properties, listed in the following lemma.

LEMMA 3   Let B be a real matrix satisfying Assumption (R). Let b be an eigenvalue of B, with modulus more than one, and pose $v = 1$ if b is real, $v = 2$ otherwise. Let k be an integer such that $k \geq 2$ if b is real, and $|b| \cos(\pi/k) > 1$ if b is complex. There exists a matrix path $M(\alpha)$, where $\alpha \in] - \varepsilon, \varepsilon[$, such that:

(a) $M(0)$ has a single eigenvalue μ_1 equal to $1/b$. Moreover, for any eigenvalue μ' of $M(0)$, $\mu' \neq \mu_1$, $\mu' \neq \bar{\mu}_1$, and for any eigenvalue b' of B, one has $\mu'b' \neq 1$; lastly, $M(0)$ is diagonalizable in a basis of eigenvectors $\{v_1, \ldots, v_k\}$ (where v_1 is associated with μ_1, and $v_2 = \bar{v}_1$ is associated with $\bar{\mu}_1$ if b is complex).

(b) For any $\alpha \neq 0$, for any eigenvalue μ of $M(\alpha)$, and any eigenvalue b' of B, $\mu b' \neq 1$.

(c) In the basis $\{v_1, \ldots, v_k\}$, the matrix $M'(0) = (dM/d\alpha)(0)$ has a nonzero upper diagnoal term ("transversal crossing").

(d) The linear system associated with $M(0)$ and B (as in Section 3) has (all its) SSE of order k.

The proof of the lemma is in the Appendix. Basically, (a) states that an eigenvalue μ_1 of $M(\alpha)$ crosses the inverse of an eigenvalue b of B at $\alpha = 0$; the crossing is of minimal dimension v, with $v = 1$ if b is real, and $v = 2$ if b is complex (since, in that case, $\bar{\mu}_1$ crosses $1/\bar{b}$ as well). In addition, $M(0)$ is diagonalizable. Also, (b) ensures that such a crossing cannot occur, along the path, but for $\alpha = 0$, and (c) guarantees that the crossing is "transversal"; this technical property will be essential for the existence of a bifurcation. Lastly, (d) will imply, by continuity, that the local SSE of the nonlinear system are of order k.

From now on, we consider a path satisfying the above conditions.

We can now investigate the existence of SSE around the stationary state. First, remember that a SSE of cardinal k is a zero of the vector field $\hat{Z}^k$, different from the stationary equilibrium $(\bar{p}, \ldots, \bar{p})$. To emphasize the *local* nature of the analysis, we define a mapping F:

$$]-\varepsilon, \varepsilon[\times \mathcal{O} \to \mathbb{R}^{nk},$$

$$(\alpha, u) \to F(\alpha, u) = (I_k \otimes \partial_0 Z_{(\bar{p})})^{-1} \cdot \hat{Z}^k(\bar{p} + u, M(\alpha)),$$

where $\mathcal{O}$ is an open neighborhood of zero in $\mathbb{R}^{nk}$ (and, for simplicity, $\bar{p}$ also denotes the vector $(\bar{p}, \ldots \bar{p})$). Of course, F is zero if and only if $\hat{Z}^k$ is zero; hence, a SSE is a zero of F different from zero. We know that $F(\alpha, 0) = 0$ for all α; moreover,

$$D_u F(\alpha, u) = (I_k \otimes \partial_0 Z)^{-1} \cdot D_p \hat{Z}^k(\bar{p} + u, M(\alpha)).$$

From Lemmas 1 and 2 of Section 2, it follows that zero is an eigenvalue of $D_u F(\alpha, u)$ with order v if and only if the equation $1 - \mu' \cdot b' = 0$ has v pairs of solution (μ', b')—where μ' (resp. b') belongs to the spectrum of $M(\alpha)$ (resp. B). In particular, from the properties of the path, $D_u F(\alpha, u)$ is invertible for $\alpha \neq 0$; for $\alpha = 0$, $D_u F$ is of rank $nk - v$, with v as defined in Lemma 3 ($v = 1$ if b is real, $v = 2$ if b is complex); technically, v will be the *codimension* of the bifurcation.

Our task, now, is to study the behavior of F around the singularity $(0, 0)$. Such a problem is however especially difficult because of the high dimension (namely nk) of the space. Hence, the first step will be to *reduce* the dimension of the space we consider; actually, we shall end with a space of minimal dimension, i.e. of dimension v (which is, in a sense, the "true" dimension of the singularity). This can be done in a number of ways. We shall use here the Lyapunov-Schmidt procedure.

From Lemma 1, we know that

$$D_u F(\alpha, 0) = I_{nk} - M(\alpha) \otimes B. \tag{4.1}$$

Let $\{w_1, \ldots, w_n\}$ be a basis of eigenvectors of B (B is diagonalizable by GR); here, w_1 is associated with b (and $w_2 = \bar{w}_1$ with $\bar{b}$ if b is complex). The set of nk vectors $\mathcal{B} = \{v_i \otimes w_j, i = 1, \ldots, k; j = 1, \ldots, n\}$ (where, as in Lemma 3, the v_i are the eigenvectors of $M(0)$) form a basis of $\mathbb{R}^{nk}$ in which $D_u F(0, 0)$ is diagonal. Moreover,

$$[D_u F(0, 0)](v_1 \otimes w_1) = v_1 \otimes w_1 - (M(0)v_1) \otimes (Bw_1)$$
$$= 0 \text{ by definition of } v_1 \text{ and } w_1.$$

Hence the vector $v_1 \otimes w_1$ (resp. the vectors $v_1 \otimes w_1$ and $v_2 \otimes w_2$) span the *kernel* N of $D_u F(0, 0)$ if b is real (resp. if b is complex); and the remaining vectors of $\mathcal{B}$ span the *image* R of $D_u F(0, 0)$. Hence, if the basis is ordered as $\{v_1 \otimes w_1, v_2 \otimes w_2, v_1 \otimes w_2, \ldots\}$, the matrix of $D_u F(0, 0)$ in this basis writes down:

$$D_u F(0, 0)_{\mathcal{B}} = \begin{pmatrix} 0 & \vdots & 0 \\ \cdots & \vdots & \cdots \\ 0 & \vdots & D\tilde{F} \end{pmatrix}$$

where the three zero blocks are of respective dimension $v \times v$, $v \times (nk - v)$, $(nk - v) \times v$, and where the $(nk - v) \times (nk - v)$ matrix $D\tilde{F}$ is of full rank. In the remainder of the proof, we shall always refer to the basis $\mathcal{B}$.

The idea, now, is to use the implicit function theorem. Of course, the latter cannot be applied to F, since $(0, 0)$ is singular—this is precisely why a bifurcation may occur. Hence, we define the mapping G by

$$]-\varepsilon, \varepsilon[\times N \times R \times N \rightarrow \mathbb{R}^{nk}$$
$$(\alpha, n', r, n) \rightarrow G(\alpha, n', r, n) = F(\alpha, n+r) + n' \qquad (4.2)$$

(where N and R have been defined above).
    Note, first that

$$G(\alpha, 0, 0, 0) = 0 \quad \text{for all } \alpha. \qquad (4.3)$$

    Also, with standard notations (and of course in the basis $\mathscr{B}$):

$$D_{n',r}G(0, 0, 0, 0) = \begin{pmatrix} I_v & \vdots & 0 \\ \cdots & \vdots & \cdots \\ 0 & \vdots & D\tilde{F} \end{pmatrix}$$

    This matrix is now invertible. Thus, we can apply the implicit function theorem to the equation $G(\alpha, n', r, n) = 0$ (considered as implicit in (n', r) around zero).
    There exists (locally) two C^1 functions $n'(\alpha, n)$ and $r(\alpha, n)$ such that

$$\forall (\alpha, n), \quad G(\alpha, n'(\alpha, n), r(\alpha, n), n) = 0 \qquad (4.4)$$

which is equivalent to

$$\forall (\alpha, n), \quad F(\alpha, n + r(\alpha, n)) + n'(\alpha, n) = 0.$$

    A consequence is that $F(\alpha, n + r(\alpha, n)) = 0$—which is what we are looking for—if and only if:

$$n'(\alpha, n) = 0. \qquad (4.5)$$

    The latter is called the *bifurcation equation*.[10] Now, the Lyapunov-Schmidt procedure is almost over. Our initial task—studying the zeros of F—has been transformed into the (equivalent) problem of studying the zeros of n'. But the major gain, now, is that n' maps the two- (resp. three-) dimensional space $]-\varepsilon, \varepsilon[\times N$ to the one- (resp. two-) dimensional space N if b is real (resp. complex). That is, starting from an equation in $\mathbb{R}^{nk}$, we end with an (equivalent) equation in $\mathbb{R}^v$, the zeros of which we shall now study.

We simply need some information upon the derivatives of n' at the origin. First, from (4.3), it is obvious that

$$\forall \alpha, \quad \begin{cases} n'(\alpha, 0) = 0, \\ r(\alpha, 0) = 0. \end{cases}$$

In particular $(\partial n'(0, 0)/\partial \alpha) = 0$, $(\partial^2 n'(0, 0)/\partial \alpha^2) = 0$. Also, differentiating (4.4) leads to

$$0 = D_n G_{(\alpha, n)} = D_u F_{(\alpha, n+r(\alpha, n))} \cdot \begin{pmatrix} I \\ D_n r \end{pmatrix} + \begin{pmatrix} D_n n' \\ 0 \end{pmatrix}. \tag{4.6}$$

Moreover, we may notice that

$$D_n n'(0, 0) = 0 \quad (\text{in } \mathbb{R}^v),$$
$$D_n r(0, 0) = 0 \quad (\text{in } \mathbb{R}^{nk-v});$$

indeed, at $(0, 0)$, one gets

$$0 = D_u F_{(0, 0)} \cdot \begin{pmatrix} I_v \\ D_n r \end{pmatrix} + \begin{pmatrix} D_n n' \\ 0 \end{pmatrix}$$

$$= \begin{bmatrix} 0 & 0 & \cdots & 0 \\ 0 & & & \\ \vdots & & D\tilde{F} & \\ 0 & & & \end{bmatrix} \begin{bmatrix} I_v \\ D_n r(0) \end{bmatrix} + \begin{bmatrix} D_n n'(0) \\ 0 \end{bmatrix}$$

$$= \begin{bmatrix} D_n n'(0) \\ D\tilde{F} \cdot D_n r(0) \end{bmatrix} = \begin{bmatrix} 0 \\ 0 \end{bmatrix},$$

which leads to

$$\begin{cases} D_n n'(0, 0) = 0, \\ D\tilde{F} \cdot D_n r(0, 0) = 0. \end{cases}$$

Since $D\tilde{F}$ is invertible, this gives

$$\begin{cases} D_n n'(0, 0) = 0, \\ D_n r(0, 0) = 0. \end{cases}$$

Lastly, differentiating (4.6) with respect to α leads to

$$\begin{pmatrix} 0 \\ 0 \end{pmatrix} = D^2_{\alpha u} F_{(\alpha,\, n+r(\alpha,\, n))} \begin{pmatrix} I_v \\ D_n r \end{pmatrix} + D_u F_{(\alpha,\, n+r(\alpha,\, n))} \begin{pmatrix} 0 \\ D^2_{\alpha n} r \end{pmatrix} + \begin{pmatrix} D^2_{\alpha n} n' \\ 0 \end{pmatrix}.$$

At $(0, 0)$, we have

$$\begin{cases} D_n r = 0, \\ D_u F = \begin{bmatrix} 0 & 0 \\ 0 & D\tilde{F} \end{bmatrix}. \end{cases}$$

Hence, at $(0, 0)$:

$$D^2_{\alpha u} F_{(0,\,0)} \cdot \begin{pmatrix} I_v \\ 0 \end{pmatrix} + \begin{pmatrix} 0 & 0 \\ 0 & D\tilde{F} \end{pmatrix} \begin{pmatrix} 0 \\ D^2_{\alpha n} r \end{pmatrix} + \begin{pmatrix} D^2_{\alpha n} n' \\ 0 \end{pmatrix} = \begin{pmatrix} 0 \\ 0 \end{pmatrix},$$

i.e.,

$$D^2_{\alpha u} F \begin{pmatrix} I_v \\ 0 \end{pmatrix} + \begin{pmatrix} I_v & 0 \\ 0 & D\tilde{F} \end{pmatrix} \begin{pmatrix} D^2_{\alpha n} n' \\ D^2_{\alpha n} r \end{pmatrix} = \begin{pmatrix} 0 \\ 0 \end{pmatrix}.$$

In particular, $D^2_{\alpha,\, n} n'(0, 0)$ is the $(v \times v)$ upper diagonal block of $-D^2_{\alpha u} F(0, 0)$. The basic property of the latter is given by the following lemma.

LEMMA 4   The matrix $D^2_{\alpha,\, n} n'(0, 0)$ is of full rank.

Proof   In the basis $\mathscr{B}$, the components of the upper diagonal block of $D^2_{\alpha,\, u} F(0, 0)$ are the components of the image of $v_1 \otimes w_1$ (resp. $v_1 \otimes w_1$ and $v_2 \otimes w_2$). Since $D_u F(\alpha, 0) = I_{nk} - M(\alpha) \otimes B$, $D^2_{u,\, \alpha} F(0, 0) = -M'(0) \otimes B$. Hence,

$$[D^2_{\alpha,\, u} F(0, 0)] \cdot (v_1 \otimes w_1) = -b(M'(0) \cdot v_1) \otimes w_1.$$

To decompose this vector in $\mathscr{B}$, it is sufficient to decompose $M'(0) \cdot v_1$ in $\{v_1, \dots, v_k\}$. This decomposition is exactly given by the first column of the matrix of $M'(0)$ in $\mathscr{B}$. By Lemma 3, the first component (i.e., upon v_1), say m'_1, is nonzero. Hence the component of $[D^2_{u,\, \alpha} F(0, 0)](v_1 \otimes w_1)$ over $v_1 \otimes w_1$ is $-m'_1 b \neq 0$. This ends the proof for $v = 1$. For $v = 2$, note that the component of $[D^2_{u,\, \alpha} F(0, 0)](v_1 \otimes w_1)$ upon $\bar{v}_2 \otimes \bar{w}_2 = v_1 \otimes w_1$ is zero; and the components of $[D^2_{u,\, \alpha} F(0,$

0)]$(v_2 \otimes w_2)$ upon $v_1 \otimes w_1$ and $v_2 \otimes w_2$ are respectively 0 and $-\bar{m}'_1 \bar{b}$. Hence,

$$D^2_{\alpha,n} n'(0,0) = \begin{pmatrix} -m'_1 b & 0 \\ 0 & -\bar{m}'_1 \bar{b} \end{pmatrix}$$

is of full rank.

To summarize, we have shown that

$$\begin{cases} D_n n'(0,0) = 0, \\ D_\alpha n'(0,0) = 0, \\ \text{Rank } D^2_{\alpha,n} n'(0,0) = v. \end{cases}$$

We may now consider independently the two cases $v = 1$ and $v = 2$.

(ii)   Proof of Theorem 3 ($v = 1$)

Since $D^2_{\alpha,n} n'(0,0)$ is nonzero, Morse's Lemma (see Milnor (1965)) can be applied to n'. For some neighborhood $\mathcal{V}$ of (0, 0) there exists a local diffeomorphism φ:

$$\mathcal{V} \to \mathcal{V},$$

$$(\alpha, n) \to (\varphi_1, \varphi_2),$$

such that

$$n'(\alpha, n) = [\varphi_1(\alpha, n)]^2 \pm [\varphi_2(\alpha, n)]^2.$$

But since $n'(\alpha, 0) = 0$, the case $(\varphi_1)^2 + (\varphi_2)^2$ is excluded; indeed, that would imply $\varphi_1(\alpha, 0) = 0$ and $\varphi_2(\alpha, 0) = 0$ for all α, and φ would not be a diffeomorphism.

Hence, it must be the case that

$$n'(\alpha, n) = [\varphi_1(\alpha, n)]^2 - [\varphi_2(\alpha, n)]^2.$$

This shows that, for any (α, n) close enough to (0, 0), the equation $n'(\alpha, n) = 0$ has two branches of solution in the (α, n) plane near (0, 0), corresponding respectively to

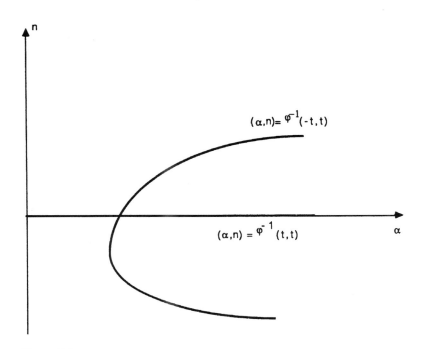

Figure 7.2

$$\varphi_1(\alpha, n) = \varphi_2(\alpha, n)$$

and

$$\varphi_1(\alpha, n) = -\varphi_2(\alpha, n)$$

Those branches can be described parametrically by

$$(\alpha_1, n_1) = \varphi^{-1}(t, t)$$

and

$$(\alpha_2, n_2) = \varphi^{-1}(-t, t),$$

where t is close to 0, and $\varphi = (\varphi_1, \varphi_2)$. Those two branches are different (but for $t = 0$) since φ is a diffeomorphism. One of them corresponds to the stationary solution (i.e., $n_1 = 0$ for all t); the other must be a SSE (cf. Figure 7.2).

(iii)   Proof of Theorem 4 (ν = 2)
This case is slightly more difficult than the former, since there is no analogy to the Morse Lemma in dimension higher than 1.
   Let us set

$$n' = \begin{pmatrix} n'_1 \\ n'_2 \end{pmatrix},$$

with $n'_i(\alpha, n) \in \mathbb{R}$, $i = 1, 2$.

$n'_i(\alpha, n) = 0$, since n'_i is C^1, defines a smooth surface (Σ_i) in $\mathbb{R}^3$.
$n'(\alpha, n) = 0$ is exactly the intersection $(\Delta) = (\Sigma_1) \cap (\Sigma_2)$.

   As in the case $\nu = 1$, we shall show that (Δ) is composed of two branches of solution. The proof is now in two steps.

First Step $*(\Sigma_1) \cap (\Sigma_2) \supset \{(\alpha, 0, 0), \alpha \in] - \varepsilon, \varepsilon[\}$. This is obvious since $n(\alpha, 0, 0) = 0\ \forall \alpha$.
   *This intersection is transversal at $(\alpha, 0, 0)$. Indeed, set $\alpha \neq 0$. A normal vector to (Σ_i) is defined by

$$\begin{pmatrix} \dfrac{\partial n'_i}{\partial \alpha} \\ \dfrac{\partial n'_i}{\partial n_1} \\ \dfrac{\partial n'_i}{\partial n_2} \end{pmatrix}.$$

But at $(\alpha, 0, 0)$, we have $(\partial n'_i / \partial \alpha) = 0$. The intersection of (Σ_1) and (Σ_2) is transversal at $(\alpha, 0, 0)$ *if and only if* the normal vectors to (Σ_1) and (Σ_2), at this point are not colinear. Hence, we have to check that the matrix

$$\begin{bmatrix} 0 & 0 \\ \dfrac{\partial n'_1}{\partial n_1} & \dfrac{\partial n'_2}{\partial n_1} \\ \dfrac{\partial n'_1}{\partial n_2} & \dfrac{\partial n'_2}{\partial n_2} \end{bmatrix}_{(\alpha,0,0)}$$

is of rank 2 for $\alpha \neq 0$. But this matrix is precisely equal to

$$\begin{bmatrix} 0 \\ D_n n'(\alpha, 0, 0) \end{bmatrix}.$$

At $(0, 0, 0)$, $D_n n'(0, 0, 0) = 0$; and we know that $D^2_{\alpha n} n'(0, 0, 0)$ is of full rank. We can see that $D_n n'(0, 0, 0) = 0$ gives (denoting $|D|$ the determinant of D):

$$|D_n n'(0,0,0)| = 0,$$

$$\frac{d}{d\alpha} |D_n n'(0,0,0)| = 0, \quad \text{and}$$

$$\frac{d^2}{d\alpha^2} |D_n n'(0,0,0)| = 2|D^2_{\alpha,n} n'(0,0,0)|.$$

Thus, for small enough values of α, $|D_n n'(\alpha, 0, 0)|$ will not be null; that is, $D_n n'(\alpha, 0, 0)$ is of full rank, which proves that the intersection is transversal.

Second Step   *We now show that (Σ_1), defined by $n'_1 = 0$, is diffeomorphic to a cone. Indeed, the Morse Lemma can be written for (Σ_1) and gives:

$$n'_1(\alpha, n_1, n_2) = \varphi_1^2 \pm \varphi_2^2 \pm \varphi_3^2.$$

But since $n'_1(\alpha, 0, 0) = 0 \ \forall \alpha$, the case $n'_1 = \varphi_1^2 + \varphi_2^2 + \varphi_3^2$ is excluded.

Hence, we must have at least one minus sign, which shows that, in the new coordinates $(\varphi_1, \varphi_2, \varphi_3)$, (Σ_1) is a cone, with vertex at $(0, 0, 0)$, say,

$$n'_1 = \varphi_1^2 + \varphi_2^2 - \varphi_3^2.$$

Take, now, some fixed h_0; we shall study the intersection of (Σ_1) and (Σ_2) in the plan $\varphi_3 = h_0$. In this plan, $n'_1 = 0$ defines a circle (Γ): $\varphi_1^2 + \varphi_2^2 = h_0^2$.

Now, set $\bar{n}_2$ to be the restriction of n'_2 to the circle Γ. Then $\bar{n}_2$ is a smooth mapping of the circle to the real line. By transversality, 0 is a regular value for this map. Thus, degree theory (see Hirsch (1976,

Chapter 5)) tells us that the inverse image of 0 is either empty, or is composed of an even number of points. But since $n_2'(\alpha, 0, 0) = 0$, this set is not empty. Hence there exists at least one other point of intersection; for this point, we have $n_2' = 0$ (and also $n_1' = 0$ by construction). Varying h_0 generates a whole branch of solutions, distinct from the "trivial" one $(\alpha, 0, 0)$.   *Q.E.D.*

The approach developed above may also help understanding the general idea, formally expressed by Theorem 2, that around the stationary state, the solutions of the nonlinear bifurcation equation "behave like" the solutions of the tangential linear equation. Again, we shall simply mention a few hints. Consider, first, the "real crossing" case $(v = 1)$, and linearize the system at the stationary point. From Section 3, the price vectors of any SSE within the linearized system must belong to the stable subspace of the deterministic dynamics. Consider, now, the nonlinear system, and pick up some SSE with support "close to" the stationary equilibrium; then the corresponding SSE price vectors tend to the stable manifold of the linearized system—and, more precisely, to the eigenvector of the linearized system corresponding to the eigenvalue b. Indeed, take $\alpha \in\ ] - \varepsilon, \varepsilon[$ and $\tilde{n} \in N$, both of them being close to zero, such that $\tilde{n} + r(\alpha, \tilde{n})$ is a zero of F (hence supports a SSE; see footnote 5 above). When α and $\tilde{n}$ tend to zero, so does $r(\alpha, \tilde{n})$. However, since $(\partial r(0, 0)/\partial \alpha) = 0$ and $D_n r(0, 0) = 0$, $r(\alpha, \tilde{n})$ tends to be of second order with respect to $\tilde{n}$; hence the vector $\tilde{n} + r(\alpha, \tilde{n})$, when infinitesimal, tends to belong to N. This means that it is colinear to $v_1 \otimes w_1$; in other terms, each p_i of the support can be written (at the limit) $v_1^i \cdot w_1$, hence is colinear to w_1. But w_1 is precisely the eigenvector of B associated with b; hence the conclusion.

Consider, now, the case of a complex eigenvalue. The same argument applies; it shows that, at the limit, the support of the SSE tends to belong to the stable manifold of B associated with b and $\bar{b}$—i.e., generated by w_1 and $w_2 = \bar{w}_1$. Note, however, that while the latter is two-dimensional, the nonlinear bifurcation solutions generically consist of (a finite number of) *curves*—i.e., *one-dimensional* manifolds. Hence, the limit will generically be (a finite number of) particular *vectors* on the stable plane.[11] This conclusion is not surprising: it simply reflects the fact that the matrix path is unidimensional. In general, a different path would lead to a different limit SSE in the linear system.

Lastly, an immediate consequence of this continuity property is that the local SSE just exhibited are of *order k*, since they are "close to" the SSE of the linear model—the latter being of order k from Lemma 3.

5 Conclusion

The conclusions that have been established above do provide a formal basis, within the framework we consider, to the general conjecture that has been stated in the introduction. As mentioned above, a related goal motivated a contribution by Woodford (1986), that focused attention on a model with predetermined variables. Although such a framework is potentially more general than the simple setting (borrowed from Guesnerie (1986)) adopted here, the two contributions are more complementary than substitute. Specifically, our main findings can be listed, and compared with Woodford's results in the paper already quoted (Woodford (1986)), in the following way.

Our basic result—indeterminacy implies the existence of local SSE—can also be deduced from Woodford's results. A specific contribution of our approach is to show that the structure of local SSE displays qualitative differences (reflecting the qualitative differences of the bifurcation) according to whether the relevant eigenvalues are real or complex; this last result is original.

More specifically, we prove the existence of local SSE that are based on the current state of a *Markovian* extrinsic process; in contrast, Woodford exhibits local SSE based upon the whole (infinite) history of some a priori given extrinsic random process. Since the general class of processes considered by Woodford includes the subclass of Markovian processes, our conclusion about the existence of Markovian SSE does imply the existence of SSE in Woodford's (general) sense. But the converse is not true; specifically, Woodford's approach (apparently) does not allow establishment of whether the particular SSE for which existence can be proved belong to the Markovian subclass.

We also establish that indeterminacy plus additional conditions imply the existence of SSE with *finite* support (the additional conditions are related to the cardinality of the support). Again, this is an original conclusion; some arguments suggesting that the special case of finite SSE may be of specific interest have been given in the introduction.

Our results provide a direct *characterization* of the Markovian processes triggering local SSE, and in that sense a complete answer to what we termed the characterization problem. Woodford's approach rather leads to an indirect characterization; in particular, the sunspot solutions are approximated by a vector moving average representation of the kind commonly used in time series econometrics. Clearly, both characterizations are of independent interest.

It must however be stressed that our results do *not* totally settle the problem of local SSE. Specifically, the conditions we derive are sufficient,[12] but, as it could easily be shown, they are necessary only for the specific subclass of processes (namely, finite Markov chains of given order) we consider. However, to the best of our understanding, the last version of Woodford's paper allows establishment that indeterminacy of the equilibrium is a necessary condition for the existence of Markovian sunspots of finite order (thanks to results on the representation of random processes).

Lastly, the techniques used here and those used in Woodford appear to be sufficiently different to be of independent interest.

The evaluation of our research strategy—that leads us to test the method in the present framework rather in some more complex one—relies upon subjective opinions, rather than objective evidence, on the optimal compromise between simplicity and generality. We mention in the text some obvious directions of generalization; this will be the topic of forthcoming research. Also, it must be remembered that, even in our framework, SSE that are not local in the sense given above are far from fully understood. Clearly, there is room for further investigations, and not only in more complex settings than the one we considered in this chapter.

Appendix

Proof of Lemma 3

The proof relies upon the following basic result.

LEMMA 5   Let M be a $(n \times n)$ Markov matrix with positive components; let $(1, \mu_2, \ldots, \mu_k)$ be the real eigenvalues of M, and $(v_1, \bar{v}_1, \ldots, v_l, \bar{v}_l)$ the complex eigenvalues (with $k + 2l = n$). There exists $\varepsilon > 0$ such that, for any real vector $(\mu_2', \ldots, \mu_k')$ and any complex vector $(v_1', \ldots, v_l')$ such that $|\mu_m' - \mu_m| < \varepsilon$ for $m = 2, \ldots, k$ and $|v_j' - v_j| < \varepsilon$ for $j = 1, \ldots, l$, there exists a Markov matrix M', with positive coefficients, the spectrum of which is $(1, \mu_2', \ldots, \mu_k', v_1', \bar{v}_1', \ldots, v_l', \bar{v}_l')$.

Proof   Set $v_j = v_j^1 + i v_j^2$. We know, from the theory of Jordan reduction, that there exists an invertible matrix P_0 such that $M = P_0^{-1} \cdot J_0 \cdot P_0$, where

$$J_0 = \begin{pmatrix} 0 & & & & & & & & \\ u_2 & \mu_2 & & & & & & & \\ & & \ddots & & & & 0 & & \\ & & u_k & \mu_k & & & & & \\ & & & & v_1^1 & v_1^2 & & & \\ & & & & -v_1^2 & v_1^1 & & & \\ & & 0 & & & & \ddots & & \\ & & & & & & & v_l^1 & v_l^2 \\ & & & & & & & -v_l^2 & v_l^1 \end{pmatrix}.$$

Moreover, we can assume that the sum of the first line of P_0 is nonzero (if not, just multiply one of the eigenvectors by some λ).

We now show that there exist a lower triangular, invertible matrix $G = (g_{ij})$ such that

$$GP_0 \begin{pmatrix} 1 \\ \vdots \\ 1 \end{pmatrix} = \begin{pmatrix} 1 \\ 0 \\ \vdots \\ 0 \end{pmatrix}.$$

Indeed, set

$$\begin{pmatrix} p_1 \\ \vdots \\ p_n \end{pmatrix} = P_0 \cdot \begin{pmatrix} 1 \\ \vdots \\ 1 \end{pmatrix},$$

with $p_1 \neq 0$. Define $g_{11} = 1/p_1$, and $g_{ij} = 0$ for $j > i$; for $j < i$, pose $g_{ij} = 1/p_j$ if $p_i \cdot p_j \neq 0$, $g_{ij} = 0$ otherwise; lastly, $g_{ii} = -(1/p_i)\Sigma_{j=1}^{i-1} p_j g_{ij}$ if $p_i \neq 0$, $g_{ii} = 1$ otherwise.

Note that $g_{ii} \neq 0$. Then G satisfies the announced condition, and is invertible since all diagonal elements are nonzero.

Set $GP_0 = P$; then $P_0 = G^{-1}P$, where G^{-1} is lower triangular, and

$$M = P^{-1}GJ_0G^{-1}P = P^{-1}JP,$$

where $J = GJ_0G^{-1}$.

Since G is lower triangular, J is lower triangular but for the terms of the ith row and $(i + 1)$th column where $i = k + 1, \ldots, k + 2l - 1$.

Now, for any $(\mu'_2, \ldots, \mu'_k, v'_1, \ldots, v'_l)$ satisfying $|\mu_i - \mu'_i| < \varepsilon$ and $|v_j - v'_j| < \varepsilon$, pose $\varepsilon_i = \mu_i - \mu'_i$, $\xi_j = v_j - v'_j = \xi_j^1 + i\xi_j^2$, and define M_ε by

$$M_\varepsilon = M + P^{-1} J_\varepsilon P,$$

where

$$J_\varepsilon = \begin{pmatrix} 0 & & & & & & & & \\ & \varepsilon_1 & & & & & & & \\ & & \ddots & & & & 0 & & \\ & & & \varepsilon_k & & & & & \\ & & & & \xi_1^1 & \xi_1^2 & & & \\ & & & & -\xi_1^2 & \xi_1^1 & & & \\ & & 0 & & & & \ddots & & \\ & & & & & & & \xi_l^1 & \xi_l^2 \\ & & & & & & & -\xi_l^1 & \xi_l^1 \end{pmatrix}.$$

Then:

M_ε has real terms.

The spectrum of M_ε is exactly $(1, \mu'_2, \ldots, \mu'_k, v'_1, \bar{v}'_1, \ldots, v'_l, \bar{v}'_l)$ (just remark that $M_\varepsilon = P^{-1}(J + J_\varepsilon)P$; the k first diagonal terms and the $l(2 \times 2)$ diagonal blocs of J are the same as J_0, since the spectrum of J and J_0 are identical; then $J + J_\varepsilon$ has the same form as J, with the k first diagonal terms equal to 1, $\mu_2 + \varepsilon_2, \ldots, \mu_k + \varepsilon_k$, and the l last diagonal blocks equal to

$$\begin{pmatrix} v_1^1 + \xi_1^1 & v_1^2 + \xi_1^2 \\ -v_1^2 - \xi_1^2 & v_1^1 + \xi_1^1 \end{pmatrix}, \ldots, \begin{pmatrix} v_l^1 + \xi_l^2 & v_l^2 + \xi_l^2 \\ -v_l^2 - \xi_l^2 & v_l^1 + \xi_l^1 \end{pmatrix};$$

hence the conclusion).

For ε small enough, $\| M - M_\varepsilon \|$ is arbitrarily small; in particular, for ε small enough, all coefficient of M_ε are positive.

Lastly,

$$M_\varepsilon \cdot \begin{pmatrix} 1 \\ \vdots \\ 1 \end{pmatrix} = M \begin{pmatrix} 1 \\ \vdots \\ 1 \end{pmatrix} + P^{-1} J_\varepsilon P \begin{pmatrix} 1 \\ \vdots \\ 1 \end{pmatrix} = \begin{pmatrix} 1 \\ \vdots \\ 1 \end{pmatrix},$$

since

$$P \begin{pmatrix} 1 \\ \vdots \\ 1 \end{pmatrix} = \begin{pmatrix} 1 \\ \vdots \\ 0 \end{pmatrix} \quad \text{and} \quad J_\varepsilon \cdot \begin{pmatrix} 1 \\ 0 \\ 0 \end{pmatrix} = 0.$$

Hence M_ε is a Markov matrix, which closes the proof.

We can now end the proof of Lemma 3. For b real, it is well known that we can find a matrix $M(0)$ with positive components, such that $1/b$ is an eigenvalue of $M(0)$. From the proof of Theorem 1, we know that the same is true if b is complex. From Lemma 5, we can choose the eigenvalues of $M(0)$ to be different (and different from the inverse of the eigenvalues of B), which proves (a). Now, (b) and (c) are immediate consequences of Lemma 5.

Notes

1. We are indebted to I. Ekeland, J. M. Grandmont, R. Radner, and to the Editor and three anonymous referees for helpful comments and advices. Errors are ours.

2. It includes in particular the standard OLG model with representative consumer and separable preferences. However, although the state variable might be capital (see Woodford (1988a)), the standard optimal growth model dose not enter this class.

3 We adopt here the terminology of Woodford (1984). Roughly speaking, the steady state is indeterminate when it is not a locally unique perfect foresight equilibrium, i.e., when it is attracting in the local perfect foresight dynamics (see Geanakoplos and Polemarchakis (1991) for a precise definition).

4. Farmer and Woodford (1989) made clear that it was indeed indeterminacy, rather than backward-bending labor supply, that was responsible for local sunspot equilibria. A fuller understanding of the question for one-dimensional models of OLG type has obtained from papers of, for example, Azariadis and Guesnerie (1986), Grandmont (1986), Chiappori and Guesnerie (1989).

5. If the deterministic dynamics are written in the "forward" sense—i.e. future state is given as a function of the present state—then indeterminacy requires the eigen-

value to be of absolute value less than one. In this chapter, we shall use the inverse normalization, hence, in our approach, indeterminacy is linked with the existence of eigenvalues *outside* the unit disk.

6. See, for instance, Woodford (1990a).

7. Note that a "quantity consistency" axiom appeared (as Axiom A1) in the just quoted studies. Quantity consistency is here a consequence of a definition of $\tilde{Z}$ (which stipulates that it only depends on the probability distribution of future prices). Formally, it implies the following relationship for functions $\tilde{Z}^k$. Assume that $p = (p_1, \ldots, p_k) \in P^k$ is such that $p_i = p_j$ for the pair i, j (with, say, $i < j$). Define p' in P^{k-1} by $p' = p_{-j} = (p_1, \ldots, p_{j-1}, p_{j+1}, \ldots, p_k)$. Then, for any p_0 and λ in S^{k-1},

$$\tilde{Z}^k(p_0, p, \lambda) = \tilde{Z}^{k-1}(p_0, p', \lambda')$$

where $\lambda' = (\lambda_1, \ldots, \lambda_{i-1}, \lambda_i + \lambda_j, \lambda_{i+1}, \ldots, \lambda_{j-1}, \lambda_{j+1}, \ldots, \lambda_k) \in S^k$.

8. This result has been independently established by J. M. Grandmont.

9. Some references dealing with the same situations (i.e., bifurcations of codimension two with semi-simple eigenvalues) are Chow and Hale (1982, Ch. 5, pp. 188 and seq.) and McLeod and Sattinger (1973). Their sufficient conditions, however, turn out to be quite difficult to interpret and apply within our framework.

10. To summarize the interest of this equation, assume that, for α given, there exists a $\tilde{n}$ such that $n'(\alpha, \tilde{n}) = 0$. Define $\tilde{r} = r(\alpha, \tilde{n})$. Then, by definition of $n'(\cdot)$ and $r(\cdot)$:

$$F(\alpha, \tilde{n} + r(\alpha, \tilde{n})) = -n'(\alpha, \tilde{n}) = 0$$

or

$$F(\alpha, \tilde{n} + \tilde{r}) = 0.$$

Pose $\tilde{p} = \bar{p} + (\tilde{n} + \tilde{r})$; then $\tilde{p}$ is a zero of $\hat{Z}^k$ different from $\bar{p}$, hence a SSE associated with matrix $M(\alpha)$. In other words, any solution of the bifurcation equation can be immediately transformed into a SSE.

11. A very special (and nongeneric) case is when the bifurcation equation is invariant under a continuous transformation group. It can be shown, in that case, that the bifurcation solutions no longer consist of separate curves, but form sheets. Since this situation is highly nongeneric in our context, we shall not study it here; the reader is referred to McLeod and Sattinger (1973) (though the latter use a different approach, based upon finite-dimensional degree theory).

12. For an early discussion of this point, see Laitner (1985).

IV

Variations and Extensions

8 Stability of Cycles with Adaptive Learning Rules

Roger Guesnerie and
Michael Woodford

1 Introduction

This chapter considers the problem of stability of learning procedures in a dynamical system that is one-dimensional and one-step
forward-looking. Such dynamical systems have often been studied
in the economic literature when, for example, they are associated
with simple versions of the overlapping generations model.

In this chapter, and this is its main specificity, attention is focused
on a simple category of learning rules, that is, adaptive learning
rules. With such learning rules, which have been introduced in
the early literature on learning, expectations are revised according
to the gap between previous expectations and realizations. The
rules depend on a single parameter α, which describes how quickly
expectations react to present conditions. The coefficient α then
reflects the relative weight of present observations and of an aggregate index of past observations.

The study of this simple class of learning rules had two main
purposes.

First, interest in simple learning rules has remained vivid in the
recent literature (see, e.g., the least squares learning of Marcet and
Sargent, 1989a,b). In this chapter, by focusing attention on a simple
class of adaptive rules, for which the trade-off between present and
(aggregate) past observations can be parametrized, one can expect

both to exhibit more precise results and to develop intuition that cannot be grasped through the complexity of more general learning procedures.

Second, the present study is intended to be a first step toward a study of learning stability where sunspot equilibria rather than purely periodic equilibria are considered. Results on this subject have been obtained by Mike Woodford (1990). The adaptive learning procedures considered here, which later will be compared to the ones analyzed in Woodford's article, provide a potentially more general setting that is well-designed to test the robustness of previous results.

The study proceeds as follows:

· Section 2 presents the model.

· In Section 3, we first exhibit a necessary condition for learning stability and then a sufficient condition. The latter result is reminiscent of the results obtained by Grandmont and Laroque (1986, 1990) for general, but not directly comparable, learning rules in a similar setting.

· In Section 4, we exploit fully the possibilities offered by the specific structure under scrutiny and we exhibit a necessary and sufficient condition for learning stability.

2   The Model

We are considering a one-dimensional one-step forward-looking dynamical system. The dynamics of the system are governed by

$$p_t = \varphi(p_{t+1}^e). \tag{1}$$

The level of the state variable today, p_t, depends on the expected level of the state variable tomorrow, p_{t+1}^e (expectations are point expectations commonly held by all actors in the system). Many dynamic models of the economic literature can be studied under the reduced form (1). In particular, in simple versions of the overlapping generations model, p_t can be identified with the money price level at period t, and p_{t+1}^e is the expected price level for period $t + 1$. (See Chiappori and Guesnerie, 1989.)

It is useful to recall some classical definitions.

· A *perfect foresight equilibrium* consists of a sequence $\{p_t\}$ such that

$$p_t = \varphi(p_{t+1}). \tag{1'}$$

· A *steady-state equilibrium* is associated with $\bar{p}$ such that

$$\bar{p} = \varphi(\bar{p}).$$

· A *periodic equilibrium* of order k consists of $\bar{p}_1, \ldots, \bar{p}_k$ such that

$$\bar{p}_1 = \varphi(\bar{p}_2), \ldots, \bar{p}_{k-1} = \varphi(\bar{p}_k), \quad \bar{p}_k = \varphi(\bar{p}_1). \tag{2}$$

· Equivalently, if one denotes φ^k the kth iterate of φ, then

$$\bar{p}_1 = \varphi^k(\bar{p}_l), \quad l = 1, \ldots, k. \tag{3}$$

An important issue in the study of stationary equilibria (steady-state or periodic equilibria) is whether they are determinate or indeterminate. A stationary equilibrium is determinate if there is no perfect foresight equilibrium (in the sense of the previous definition (1')) that is close (for some adequate topology on the space of infinite sequences) to the stationary equilibrium. (See Woodford, 1984, for a comprehensive discussion of the concept.)

Determinacy normally obtains whenever there exists *no* other perfect foresight equilibrium $\{p_t\}$ that converges to the stationary equilibrium under consideration. This latter fact is itself a consequence of local asymptotic stability of the equilibrium with respect to φ (or φ^k).

When the function φ of the reduced form (1) is differentiable, then the following criteria for asymptotic stability (and then for determinacy) are well known.

· A steady-state $\bar{p}$ is *determinate* if $|\varphi'| < 1$, where φ' is the derivative of φ at $\bar{p}$.

· A periodic equilibrium $(\bar{p}_1, \ldots, \bar{p}_k)$ is *determinate* if $|\varphi'_1 \times \varphi'_2 \times \ldots \times \varphi'_k| < 1$,

where $\varphi'_1, \varphi'_2, \ldots, \varphi'_k$ are the derivatives of φ, respectively, at $\bar{p}_1$, $\bar{p}_2, \ldots, \bar{p}_k$.

Equivalently, the criterion says that the absolute value of the derivative of φ^k at (any) $\bar{p}_l$ is smaller than 1.

We are now going to provide another interpretation of the previous conditions for determinacy.

Normalize p on $[0, 1]$ and consider ψ^1 a vector field on $[0, 1]$: $\psi^1 : p \to p - \varphi(p)$.

The Poincaré–Hopf index of the vector field ψ^1 in $\bar{p}$ is +1 iff the derivative of ψ^1 is positive iff $\varphi' < 1$.

Note that if the vector field is "pointing outward"—as it typically is in standard economic specifications reducible to form (1)—a Poincaré–Hopf index (from now on PH index) of −1 would signal other zeros of ψ and then other steady states. On the contrary, a PH index of +1 does not "signal" other steady states.

In the general case, consider ψ^k a vector field on $[0, 1]^k$:

$$\psi^k : (p_1, p_2, \ldots, p_k) \to (p_1 - \varphi(p_2), p_2 - \varphi(p_3), \ldots, p_k - \varphi(p_1)).$$

The PH index of the vector field ψ^k at $(\bar{p}_1, \bar{p}_2, \ldots, \bar{p}_k)$, a zero of ψ^k, is +1 iff the determinant of the Jacobian matrix associated with ψ^k at $(\bar{p}_1, \bar{p}_2, \ldots, \bar{p}_k)$ is positive. In fact, the value of the determinant is easily computed and equals $1 - \varphi'_1 \ldots \varphi'_k$. Hence the PH index is +1 iff $\varphi'_1 \ldots \varphi'_k < 1$.

From now on, we denote $\varphi'_1, \ldots, \varphi'_k$ as v^k. We should recall

the PH index of ψ^k is $+1 \Leftrightarrow v^k < 1$. $\qquad\qquad (4)$

Note that, as in the one-dimensional case, if the vector field ψ^k points outward, a PH index of −1 in one zero of the vector field signals the existence of other zeros.

Let us now come to the learning dynamics we are going to consider. It is described by

$$p_{t+1}^e = \alpha p_{t+1-k} + (1-\alpha)p_{t+1-k}^e, \quad \alpha \in [0,1]. \tag{5}$$

The price expected at time $t + 1$ is a convex combination of the
actual and *expected* prices k periods before. The learning rule can be
rewritten as a function of past observations alone. Putting

$$p_{nk+l}^e = \alpha p_{(n-1)k+l} + \alpha(1-\alpha)p_{(n-2)k+l} + \alpha(1-\alpha)^2 p_{(n-3)k+l} + \ldots$$
$$l = 1, \ldots, k. \tag{5'}$$

We note here that the rule does not belong to the class of finite
memory learning rules considered by Grandmont and Laroque
(1986, 1988). However, adapting previous definitions of these
authors, the rule would detect cycles of order k: If a cycle $\bar{p}_1, \ldots, \bar{p}_k$
repeats itself an infinity of times before time t, agents will forecast
a new cycle from time t on. Note, nevertheless, that there is no sense
in which the rule detects cycles of period $2k$.

The rule is an adaptation of learning rules that are standard in
the case of a steady state to the case where agents do not rule out
the possibility of occurrence of periodic equilibria of period k. In
some basic sense, this rule is ad hoc, as any other learning rule. It
has the merit of simplicity and also can be justified by agents'
beliefs, which, although they fall short of being "fully rational," are
"reasonable." For example, agents believe that the process generating prices is (potentially) periodic with period k, so that prices are
drawn from the same distribution every kth period, whereas the distributions drawn from in any k successive periods need have no
connections with one another. Given this belief, agents attempt
separately to estimate $\bar{p}_1$, the average of p_t in any period where
$t = nk + 1$, $\bar{p}_2$ the average value of p_t in any period where $t = nk + 2$,
and so on. The estimate of $\bar{p}_1$ is updated each time a new observation occurs in a period where $t = nk + 1$, using an "adaptive

expectations" formula of the type used by Cagan, Nerlove, and others. The weighting of periods made explicit in (5') does not treat present and past symmetrically. It can be justified by a belief that permanent changes in the true value of $\bar{p}_1$ occur occasionally so that more recent observations are of greatest value in helping to estimate the current value. With such beliefs, the size of α that makes sense depends upon one's belief about how frequently the permanent changes occur and how large the variance of such changes, relative to the variance in the prices drawn from the distribution when $\bar{p}_1$ is fixed.

The learning dynamics of the system obtains from the superposition of the equilibrium rule (1) and the learning rule (5):

$$p_t = \varphi(p_{t+1}^e), \tag{1}$$

$$p_{t+1}^e = \alpha p_{t+1-k} + (1-\alpha)p_{t+1-k}^e. \tag{5}$$

Consider a periodic solution of order k of equations (2) ($\bar{p}_1, \ldots,$ $\bar{p}_k$). Then $p_t = \bar{p}_{t(\text{mod } k)}$, $p_t^e = \bar{p}_{t(\text{mod } k)}$ is also a periodic solution of equations (1) and (5). The central question of this chapter can now be precisely formulated: Under which conditions is such a periodic equilibrium locally stable under the learning dynamics, (1) and (5)?

In order to answer the question, let us eliminate expectations from (1) and (5) and let us focus attention on the dynamics of actual prices. Combining (1) and (5) yields:

$$p_t = \varphi[\alpha p_{t+1-k} + (1-\alpha)\varphi^{-1}(p_{t-k})]. \tag{6}$$

Adding

$$p_{t-1} = p_{t-1},$$

$$\vdots$$

$$p_{t+1-k} = p_{t+1-k},$$

we can write

$$\begin{pmatrix} p_t \\ \vdots \\ p_{t+1-k} \end{pmatrix} = \Phi \begin{pmatrix} p_{t-1} \\ \vdots \\ p_{t-k} \end{pmatrix}.$$

Hence, the evolution of actual prices is associated with a dynamical system in the space IR^k. It is easy to check that a periodic equilibrium $(\bar{p}_k, \ldots, \bar{p}_1)$ of order k (solution of (2)) is also a fixed point of the kth iterate of the map Φ (we denote it Φ^k). Local stability of the learning dynamics depends upon the stability of Φ^k and, hence, on the eigenvalues of the Jacobian matrix of Φ^k at the fixed point. The next section is devoted to the study of the latter question.

3 Preliminary Results

Let $(\bar{p}_k, \ldots, \bar{p}_1)$ be a periodic equilibrium of order k and let $D(\Phi^k)$ be the Jacobian of the kth iterate of the map Φ just defined before in equations (6'). Lemma 1 gives an explicit form of $D(\Phi^k)$.

LEMMA 1   For $k \geq 3$,

$$D(\Phi^k) = \begin{pmatrix} 1-\alpha & 0 & 0 & \cdots & \alpha^2\varphi_1'\varphi_k' & \alpha(1-\alpha)\varphi_1' \\ \alpha\varphi_2' & 1-\alpha & 0 & \cdots & 0 & 0 \\ 0 & \alpha\varphi_3' & 1-\alpha & \cdots & 0 & 0 \\ & & & & \alpha\varphi_k' & 1-\alpha \end{pmatrix},$$

where $\varphi_1', \ldots, \varphi_k'$ are the derivatives of φ at $\bar{p}_1, \ldots, \bar{p}_k$. Also

$$D(\Phi^2) = \begin{pmatrix} 1-\alpha+\alpha^2\varphi_1'\varphi_2' & \alpha(1-\alpha)\varphi_1' \\ \alpha\varphi_2' & (1-\alpha) \end{pmatrix},$$

$$D(\Phi) = \begin{pmatrix} 1-\alpha \\ 1-\varphi'\alpha \end{pmatrix}.$$

Proof   We have

$$
\begin{pmatrix} \bar{p}_k \\ \vdots \\ \bar{p}_1 \end{pmatrix} = \Phi \times \Phi \dots \Phi \begin{pmatrix} \bar{p}_k \\ \vdots \\ \bar{p}_1 \end{pmatrix}.
$$

Let $D\Phi_j$ be the derivative $D\Phi$ evaluated at

$$
\begin{pmatrix} \bar{p}_{j-2(\mathrm{mod}\ k)} \\ \vdots \\ \bar{p}_{j-(k+1)(\mathrm{mod}\ k)} \end{pmatrix}.
$$

Then $D\Phi^k = D\Phi_1 \times D\Phi_2 \dots D\Phi_k$. Note that

$$
D\Phi_j = \begin{pmatrix} 0 \text{---} 0 & \alpha\varphi_j' & 1-\alpha \\ & I_{k-1} & & 0 \end{pmatrix},
$$

where $\varphi_j' = \varphi'(\bar{p}_j)$.

Let us proceed by induction (for $k \geq 3$) and assume that the product of the first p terms, for any $1 \leq p \leq k - 2$, is

$$
\begin{bmatrix}
0 \text{---} 0 & \alpha\varphi_1' & 1-\alpha & 0 & \text{---} & 0 \\
 & 0 & \alpha\varphi_2' & 1-\alpha & & | \\
 & 0 & & & & | \\
 & & & & & 0 \\
 & & & & \alpha\varphi_p' & 1-\alpha \\
I_{k-p} & & & & 0 & 0 \\
 & & & & & 0
\end{bmatrix}.
$$

One then shows that the product of the $p + 1$ terms is

$$\begin{bmatrix} 0 ——0 & \alpha\varphi_1' & 1-\alpha & 0 & — & 0 \\ & 0 & \alpha\varphi_2' & 1-\alpha & & 0 \\ & & & & & | \\ & & & \alpha\varphi_{p+1}' & 1-\alpha \\ & & & 0 & 0 \\ I_{k-p-1} & — & — & — \end{bmatrix}.$$

The last iteration consists in the multiplication of

$$\begin{bmatrix} \alpha\varphi_1' & 1-\alpha & 0 & — & — & — & 0 \\ 0 & \alpha\varphi_2' & 1-\alpha & & & & | \\ | & & & & & & | \\ 0 & & & & \alpha\varphi_{k-1}' & 1-\alpha \\ 1 & 0 & — & — & — & 0 & 0 \end{bmatrix} \begin{bmatrix} 0 & — & — & — & 0 & \alpha\varphi_k' & 1-\alpha \\ 1 & & & & & 0 & 0 \\ | & & & & & \\ | & & & & & \\ 0 & — & — & — & — & 1 & 0 \end{bmatrix}.$$

The cases where $k = 2$ and $k = 1$ are treated directly. The conclusion follows. □

Lemma 2 exhibits the "characteristic polynomial" of $D(\Phi^k)$.

LEMMA 2 The zeros of the characteristic polynomial associated with $J(\Phi^k)$ are the zeros of

$$P(\lambda) = (\lambda - (1-\alpha))^k - \lambda\alpha^k v^k,$$

where v^k is defined (as before) by $v^k = \varphi_1' \dots \varphi_k'$.

Proof The characteristic polynomial is defined by

$$\det(D(\Phi^k) - \lambda I) = 0.$$

Developing (for example) with respect to the first line yields (for $k \geq 3$)

$$(1-\alpha-\lambda)^k + (-1)^k(1-\alpha-\lambda)\alpha^k v^k + (-1)^{k+1}(1-\alpha)\alpha^k v^k,$$

that is,

$$(1-\alpha-\lambda)^k + (-1)^{k+1}\lambda\alpha^k v^k,$$

the zeros of which are the same as those of

$$P(\lambda) = (\lambda - (1-\alpha))^k - \lambda \alpha^k v^k.$$

The same result obtains for $k = 2, 1$.   □

It should be noted here that the characteristic polynomial and hence the eigenvalues of $D\Phi^k$ depend upon the parameter of the learning rule (α), and upon the characteristics of the original dynamical systems only through v^k.

Let us recall that, as shown in Section 2:

$|v^k| < 1 \Leftrightarrow$ determinacy of the system (1'),

$v^k < 1 \Leftrightarrow$ the PH index of the mapping ψ^k is +1.

A necessary (Proposition 1) and a sufficient (Proposition 2) condition for stability can be stated as follows:

PROPOSITION 1   A necessary condition for local stability is that $v^k < 1$, that is, that the PH index of the k-period cycle, defined with respect to the map ψ^k, is +1.

Proof   A necessary condition for stability is that

$$\text{Sign } P(\lambda = 1) = \text{Sign } P(\lambda = +\infty).$$

But Sign $P(\lambda = +\infty)$ is positive and Sign $P(\lambda = 1)$ is the sign of $1 - v^k$. The conclusion follows.   □

PROPOSITION 2   A sufficient condition for local stability is that $|v^k| < 1$, that is, that perfect foresight dynamics be determinate near the period k cycle.

Proof   We must show that $|v^k| < 1$ implies that $P(\lambda) = 0$ cannot have a solution outside the unit circle.

We will show that

$$|\lambda - (1-\alpha)|^k = |\lambda| |\alpha^k v| \tag{7}$$

is impossible whenever $|\lambda| \geq 1$.

Let us put $|\lambda| = 1 + \epsilon, \epsilon \geq 0$,

$$|\lambda - (1-\alpha)| \geq |\lambda| - 1 - \alpha = \epsilon + \alpha,$$

and

$$|\lambda - 1 - \alpha|^k \geq (\epsilon + \alpha)^k.$$

If the equation $(\epsilon + \alpha)^k = (1 + \epsilon)\alpha^k|v^k|$ has no solution for $\varepsilon > 0$, then (7) has no solution for $|\lambda| \geq 1$.

Let us consider the curves $y = (\epsilon + \alpha)^k$ and $y = (1 + \epsilon)\alpha^k|v^k|$ depicted in Figure 8.1. Considering the diagram and the convexity of x^k, one concludes that the two curves will have no intersection point for $\varepsilon > 0$ whenever $|v^k|$ is smaller than 1 and the slope of the curve at A is larger than the slope of the line. The latter inequality, $k\alpha^{k-1} > \alpha^k|v^k|$, holds when $|v^k| < 1$.   □

Let us comment briefly on the results:

The sufficient condition given in Proposition 2 is remarkably simple and the statement speaks for itself. The fact that determinacy of the dynamic system and convergence of the learning dynamics have a relationship is intuitively plausible. For example, in the limit case, where the weight of the past in the formulation of expectations vanishes ($\alpha = 1$), the learning dynamics reduces to $p_t = \varphi(p_{t+1-k})$ and its local stability is equivalent to the fact that $|v^k| < 1$, that is, equivalent to determinacy. This equivalence ceases to hold when $\alpha \neq 1$, but it is remarkable that determinacy remains a sufficient condition for stability whatever α.

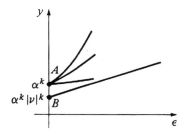

Figure 8.1

In the literature, the role of v^k for local stability has been ascertained for learning rules with finite memory but with more general functional forms. In fact, an extension of the proposition in Grandmont and Laroque to general learning rules with finite memory would imply our Proposition 2 as a particular case. (We leave it to the reader to check precisely this assertion.) We do not know whether such extensions are true, but they are intuitively plausible.

Proposition 1 is also extremely simple. One of its consequences is not so transparent and deserves some comments. Consider the vector field ψ^k. Assume that the system under consideration has a unique steady state and assume that the PH index of ψ^k in this steady state is -1. Then if the vector field points outward, the fact that the PH index in the steady state is -1 implies that the vector field has other zeros and these zeros are necessarily truly periodic equilibria. Note that two of these zeros, at least, have necessarily an index of $+1$ and satisfy the necessary condition for local stability of any α-learning rule. In this case, we would say that the Poincaré–Hopf method "detects cycles" (in the economic literature, the PH method has mainly been used to detect sunspots; see Azariadis and Guesnerie, 1982a,b, 1986; Spear, 1984; Guesnerie, 1986; Chiappori and Guesnerie, 1989). The remarkable fact is that *when the PH method detects cycles* from a given steady state, *the given steady state is unstable for a learning process* (which considers the possibility of cycles) *whereas some of the detected cycles are good candidates for stability.*

The latter result is reminiscent of some the findings of Woodford, who considers learning rules that are compatible with sunspots beliefs. There is no immediate correspondence between Woodford's framework and ours. However, our problems become quite similar when, on the one hand, the sunspot matrices tend to cycle matrices in Woodford's model and, on the other hand, $\alpha \to 0$ in our model. Indeed, the findings on the stability of equilibria detected by PH methods drawn from Proposition 2 and from Woodford's results, in the limit case just sketched, do coincide.

4   Necessary and Sufficient Conditions for Stability

Both Propositions 1 and 2 are, in fact, special cases of the following more general characterization:

THEOREM 1   Given $k \geq 2$ and $0 < \alpha < 1$, there exists a critical value $v^*(k, \alpha)$ such that a k cycle will be locally stable under the learning dynamics if and only if $v^*(k, \alpha) < v^k < 1$. Furthermore, for all k and α, $-\infty < v^*(k, \alpha) < -1$.

Proof of this requires that we first establish some preliminary lemmas.

From now on, we denote v^k by v (dropping the upper index). A lower index will be used sometimes for denoting specific values of v. Recall that (ignoring nongeneric cases) a k cycle is locally stable if and only if all k roots of the polynomial

$$[\lambda - (1 - \alpha)]^k = \alpha^k v \lambda \tag{7}$$

have modulus less than 1. From this, it is obvious that, for a given k and α, stability depends only upon the value of v. Accordingly, we wish to study how the set of roots of (7) changes as we vary v. Let us define $B(k, \alpha)$ as the set of negative *bifurcation values* for v, given k and α, that is, as the set of values $v < 0$ for which there exists a (possibly complex) λ with $|\lambda| = 1$ that satisfies (7). Only at such a value of v can the number of roots with modulus less than 1 change. We need only consider negative bifurcation values, since Propositions 1 and 2 have already established that all k roots have modulus less than 1 for all $-1 < v < 1$, whereas less than k roots have this property for all $v > 1$.

LEMMA 3   If k is even, $B(k, \alpha)$ is a set of $k/2$ distinct values. Let $k \geq 2$ and $0 < \alpha < 1$. Then

$$-\left(\frac{2-\alpha}{\alpha}\right)^k = v_{k/2} < \ldots < v_2 < v_1 < -1.$$

At each of the higher values, v_1 through $v_{k/2-1}$, there is a complex pair of roots of (7) with $|\lambda| = 1$. At $v_{k/2}$, there is a real root $\lambda = -1$. If k is odd, $B(k, \alpha)$ is a set of $(k-1)/2$ distinct values,

$$-\left(\frac{2-\alpha}{\alpha}\right)^k < v_{(k-1)/2} < \ldots < v_2 < v_1 < -1$$

at each of which there is a complex pair of roots with $|\lambda| = 1$.

Proof   If $|\lambda| = 1$, we can write $\lambda = e^{i\theta}$ for some $-\pi < \theta \leq \pi$. Then $v \in B(k, \alpha)$ if and only if the equation

$$\left[e^{i\theta} - (1-\alpha)\right]^k = \alpha^k v e^{i\theta} \tag{8}$$

has a solution $-\pi < \theta \leq \pi$. Let us also adopt the notation

$$\left[e^{i\theta} - (1-\alpha)\right] = x e^{i\phi}, \quad -\pi < \phi \leq \pi.$$

This defines two continuous functions, $x(\theta, \alpha)$ and $\phi(\theta, \alpha)$, on the domain $-\pi < \theta \leq \pi$. For future reference, it should be noted that these functions are defined by

$$x(\theta, \alpha) = [2(1-\alpha)(1-\cos\theta) + \alpha^2]^{1/2}, \tag{9}$$

$$\tan\phi(\theta, \alpha) = \frac{\sin\theta}{\cos\theta - (1-\alpha)}, \tag{10}$$

where the solution to (10) is selected from the interval $0 \leq \phi < \pi$ for $0 \leq \theta < \pi$, from the interval $-\pi < \phi \leq \pi$ for $-\pi < \theta \leq 0$, and the solution is chosen to be $\phi = \pi$ in the case $\theta = \pi$. (Under these selection rules, $\phi(\theta, \alpha)$ is a smooth function of both arguments, even though the right-hand side of (10) is discontinuous.) By adopting this change of variable, (8) is equivalent to

$$x(\theta, \alpha)^k = -\alpha^k v, \tag{11}$$

$$k\phi(\theta, \alpha) = \theta + \pi (\text{mod } 2\pi). \tag{12}$$

(In deriving (11) and (12), we are restricting attention to the case $v < 0$.)

Now for each θ that solves (12), there exists a unique $v < 0$ that solves (11), because $x(\theta, \alpha) > 0$ for all values of its arguments. Hence, the set $B(k, \alpha)$ can be identified with the set of angles $-\pi < \theta \le \pi$ that solves (12). We turn to a consideration of the solutions of (12).

It should be noted that (10) implies that the function $\phi(\theta, \alpha)$ has the following properties:

$$\phi(-\theta, \alpha) = -\phi(\theta, \alpha), \tag{13}$$

$$\theta \le \phi(\theta, \alpha) < \theta + \frac{\pi}{2}, \quad \text{for } 0 \le \theta \le \pi, \tag{14}$$

$$\theta - \frac{\pi}{2} < \phi(\theta, \alpha) \le \theta, \quad \text{for } -\pi \le \theta \le 0, \tag{15}$$

$$\lim_{\theta \to -\pi} \phi(\theta, \alpha) = -\pi, \qquad \phi(0, \alpha) = 0, \qquad \phi(\pi, \alpha) = \pi, \tag{16}$$

$$\frac{1}{2-\alpha} \le \phi_\theta(\theta, \alpha) \le \frac{1}{\alpha}, \tag{17}$$

$$\lim_{\theta \to -\pi} \phi_\theta(\theta, \alpha) = \frac{1}{2-\alpha}, \qquad \phi_\theta(0, \alpha) = \frac{1}{\alpha}, \qquad \phi_\theta(\pi, \alpha) = \frac{1}{2-\alpha}, \tag{18}$$

$$\phi_{\theta\theta}(\theta, \alpha) < 0, \quad \text{for } 0 \le \theta \le \pi, \tag{19}$$

$$\phi_{\theta\theta}(\theta, \alpha) > 0, \quad \text{for } -\pi \le \theta \le 0. \tag{20}$$

(The general shape of the function $\phi(\theta, \alpha)$ as a function of θ is indicated in Figure 8.2.)

Now for $k \ge 2$, the left-hand side of (12) is a monotonically increasing function on the interval $[-\pi, \pi]$, taking values from $-k\pi$ to $k\pi$, with a slope always greater than 1, since

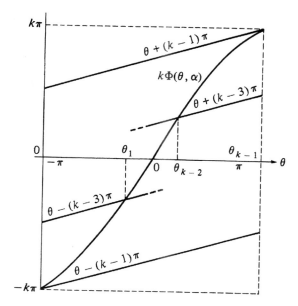

Figure 8.2

$$k\phi_\theta \geq \frac{k}{2-\alpha} > 1,$$

from (17). The right-hand side of (12) consists of a family of parallel straight lines of slope 1. If k is even, the line $\theta + (k - 1)\pi$ intersects the curve $k\phi(\theta, \alpha)$ at $\theta = \pi$, and is above it everywhere on the interval $(-\pi, \pi)$, whereas the line $\theta - (k - 1)\pi$ intersects the curve $k\phi(\theta, \alpha)$ at $\theta = -\pi$, and is below it everywhere on the interval $(-\pi, \pi)$. (See Figure 1.) It follows that each of the lines $\theta + (2n - 1)\pi$, $(4 - k)/2 \leq n \leq k/2$, intersects the curve $k\phi(\theta, \alpha)$ at exactly one point in the interval $[-\pi, \pi]$. Let the point of intersection of the line $\theta + (2n - 1)\pi$ be denoted θ_s, where $s = n + k/2 - 1$. One obtains a sequence of $k - 1$ intersection points $-\pi < \theta_1 < \theta_2 < \ldots < \theta_{k-1} = \pi$, with the further property that $\theta_{k-1-s} = -\theta_s$.

Similarly, if k is odd, the curve $k\phi(\theta, \alpha)$ lies between the lines $\theta + (k - 2)\pi$ and $\theta + k\pi$ at $\theta = \pi$, and between the lines $\theta - k\pi$ and

$\theta - (k - 2)\pi$ at $\theta = -\pi$. It follows that each of the lines $\theta + (2n - 1)\pi$, $(3 - k)/2 \le n \le (k - 1)/2$, intersects the curve at exactly one point in $(-\pi, \pi)$. Let the point of intersection of the line $\theta + (2n - 1)\pi$ be denoted θ_s, where, in this case, $s = n + (k - 1)/2$. One obtains again a sequence of $k - 1$ intersection points, where now $-\pi < \theta_1 < \theta_2 < \ldots < \theta_{k-1} < \pi$, and $\theta_{k-s} = -\theta_s$.

It follows from (9) that $x(-\theta, \alpha) = (\theta, \alpha)$. Hence, when k is even, θ_s and θ_{k-1-s} result in the same value of v as a solution to (11). Hence, the number of distinct bifurcation values in the set $B(k, \alpha)$ is only $k/2$. Let these values be denoted v_j, $j = 1, \ldots, k/2$, where

$$v_j(k, \alpha) = \frac{-x^k(\theta_{k/2+j-1}, \alpha)}{\alpha^k}.$$

Because $x(\theta, \alpha)$ is a monotonically increasing function of θ, for $0 \le \theta \le \pi$, the bifurcation values can be ordered as indicated in the statement of the lemma, and $\theta_{k-1} = \pi$ implies that $v_{k/2} = -((2 - \alpha)/\alpha)^k$. Furthermore, (9) implies that for all $0 < |\theta| < \pi$, so that $((2 - \alpha)/\alpha)^k < v_j < -1$,

$$\alpha < x(\theta, \alpha) < 2 - \alpha \quad \text{for } 1 \le j \le \frac{k}{2} - 1.$$

Finally, $\theta_{k-1} = \pi$ implies the existence of a root $\lambda = e^{i\pi} = -1$ corresponding to $v_{k/2}$, whereas $0 < |\theta_s| < \pi$ for $s \ne k - 1$ implies that $\lambda = e^{i\theta}$ is complex at each of the other bifurcation values. The existence of a pair of angles $(\theta_s, \theta_{k-1-s})$ for each of the other bifurcation values for v indicates the existence of a complex conjugate pair of roots $(\lambda, \bar{\lambda})$.

Similarly, when k is odd, θ_s and θ_{k-s} result in the same value of v, so that the number of distinct bifurcation values is only $(k - 1)/2$. These values are given by

$$v_j(k, \alpha) = \frac{-x^k(\theta_{(k-1)/2+j}, \alpha)}{\alpha^k},$$

for $j = 1, \ldots, (k - 1)/2$, and, in this case, each corresponds to a complex conjugate pair of roots $(\lambda, \bar{\lambda})$, since $0 < |\theta_s| < \Pi$ for all $1 \leq s \leq k - 1$. Again, the monotonicity at $x(\theta, \alpha)$ allows the bifurcation values to be ordered as in the statement of the lemma, and the fact that $\alpha < x(\theta_s, \alpha) < 2 - \alpha$ implies the bounds.   □

LEMMA 4   Let $k \geq 2$ and $0 < \alpha < 1$. Then as v passes from above to below the negative bifurcation value v_j, for $1 \leq j \leq k/2 - 1$ in the case that k is even, or for $1 \leq j \leq (k - 1)/2$ in the case that k is odd, a single complex conjugate pair of roots $(\lambda, \bar{\lambda})$ of (7) crosses the unit circle from inside (i.e., their modulus crosses the value 1 from below), while all other roots of (7) remain either inside or outside the unit circle. As v passes from above to below the bifurcation value $v_{k/2}$, in the case that k is even, a single real root λ of (7) passes through the value -1 from above, while all other roots remain either inside or outside the unit circle.

Proof   See Appendix A.

Proof of Theorem 1   Proposition 2 has already established that not all roots of (7) have modulus less than 1 if $v > 1$, and Proposition 1 has already established that all k roots have modulus less than 1 if $-1 < v < 1$. Since by Lemma 1, no bifurcation values occur between v_1 and -1, all k roots must have modulus less than 1 for all $v_1 < v < 1$. From Lemma 2, it follows furthermore that there are exactly $k - 2$ roots with modulus less than 1 for all $v_2 < v < v_1$, exactly $k - 4$ such roots for all $v_3 < v < v_2$, and so on, until, if k is odd, there is exactly one such root for all $-\infty < v < v_{(k-1)/2}$; or, if k is even, exactly two such roots for all $-\infty < v < v_{k/2}$. Hence, whether k is odd or even, all k roots have a modulus less than 1 if and only if $v_1 < v < 1$, and the theorem follows given the identification

$$v^*(k, \alpha) = v_1(k, \alpha).$$

Note that whether k is odd or even,

$$v^*(k, \alpha) = \frac{-x(\theta^*(k, \alpha); \alpha)^k}{\alpha^k},$$ (21)

where $\theta^*(k, \alpha)$ is the unique solution to

$$k\phi(\theta, \alpha) = \theta + \pi$$ (22)

in the interval $-\pi < \theta \le \pi$. □

A few remarks are in order relating to the result just obtained. First of all, it will be observed that the assumption $k \ge 2$ is required in the proof of both Lemmas 1 and 2. In fact, the theorem is not true in the case $k = 1$, that is, the case of steady-state equilibrium. In that case, it is easily seen that (7) has one solution,

$$\lambda = \frac{1-\alpha}{1-\alpha v}.$$

The stability condition is $|\lambda| < 1$, which is true if $v < 1$ *or* if $v > ((2 - \alpha)/\alpha)$. Hence, when $k = 1$, unlike any of the cases $k \ge 2$, the region of stability for v is not a single connected interval; it has neither a lower nor an upper bound, and, in particular, 1 is not the upper bound.

It is also worth commenting briefly upon what happens when a k-cycle loses stability due to v being moved outside the region of stability defined in the theorem. Specifically, consider a smooth one-parameter family of economies, indexed by a parameter μ, with an equilibrium condition

$$p_t = \varphi(p_{t+1}^e, \mu).$$

Suppose that $(\bar{p}_1(\mu), \ldots, \bar{p}_k(\mu))$ describes a smooth family of equilibrium k-cycles, one for each value of μ in some interval, and consider how $v(\mu)$, evaluated at this particular k-cycle, varies as μ varies.

At a value of μ such that $v(\mu) = 1$, (7) has a root $\lambda = 1$, and as a result, the derivative condition

$\text{Det}\left[D\Phi^k - I\right] \neq 0,$

needed in order to use the inverse function theorem to prove that the fixed point of the map $\Phi^k(\mu)$ is locally unique, fails when $v(\mu) = 1$. Typically (although this depends upon higher derivative conditions that we do not discuss here), there will be another family of k-cycles (fixed points of $\Phi^k(\mu)$) that intersects the family under investigation at that particular value of μ. In this case, the loss of stability of the family of k-cycles under investigation as $v(\mu)$ goes above 1 for that family may coincide with the existence of one or more nearby k-cycles that are stable (because for them $v < 1$) for the same values of μ.

In the case of a value of μ such that $v(\mu) = v^*(k, \alpha)$, more complicated bifurcations are possible. When $k = 2$, as $v(\mu)$ passes through the value $v^*(2, \alpha)$, a root of (7) passes through the value -1. In such a case, one typically (again depending upon some higher derivatives) has a *flip bifurcation*, in which a cycle of period $2k$ (of the learning dynamics) comes into existence for μ on one side or the other of the critical value. It is possible that as the k-cycle loses stability, a stable nearby $2k$-cycle comes into existence, to which the learning dynamics are attracted instead. Since we have assumed a learning rule that is consistent with all cycles of period k, but not with cycles of period $2k$, the $2k$ cycle of the *learning* dynamics will not generally correspond to a $2k$ cycle of the *perfect foresight* dynamics. When $k > 2$, as $v(\mu)$ passes through the value $v^*(k, \alpha)$, a complex conjugate pair of roots passes through the unit circle. In such a case, one typically has a discrete-time *Hopf bifurcation*, in which an invariant circle of the learning dynamics comes into existence. It is possible that as the k cycle loses stability, the learning dynamics are attracted instead to quasiperiodic motion on a nearby invariant circle. Again, this will not generally involve expectations becoming correct even asymptotically.

The following result indicates how the speed of adjustment of the learning rule affects the size of the region of stability for a k cycle:

PROPOSITION 3   Given $k \geq 2$, the critical value $v^*(k, \alpha)$ is a continuous monotonically increasing function of α, with limiting values

$$\lim_{\alpha \to 0} v^*(k, \alpha) = -\left(\cos\frac{\pi}{k}\right)^{-k},$$

$$\lim_{\alpha \to 1} v^*(k, \alpha) = -1.$$

Proof See Appendix B.

It is also of some interest to consider how $v^*(k, \alpha)$ is affected by variation in k, for given α. It is clear from (22), together with the fact that $k\phi_\theta > 1$, that increasing k causes $\theta^*(k, \alpha)$ to decrease. From (9), it is then obvious that $X^*(k, \alpha)$ (as defined in Appendix B) falls as well. It is not, however, clear from (21) how $v^*(k, \alpha)$ changes. If $X^*(k, \alpha)$ did not fall, the change in the exponents in (21) would make $v^*(k, \alpha)$ lower, since $X^*(k, \alpha) > \alpha$. On the other hand, if the exponents did not change, the decrease in $X^*(k, \alpha)$ would make $v^*(k, \alpha)$ higher. The ultimate effect on $v^*(k, \alpha)$ depends upon which of these two effects is larger, and we have not been able to reach any general conclusion about this. However, it is at least possible to describe generally what must happen in the limit of very large k:

PROPOSITION 4   For given $0 < \alpha < 1$, $v^*(k, \alpha)$ approaches -1 as k is made arbitrarily large. Furthermore, the rate of convergence is given by the expression

$$v^*(k, \alpha) = -1 - \frac{(1-\alpha)\pi^2}{2k} + O(k^{-2}).$$

Proof See Appendix C.

5   Conclusion

The results of Section 4 have provided a characterization of the conditions of learning stability. The description of the areas of stability, in terms of the underlying parameters of the system, could still be slightly refined. But on the whole, the program announced in the introduction has been completed in a way that seems reasonable.

Appendix A: Proof of Lemma 4

In order to determine how the roots of (7) vary with v in a neighborhood of a bifurcation value, we must differentiate (7) at such a value of v and near some root λ. We obtain

$$\frac{d\lambda}{dv} = \frac{\alpha^k \lambda}{k[\lambda - (1-\alpha)]^{k-1} - \alpha^k v}, \tag{A.1}$$

where the right-hand side is evaluated at the particular root λ whose motion we wish to consider. Let (21) be evaluated at a bifurcation value v_j and at a root such that $|\lambda| = 1$. We are interested in the sign of

$$\frac{1}{|\lambda|}\frac{d|\lambda|}{dv} = \mathrm{Re}\left[\frac{1}{\lambda}\frac{d\lambda}{dv}\right]$$

$$= \mathrm{Re}\left[\frac{\alpha^k}{k[\lambda - (1-\alpha)]^{k-1} - \alpha^k v}\right]$$

$$= \mathrm{Re}\left[\frac{\alpha^k}{kx^{k-1}e^{i(k-1)\phi} + x^k}\right],$$

where we use (A.1), and in the final line, we again use the notation introduced in (9) and (10) for the case of a root with $|\lambda| = 1$, as well as equation (11). It follows that

$$\mathrm{sign}\frac{d|\lambda|}{dv} = \mathrm{sign}\,\mathrm{Re}\left[kx^{k-1}e^{i(k-1)\phi} + x^k\right]$$

$$= \mathrm{sign}\left[k\cos(k-1)\phi + x\right]$$

$$= \mathrm{sign}\left[k\cos(\theta + \pi - \phi) + x\right]$$

$$= \mathrm{sign}\left[x - k\cos(\phi - \theta)\right]$$

using (12).

Equations (9) and (10) imply that

$$\cos(\phi - \theta) = \frac{1 - (1 - \alpha)\cos\theta}{x}. \tag{A.2}$$

Equation (9) also implies that

$$\begin{aligned}
x^2 &= 1 + (1 - \alpha)^2 - 2(1 - \alpha)\cos\theta \\
&< 2[1 - (1 - \alpha)\cos\theta] \\
&= 2\cos(\phi - \theta)
\end{aligned}$$

using (22), so that

$$\cos(\phi - \theta) > \frac{x}{2} \ge \frac{x}{k}$$

given that $k \ge 2$. This implies $d|\lambda|/dv < 0$, so that the modulus of the eigenvalue crosses 1 from below as v crosses the bifurcation value from above. The remaining details of the statement of the lemma then follow from Lemma 1. □

Appendix B: Proof of Proposition 3

The continuity, and indeed differentiability, of $v^*(k, \alpha)$ in α follows immediately from its implicit definition by (21) and (22). In determining how it varies with α, we consider separately the cases $k = 2$ and $k \ge 3$.

If $k = 2$, $\theta^*(2, \alpha) = \pi$ for all α. It follows from (9) and (23) that

$$v^*(2, \alpha) = -\left(\frac{2 - \alpha}{\alpha}\right)^2.$$

This is a monotonically increasing function, and has the limits indicated in the statement of the proposition. (Note that $\cos(\pi/2) = 0$.)

If $k \ge 3$, we cannot solve for $\theta^*(k, \alpha)$ in closed form. However, differentiation of (22) implies that

$$\frac{\partial \theta^*}{\partial \alpha} = \frac{k \sin \theta^*}{(k-2)[1-(1-\alpha)\cos \theta^*]+\alpha(2-\alpha)}. \tag{B.1}$$

Now it follows from (16) that

$$k\phi(0, \alpha) = 0 < \pi = 0 + \pi,$$

while it follows from (4) that

$$k\phi(\text{arc } \cos(1-\alpha), \alpha) = \frac{k\pi}{2} \ge \frac{3\pi}{2} > \text{arc } \cos(1-\alpha) + \pi$$

given $k \ge 3$. Hence, the solution to (22) must lie in the interval

$$0 < \theta^*(k, \alpha) < \text{arc } \cos(1-\alpha). \tag{B.2}$$

This implies that $\sin \theta^* > 0$, so that (B.1) implies that $\partial \theta^*/\partial \alpha > 0$. Defining $X^*(k, \alpha) = x(\theta^*(k, \alpha), \alpha)$, we can differentiate (9) to obtain

$$\frac{\partial X^*}{\partial \alpha}$$

$$= \frac{1}{X^*}\left\{\frac{(1-\alpha)k\sin^2\theta^*}{(k-2)[1-(1-\alpha)\cos \theta^*]+\alpha(2-\alpha)} + [\cos \theta^* - (1-\alpha)]\right\}. \tag{B.3}$$

The first term inside the braces is positive as just noted, and the second term is also positive because of (B.2). Hence, (B.3) implies that

$$\frac{\partial X^*}{\partial \alpha} > 0.$$

Finally, differentiation of (21) yields

$$\frac{\partial v^*}{\partial \alpha} = \frac{Kv^*}{\alpha}\left[\frac{\alpha}{X^*}\frac{\partial X^*}{\partial \alpha} - 1\right]. \tag{B.4}$$

Hence, the sign of $\partial v^*/\partial \alpha$ depends upon the sign of (α/X^*) $(\partial X^*/\partial \alpha)$. Using (B.3), we obtain

$$\frac{\alpha}{X^*}\frac{\partial X^*}{\partial \alpha}$$

$$= \frac{\alpha}{(X^*)^2}\left\{\frac{(1-\alpha)k\sin^2\theta^*}{(k-2)[1-(1-\alpha)\cos\theta^*]+\alpha(2-\alpha)}+[\cos\theta^*-(1-\alpha)]\right\}$$

$$= \frac{\alpha}{[\cos\theta^*-(1-\alpha)]^2+\sin^2\theta^*}$$

$$\times\left\{\frac{[(k-1)\cos\theta^*+(1-\alpha)][\cos\theta^*-(1-\alpha)]^2+\sin^2\theta^*}{(k-1)([\cos\theta^*-(1-\alpha)]^2+\sin^2\theta^*)+k(1-\alpha)[\cos\theta^*-(1-\alpha)]}\right\}$$

$$= \frac{\alpha[(k-1)\cos\theta^*+(1-\alpha)]}{(k-1)\{[\cos\theta^*-(1-\alpha)]^2+\sin^2\theta^*\}+k(1-\alpha)[\cos\theta^*-(1-\alpha)]}$$

$$= \frac{\alpha(k-\alpha)-\alpha(k-1)(1-\cos\theta)}{\alpha(k-\alpha)+(1-\alpha)(k-2)(1-\cos\theta)}<1,$$

where we have used (9) in the third and fourth lines. Comparing this with (B.4), and recalling that $v^* < 0$, we see that $\partial v^*/\partial\alpha > 0$, as stated in the proposition.

We turn to the evaluation of the limiting values for $v^*(k,\alpha)$. Consider, first, the limit as $\alpha \to 1$. Equation (9) implies that

$$\lim_{\alpha\to 1} X^*(k,\alpha) = 1,$$

so that (21) implies

$$\lim_{\alpha\to 1} v^*(k,\alpha) = -1.$$

The limit as $\alpha \to 0$ is not so easily evaluated. The bounds in (26) imply that

$$\lim_{\alpha\to 0}\theta^*(k,\alpha) = 0,$$

so that (9) implies

$$\lim_{\alpha\to 0} X^*(k,\alpha) = 0.$$

But this cannot be substituted into (21) to yield a determinate limit, since both numerator and denominator approach zero. However, the limit can be easily evaluated in another way. Consider how the roots of (7) vary as α approaches zero. It is evident that all k roots approach 1 as $\alpha \to 0$. Furthermore, each root approaches 1 as

$$\lambda(\alpha) = 1 + \alpha\mu + O(\alpha^2),$$

where μ is a corresponding root of the equation

$$(\mu + 1)^k = v. \tag{B.5}$$

The modulus $|\lambda(\alpha)|$ approaches 1 from below if and only if Re $\mu < 0$. Hence, all roots of (7) have a modulus less than 1 as α is made very close to zero if and only if v is such that all k roots of (29) have a negative real part. But in the case that $v < 0$, the roots of (29) are

$$\mu_j = -1 + |v|^{1/k_e} \frac{i\pi(2j-1)}{k}$$

for $j = 1, \ldots, k$. Hence,

$$\mathrm{Re}\,\mu_j = -1 + |v|^{1/k} \cos\left((2j-1)\frac{\pi}{k}\right).$$

The largest such value is the one corresponding to $j = 1$ (or equivalently to $j = k$), so that a necessary and sufficient condition for $\mathrm{Re}\mu_j < 0$ for all j is that

$$-1 + |v|^{1/k} \cos\left(\frac{\pi}{k}\right) < 0$$

or, equivalently, that

$$|v| < \left(\cos\frac{\pi}{k}\right)^{-k},$$

which is to say that

$$v > -\left(\cos\frac{\pi}{k}\right)^{-k}.$$

Hence, this must be the limiting value of $v^*(k, \alpha)$ as α approaches zero.   □

Appendix C: Proof of Proposition 4

It is easily verified from (9), (18), and (22) that $\theta^*(k, \alpha)$, $X^*(k, \alpha)$, and $v^*(k, \alpha)$ are well defined (even if not meaningful) for nonintegral values of k, and that these functions so interpreted are continuous, and indeed differentiable, functions of k. Let us consider these quantities as functions of k^{-1}, as k^{-1} approaches zero.

It is evident from (22) that

$$\lim_{k^{-1} \to 0} \theta^*(k, \alpha) = 0,$$

$$\lim_{k^{-1} \to 0} k\phi(\theta^*, \alpha) = \pi.$$

Furthermore, differentiation of (22) yields

$$\frac{\partial \theta^*}{\partial k^{-1}} = \frac{k\phi(\theta^*, \alpha)}{\phi_\theta(\theta^*, \alpha) - k^{-1}}$$

and then, since

$$\lim_{k^{-1} \to 0} \phi_\theta(\theta^*, \alpha) = \phi_\theta(0, \alpha) = \frac{1}{\alpha},$$

we obtain

$$\lim_{k^{-1} \to 0} \frac{\partial \theta^*}{\partial k^{-1}} = \alpha\pi. \tag{C.1}$$

Equation (9) implies

$$\lim_{k^{-1} \to 0} X^*(k, \alpha) = x(0, \alpha) = \alpha,$$

while differentiation of (9) yields

$$\frac{\partial}{\partial k^{-1}}[\log X^*(k, \alpha)] = \frac{(1-\alpha)\sin\theta^*}{X^{*2}} \frac{\partial \theta^*}{\partial k^{-1}} \tag{C.2}$$

so that

$$\lim_{k^{-1}\to 0} \frac{\partial}{\partial k^{-1}}[\log X^*(k,\alpha)] = 0.$$

Finally, (21) implies

$$\lim_{k^{-1}\to 0}[\log(-v^*(k,\alpha))] = \lim_{k^{-1}\to 0} k\left[\log \frac{X^*(k,\alpha)}{\alpha}\right]$$
$$= \lim_{k^{-1}\to 0} \frac{\partial}{\partial k^{-1}}[\log X^*(k,\alpha)] = 0,$$

where we use l'Hospital's rule in the second line, so that

$$\lim_{k^{-1}\to 0} -v^*(k,\alpha) = -1$$

as stated in the proposition. Furthermore, differentiation of (23) yields

$$\lim_{k^{-1}\to 0} \frac{\partial v^*}{\partial k^{-1}} = \lim_{k^{-1}\to 0} v^* \frac{\partial}{\partial k^{-1}}\left[k\log \frac{X^*(k,\alpha)}{\alpha}\right]$$
$$= \lim_{k^{-1}\to 0} \frac{\partial}{\partial k^{-1}}\left[k\log \frac{X^*(k,\alpha)}{\alpha}\right].$$

Now

$$\lim_{k^{-1}\to 0} \frac{\partial}{\partial k^{-1}}\left[k\log \frac{X^*(k,\alpha)}{\alpha}\right]$$
$$= \lim_{k^{-1}\to 0}\left\{-k^2\log \frac{X^*(k,\alpha)}{\alpha} + k\frac{\partial}{\partial k^{-1}}\left[\log \frac{X^*(k,\alpha)}{\alpha}\right]\right\}$$
$$= -\lim_{k^{-1}\to 0} \frac{\partial}{\partial k^{-1}}\left[k\log \frac{X^*(k,\alpha)}{\alpha}\right] + \lim_{k^{-1}\to 0} k\frac{\partial}{\partial k^{-1}}\left[\log \frac{X^*(k,\alpha)}{\alpha}\right]$$

using l'Hospital's rule, so that

$$\lim_{k^{-1}\to 0} \frac{\partial}{\partial k^{-1}}\left[k\log\frac{X^*(k,\alpha)}{\alpha}\right] = \frac{1}{2}\lim_{k^{-1}\to 0} k\frac{\partial}{\partial k^{-1}}\left[\log\frac{X^*(k,\alpha)}{\alpha}\right]$$

$$= \lim_{k^{-1}\to 0}\left[\frac{(1-\alpha)k\sin\theta^*(k,\alpha)}{2X^*(k,\alpha)^2}\frac{\partial\theta^*}{\partial k^{-1}}\right]$$

$$= \frac{1-\alpha}{2\alpha}\lim_{k^{-1}\to 0} k\sin\theta^*(k,\alpha)$$

using (31) and (32). Finally, using l'Hospital's rule again,

$$\lim_{k^{-1}\to 0} k\sin\theta^*(k,\alpha) = \lim_{k^{-1}\to 0}\frac{\partial}{\partial k^{-1}}[\sin\theta^*(k,\alpha)]$$

$$= \lim_{k^{-1}\to 0}\left[\cos\theta^*(k,\alpha)\frac{\partial\theta^*}{\partial k^{-1}}\right]$$

$$= \alpha\pi$$

due to (32). Hence, we obtain

$$\lim_{k^{-1}\to 0}\frac{\partial v^*}{\partial k^{-1}} = \lim_{k^{-1}\to 0}\frac{\partial}{\partial k^{-1}}\left[k\log\frac{X^*(k,\alpha)}{\alpha}\right] = \frac{(1-\alpha)\pi^2}{2}.$$

This implies that $v^*(k,\alpha)$ approaches -1 at the rate stated in the proposition. □

9   Sunspot Equilibria in Systems with Memory: An Introductory Presentation

Julio Dávila and
Roger Guesnerie

1 Introduction

This chapter aims at introducing the question of existence of sunspot equilibria in systems that have a more complex structure than the simple overlapping generation model in which the dynamical sunspot phenomena have been first studied: Azariadis (1981b), Azariadis and Guesnerie (1982a), Farmer and Woodford (1984), etc. . . . Indeed, starting from this literature, sunspot equilibria have become well understood in one-dimensional one-step-forward-looking infinite horizon models and reasonably well understood in multidimensional models that remain one-step forward looking (see Chiappori and Guesnerie [1991b], Guesnerie and Woodford [1992]).

Attention in the present chapter is focused on models that are again one-step forward looking but that have memory. Most of the argument holds in settings where the state of the system at each period is essentially one-dimensional, at the exception of the last section that considers multidimensional systems.

Our objective here is twofold. We first attempt to provide simple intuition on the nature of the self-fulfillment mechanisms that sustain sunspot equilibria in the models under consideration: It is why, for example, we discuss in detail what happens in linear models. Second, we only review existing results while providing, at best, sketches of proofs.

Finally, the chapter takes the option of concentrating on a particular type of sunspot equilibria that are the subject of Dávila's work (1994, 1997). Such sunspot equilibria are particularly appealing from an economic viewpoint: For example, the sunspot equilibria of Sections 1 to 3 look like periodic equilibria in the sense that they describe oscillations of the system between 2 or k states that recur for ever; the oscillations are however not deterministic, as for standard cycles, but stochastic. The stochastic quasi-cycles that are described are reminiscent of the 2-SSE or k-SSE that were first exhibited in the OLG model; they are much simpler than the general SSE whose existence was considered in Woodford (1984) and obtain under more severe conditions, as emphasized in Section 4.

The chapter proceeds as follows:

Section 1 presents, in simple models, the fulfillment mechanisms associated with sunspot equilibria with a binary support, first without memory and then with one-period memory.

Section 2 keeps a linear setting but extends the analysis to multi-period memory and finite support of any order.

Section 3 reassesses the sunspot existence problem in the non-linear version of the model previously introduced, and reviews the results obtained by Dávila (1997).

Section 4 discusses the relationship of the previous analysis with Woodford's contribution.

Section 5 provides insights on the sunspot existence problem in settings that are similar as far as memory is concerned, but that are multidimensional: results that are, however, weaker than in the one-dimensional setting are again borrowed from Dávila (1994).

Brief concluding comments are offered.

2   Sunspot Equilibria in Simple Linear Systems

Particularly simple sunspot equilibria appearing in dynamic economic models are the so-called finite Markovian stationary sunspot
equilibrium (see Azariadis [1981b] and Azariadis and Guesnerie
[1982a,b, 1986] for the first examples and Chiappori and Guesnerie
[1991b] for an extensive survey covering these types of sunspot
equilibria and related subjects). In order to provide a simple
instance of such an equilibrium, let us consider the following one-
dimensional dynamical system

$$x_{t+1} = f(x_t). \tag{2.1}$$

Equation (2.1) says that the state of the system considered is, at any
time, a function of the previous date state. Let us simplify the
example further considering f in (2.1) to be linear, the equation
becoming thus:

$$x_{t+1} = ax_t. \tag{2.2}$$

Equation (2.2) says now that the state variable at any date is a fixed
proportion of the state variable at the previous date. It reads, too:[1]

$$x_t = \frac{1}{a} x_{t+1}, \tag{2.3}$$

Equation (2.3) can be interpreted as follows: The state of the system
at any date is determined by the perfectly foreseen next period state,
i.e., the state expected to happen, with probability 1. Such backward
dynamics obtains, for instance, as the linearization, around a steady
state, of the reduced form of the perfect foresight equilibrium
conditions of a simple overlapping generations economy: the
state variable can be chosen to be the labor supply of the young or,
equivalently, the first period consumption or the money balances
depending on the particular details of the model (see for example
Guesnerie and Woodford [1992]).

As a straightforward and natural extension, in the case where the state of the system in the next period is not known with certainty but only with some probability, equation (2.3) may be generalized to become

$$x_t = \frac{1}{a} E_t(x_{t+1}), \tag{2.4}$$

that is to say, the state of the system at any date is determined by the expectations at that time about the next period state. Again, it is the linearization, for small noise, of the equilibrium conditions involving stochastic forecasts.

For instance, at any date t, it may be foreseen that the next period state will be either x^1 with some probability π^{11} or a distinct state x^2 with the complementary probability π^{12} if at t the state is x^1, while the same distinct states will occur with some other probabilities π^{21} and π^{22} if at t the state is x^2. Then, according to (2.4), x^1 will actually be the equilibrium state at any given date, if it satisfies:

$$x^1 = \frac{1}{a}(\pi^{11}x^1 + \pi^{12}x^2) \tag{2.5a}$$

and similarly x^2 will actually be the equilibrium state at any given date if it satisfies

$$x^2 = \frac{1}{a}(\pi^{21}x^1 + \pi^{22}x^2). \tag{2.5b}$$

The equilibrium equations just described define the simplest example of a finite markovian stationary sunspot equilibrium of the system (2.4), from now on SSE, more specifically, of a markovian SSE of order 2 (a 2-SSE henceforth). Some comments on the equilibrium concept and the stochastic dynamics that it generates are now in order.

Think, as in a simple overlapping generations economy, that is taken provisionally as linear, of the state at any period as being the amount of labor supplied by the contemporary youngs. Thus the state at date t results from decisions that depend on the expectations about the next period's young labor supply,[2] i.e., about the next period state, say as in (2.4). Should there by any reason for generation t to believe that generation $t + 1$ will supply x^1 or x^2 depending on the contemporary observation of either one value, say 1, or another value, say 2, of a random signal (the "sunspot") following a Markov chain governed by (π^{ij}), then the rational choice for generation t, as it comes from (2.4), is to choose to supply x^1 (resp. x^2) if it observes the value 1 (resp. 2) of the signal at time t. Beliefs of this type, if maintained through time will generate stochastic dynamics, where x^1, x^2, will alternate for ever, perfectly correlated with the exogenous random sunspot signal 1, 2.

Note that the randomness follows from beliefs triggered by sunspot events; however, a variety of stories involving a subtler chain of beliefs might be invoked in order to sustain the sunspot equilibrium.[3]

Formally, a 2-SSE of the kind under consideration, consists of two states x^1 and x^2 and a Markov matrix Π satisfying (2.5a), (2.5b). Even if the above remarks on interpretation should be reminded, the equations can simply read as follows: The beliefs: $1 \rightarrow x^1, 2 \rightarrow x^2$, if universal, are self fulfilling.

The issue of the existence of such an equilibrium can now be briefly discussed. For the equations (2.5a), (2.5b) to be satisfied for some values of x^1, x^2 and Π, the parameter a has to be such that ax^1 and ax^2 can be written as convex linear combinations of x^1 and x^2. A careful inspection of this condition shows that: i) x^1, x^2 must have different signs, ii) a needs to have an absolute value smaller than one. Moreover, this is sufficient too, in the following sense: if $|a| < 1$, for any x^1, x^2 of different sign, one can find one Markov matrix, such that equations (2.5a) and (2.5b) are fulfilled.

Thus, *a necessary and sufficient condition for the existence of SSE of order 2, solution to (2.4), is $|a| < 1$.*[4]

Now, note an essential characteristic of the dynamics under consideration in (2.1): The state in the next period only depends upon the current state and not on the history of the system in the past. This is an obviously restrictive feature that leaves out of the scope of the example models of economies such as those in Woodford (1986) and Reichlin (1986), for instance, in which the reduced form of the equilibrium dynamics leads to a state determined at any date by both the expected next period state and the previous state. The simplest and most straightforward generalization of (2.1) in order to cope with the role of past history in determining the current state is the following:

$$x_{t+1} = f(x_t, x_{t-1}) \tag{2.6}$$

where, as in the previous example, we focus attention on the linearization of f (around some steady state), that is to say

$$x_{t+1} = a_0 x_t + a_1 x_{t-1}. \tag{2.7}$$

Again, equation (2.7) can be read as follows[5]:

$$x_t = \frac{1}{a_0} x_{t+1} - \frac{a_1}{a_0} x_{t-1} \tag{2.8}$$

meaning that the state is determined at any date by both the perfectly foreseen next period state and the previous state. Should there be any uncertainty about the next period state, equation (2.8) could be generalized to become

$$x_t = \frac{1}{a_0} E_t(x_{t+1}) - \frac{a_1}{a_0} x_{t-1}. \tag{2.9}$$

Our main concern now is the following: does such stochastic dynamics still have solutions similar to those just shown for equation (2.4)? Or, are there distinct states x^1 and x^2 and probabilities of transition between them π^{ij} such that x^i ($i = 1, 2$) is the equilibrium state if the next period state is expected to be either x^1 with probability π^{i1} or x^2 with probability π^{i2}, whichever, x^1 or x^2, may have been the previous state? If there is any such equilibrium it would be characterized by the equations

$$x^1 = \frac{1}{a_0}(\pi^{11}x^1 + \pi^{12}x^2) - \frac{a_1}{a_0}x^1$$

$$x^1 = \frac{1}{a_0}(\pi^{11}x^1 + \pi^{12}x^2) - \frac{a_1}{a_0}x^2$$

$$x^2 = \frac{1}{a_0}(\pi^{21}x^1 + \pi^{22}x^2) - \frac{a_1}{a_0}x^1$$

$$x^2 = \frac{1}{a_0}(\pi^{21}x^1 + \pi^{22}x^2) - \frac{a_1}{a_0}x^2$$

(2.10)

From the first two equations (or the last two) the answer to this question is obviously no, since necessarily x^1 and x^2 would have to be equal at any solution.[6]

In order to overcome this difficulty, we may let the probabilities of transition to depend not only on the current state but on the previous state too, letting π^{ijk} denote the probability of x^k being the next state if the current one is x^j and the previous one has been x^i.

In this modified setting, the question becomes: Are there distinct states x^1, x^2 and four points in the relative interior of the unit simplex (π^{ij1}, π^{ij2}), $i, j = 1, 2$, satisfying the following equations?

$$x^1 = \frac{1}{a_0}(\pi^{111}x^1 + \pi^{112}x^2) - \frac{a_1}{a_0}x^1$$

$$x^1 = \frac{1}{a_0}(\pi^{211}x^1 + \pi^{212}x^2) - \frac{a_1}{a_0}x^2$$

$$x^2 = \frac{1}{a_0}(\pi^{121}x^1 + \pi^{122}x^2) - \frac{a_1}{a_0}x^1$$

$$x^2 = \frac{1}{a_0}(\pi^{221}x^1 + \pi^{222}x^2) - \frac{a_1}{a_0}x^2$$

(2.11)

The first equation says that the equilibrium to-day is x^1, if the signals observed today and yesterday were 1 (in which case, the state observed yesterday was x^1), so that the transition probabilities for 1 and 2, tomorrow, will be π^{111}, π^{112}, respectively. And so on.

As above, one proceeds to an informal inspection of the compatibility of the four homogenous equations with two unknowns. We may first look at the case where a_0, a_1 have the same sign (say positive).

We first note that the signs of x^1, x^2 have to be different: If not, and if, for example, they were positive, $(a_0 + a_1)x^1$ and $(a_0 + a_1)x^2$ cannot be both convex combinations of x^1, x^2, as required by the first and the fourth equations. Now if $a_0 + a_1 > 1$, then $(a_0 + a_1)x^1 < x^1$, (if w.l.o.g $x^1 < 0$), so that neither the first nor the fourth equation can be satisfied. It follows that necessarily $a_0 + a_1 < 1$. We then check that, in this case, since both coefficients a_0, a_1 are positive and smaller than one, $a_0 x^1 + a_1 x^2$, as well as $a_0 x^2 + a_1 x^1$, belong to the segment $\{x^1, x^2\}$. It follows that if the latter condition is satisfied, for any x^1, x^2 of different signs, one can find Markov coefficients such that equations (2.12) hold true.

The argument could be pursued in the case where a_0 and a_1 have different signs. But the question can be settled in a more general and more efficient way by noticing that the existence of a solution $x^1 \neq x^2 \neq 0$, requires that the four planes in the x^1, x^2 space determined by (2.12) coincide, that is to say, that their four normal vectors coincide too,[7] for some probabilities of transition. It can be shown[8] that such a coincidence obtains if and only if, $|a_0| + |a_1| < 1$. Such stochastic dynamics solution to (2.10) is what we will refer to as a stationary sunspot equilibrium of order 2 of the system. Thus we can now state the following[9]:

PROPOSITION 2.1   There exist 2-SSE solution of (2.9) iff $|a_0| + |a_1| < 1$.

The characterization provided by the previous proposition shows that 2-SSE exist for a non-negligible set of dynamical systems (2.10).

Furthermore, following the line of argument of previous footnote (4), one can check that the dimensionality of the transition probabilities associated with SSE in a given system is one.

In Section 5, it will be seen how the set of dynamical systems that have SSE of the type under consideration relate to the set of systems of the same class with the steady state indeterminate in the perfect foresight dynamics.

3   More on Sunspot Equilibria in Linear Systems

While remaining in the model "with memory" governed by equation (2.9), we are going to consider successively the case where the sunspot phenomenon has arbitrarily many states (Subsection 3.1), and the case of "long memory" (Subsection 3.2).

3.1   Sunspot Equilibria with Arbitrarily Many States

The necessary and sufficient characterization of the systems (2.9) with 2-SSE in the previous paragraph turns out to be unchanged when we consider markovian stationary sunspot equilibria of any finite order k: as we shall show, the system (2.9) has what will be called k-SSE for any $k \geq 2$ if, and only if, it has 2-SSE.

A k-SSE solution of (2.9) will consist of k distinct states $x^1, \ldots, x^k$ and k^2 points π^{ij} (of coordinates π^{ijl}, $l = 1, \ldots, k$) in the relative interior of the $(k-1)$-dimensional unit simplex (one for each possible sequence of these states in the previous and current period) such that, for all i, j

$$x^j = \frac{1}{a_0}\left(\pi^{ij1}x^1 + \pi^{ijk}x^k\right) - \frac{a_1}{a_0}x^i \tag{3.1}$$

The equation says that state x^j occurs today, if state x^i has occurred yesterday, and if to-morrow x^l occurs with probability π^{ijl}. Again, when the equation holds true, the belief sunspot signal $i \rightarrow x^i$ is self-fulfilling, whenever the occurrence of the sunspot signal is governed by those transition probabilities π^{ijl}, that depend upon the two last values of the sunspot signal.

This can be rewritten as:

$$a_1 x^i + a_0 x^j = \pi^{ij1} x^1 + \ldots + \pi^{ijk} x^k \qquad (3.2)$$

for all $i, j = 1, \ldots, k$.

Equivalently, a k-SSE consists of k distinct states $x^1, \ldots, x^k$ whose linear combinations $a_1 x^i + a_0 x^j$ are all in the interior of their convex hull. One can show now that if the system (2.9) has k-SSE for any given $k > 2$, it must also have a 2-SSE: let x^1 and x^2 be the smallest and the biggest of the x^i; the four linear combinations $a_1 x^i + a_0 x^j$, $i, j = 1, 2$ being in the convex hull of all the k states, they must necessarily be in the convex hull of the smallest and the biggest two as well. Hence, as can be checked from equations (3.1) x^1 and x^2 are the states of a 2-SSE.

Conversely, if a system has a 2-SSE, then it has k-SSE for all $k > 2$, since given any k let $y^1, \ldots, y^k$ be k states such that $y^1 = x^1$ and any other $y^i = x^2$, x^1 and x^2 being the states of the 2-SSE. Then every $a_1 y^i + a_0 y^j$ for all $i, j = 1, \ldots, k$, is in the convex hull of $y^1, \ldots, y^k$, since all of them coincide with some $a_1 x^r + a_0 x^s$ with $r, s = 1, 2$ and the convex hull of $y^1, \ldots, y^k$ is that of x^1, x^2. Of course these $y^1, \ldots, y^k$ are not the states of a k-SSE yet, since not all of them are distinct. But the values of $y^2, \ldots, y^k$ can be perturbed slightly in order to make all of them distinct and, by continuity, keep their linear combinations $a_1 y^i + a_0 y^j$ in their convex hull still. These newly perturbed states are now those of a k-SSE. Thus the previous proposition, 2.1, holds more generally and can be restated in the following terms.

PROPOSITION 3.1   There exist k-SSE solution of (2.9) for all k iff $|a_0| + |a_1| < 1$.

3.2   Linear Systems with Long Memory

The previous argument can also be modified in order to show that similar sunspot equilibria appear as solutions to dynamical systems with arbitrarily long memory. Indeed, consider a dynamical system like

$$x_t = \frac{1}{a_0} E_t(x_{t+1}) - \frac{a_1}{a_0} x_{t-1} - \ldots - \frac{a_p}{a_0} x_{t-p} \tag{3.3}$$

in which all the p most recent states (with the expectations) determine the current one. A stationary sunspot equilibrium of any order k will consist of k distinct states $x^1, \ldots, x^k$ and probabilities of transition between them necessarily depending on the current state and all the p immediate previous ones (otherwise, for the same reasons as before, no off-diagonal solutions can be found) satisfying conditions analogous to (3.1). But we have now k^{p+1} equations, one for each history of the realizations of the sunspot signals from $t - p$ until the current period t.

The existence of such k-SSE is equivalent, in this case as well, to the coincidence of all the normal vectors of the k^{p+1} hyperplanes representing the equilibrium conditions.

It can be shown[10] that such a condition can be met if, and only if,

$$\sum_{i=0}^{p} |a_i| < 1 \tag{3.4}$$

which actually encompasses the characterizations found in the previous cases (i.e., without memory, $p = 0$, and one-step backward memory, $p = 1$).

4   Local Sunspot Equilibria in Non-Linear Systems with Memory

The argument developed in the previous paragraph in order to show the existence of finite Markovian stationary sunspot equilibria of linear dynamical systems can be transposed to show the existence of similar equilibria in nonlinear systems. One proceeds as follows:

Assume the state at a given date, x_t, is determined by both the previous state x_{t-1} and the probability distribution of the state in the next period μ_{t+1}. The reduced (non-necessarily linear) form can then be written:

$$x_t = \tilde{f}(x_{t-1}, \mu_{t+1}) \tag{4.1}$$

In the case where μ_{t+1} is a lottery on, for example, two possible states x_{t+1}^1, x_{t+1}^2, we shall denote it as: $\{x_{t+1}^1, x_{t+1}^2, m^1, m^2\}$, so that

$$x_t = \tilde{f}(x_{t-1}, \{x_{t+1}^1, x_{t+1}^2, m^1, m^2\}) \tag{4.2}$$

A 2-SSE of such a system consists, by definition, of two distinct states x^1 and x^2 and four vectors of probabilities (m^{ij1}, m^{ij2}), $i, j = 1, 2$ satisfying

$$x^1 - \tilde{f}(x^1, \{x^1, x^2, m^{111}, m^{112}\}) = 0$$

$$x^2 - \tilde{f}(x^1, \{x^1, x^2, m^{121}, m^{122}\}) = 0$$

$$x^1 - \tilde{f}(x^2, \{x^1, x^2, m^{211}, m^{212}\}) = 0 \tag{4.3}$$

$$x^2 - \tilde{f}(x^2, \{x^1, x^2, m^{221}, m^{222}\}) = 0.$$

Under some conditions to be made precise later on, each equation of (4.3) can be thought of as determining a curve in the (x^1, x^2) plane, whose position is determined by the corresponding probabilities of transition. The existence of a 2-SSE is then equivalent to the existence of probabilities (m^{ij1}, m^{ij2}), $i, j = 1, 2$, such that the four curves have a common off-diagonal intersection. Therefore, we have to look for conditions on $\tilde{f}$ in (4.2) sufficient to guarantee such an off-diagonal intersection for some probabilities, and hence sufficient for the existence of 2-SSE of system (4.2).[11]

First assume that there is a steady state $\bar{x}$ of the system. This is a state from which the system will not depart if it comes from it and is expected with certainty to be in it in the next period, so that $\bar{x}$ satisfies:

$$\bar{x} = \tilde{f}(\bar{x}, \{\bar{x}, \bar{x}, \alpha^1, \alpha^2\}) \tag{4.4}$$

for any probabilities α^1, α^2 (the lottery $\{\bar{x}, \bar{x}, \alpha^1, \alpha^2\}$ is nothing but $\bar{x}$ with certainty whichever these probabilities are).

Hence, the point $(\bar{x}, \bar{x})$ in the (x^1, x^2) plane is an intersection point of all the four curves of equations (4.3), although it is not a 2-SSE since it is not off-diagonal.

Now, in order to be sure that these equations represent curves indeed (at least in some neighborhood of the point $(\bar{x}, \bar{x})$) some assumptions have to be made on $\tilde{f}$ which can be conveniently stated in terms of the restriction of $\tilde{f}$ to certainty lotteries, i.e., lotteries that can be written as $\{x_{t+1}, x_{t+1}, \alpha^1, \alpha^2\}$.[12] Such restriction f can thus be defined as

$$f(x_{t-1}, x_{t+1}) = \tilde{f}(x_{t-1}, \{x_{t+1}, x_{t+1}, \alpha^1, \alpha^2\}) \tag{4.5}$$

for any probabilities α^1, α^2.

Notice that using this restriction to pointwise expectations, the system (4.2) reduces to its deterministic counterpart:

$$x_t = f(x_{t-1}, x_{t+1}) \tag{4.6}$$

and that hence the steady state of the dynamics with uncertain expectations is also a steady state of the dynamics with certain expectations, i.e.,

$$\bar{x} = f(\bar{x}, \bar{x}) \tag{4.7}$$

(actually this is nothing but the equation (4.4) rewritten taking into account the definition of f in (4.5)).

Assume now that

$$\partial_{1i}\tilde{f}(\bar{x}, \{\bar{x}, \bar{x}, \alpha^1, \alpha^2\}) = \alpha^i \partial_1 f(\bar{x}, \bar{x}) \tag{4.8}$$

for $i = 1, 2$, where $\partial_{1i} \tilde{f}$ denotes the partial derivative of $\tilde{f}$ with respect to x_{t+1}^i and $\partial_1 f$ that of f with respect to x_{t+1}. Such an assumption amounts to say (in infinitesimal language) that the effect on $\tilde{f}$ of a small change in a future state that may happen with some probability is equal to the probability of the change multiplied by the deterministic effect on f of the same small change.[13] Then the gradients of the left-hand sides in (4.3) can be written as

$$(1 - \partial_{-1} f(\bar{x}, \bar{x}) - m^{111}\partial_1 f(\bar{x}, \bar{x}), -m^{112}\partial_1 f(\bar{x}, \bar{x}))$$

$$(-\partial_{-1} f(\bar{x}, \bar{x}) - m^{121}\partial_1 f(\bar{x}, \bar{x}), 1 - m^{122}\partial_1 f(\bar{x}, \bar{x}))$$

$$(1 - m^{211}\partial_1 f(\bar{x}, \bar{x}), -\partial_{-1} f(\bar{x}, \bar{x}) - m^{212}\partial_1 f(\bar{x}, \bar{x})) \tag{4.9}$$

$$(-m^{211}\partial_1 f(\bar{x}, \bar{x}), 1 - \partial_{-1} f(\bar{x}, \bar{x}) - m^{222}\partial_1 f(\bar{x}, \bar{x}))$$

Where now $\partial_{-1} f$ is the partial derivative of f with respect to x_{t-1}.

Notice that the scalar product of any of these vectors with the vector $(1, 1)$ is equal to $1 - \partial_{-1} f(\bar{x}, \bar{x}) - \partial_1 f(\bar{x}, \bar{x})$. If this is not zero, or equivalently, if

$$\partial_{-1} f(\bar{x}, \bar{x}) + \partial_1 f(\bar{x}, \bar{x}) \neq 1, \tag{4.10}$$

then surely none of the gradients in (4.9) is null and hence the equations (4.3) represent indeed four smooth curves in the (x^1, x^2) plane in some neighborhood of $(\bar{x}, \bar{x})$. For the sake of consistency with the linear case let us denote $-\partial_{-1} f(\bar{x}, \bar{x})/\partial_1 f(\bar{x}, \bar{x}) = a_1$ and $1/\partial_1 f(\bar{x}, \bar{x}) = a_0$. Then the condition (4.10) becomes

$$a_0 + a_1 \neq 1. \tag{4.11}$$

The assumptions made up to this point, namely the existence of $\bar{x}$ such that (4.7), (4.8) and (4.10) hold are not stringent. Actually they are straightforward generalizations to systems with memory of conditions holding in systems without memory, for instance, simple overlapping generations economies.

Now the key idea of the argument leading to the characterization of systems like (4.2) with an off-diagonal intersection of equations (4.3), i.e., with 2-SSE, can be stated as follows. If there exist probabilities such that all the four curves in (4.3) share a common tangent T at $(\overline{x}, \overline{x})$, then they can be slightly perturbed in order to make them intersect at any point in T close enough to $(\overline{x}, \overline{x})$.[14] Thus a sufficient condition for the existence of local sunspots, i.e., of uncountably many 2-SSE of (4.1) arbitrarily close to the steady state, is the existence of probabilities such that all the gradients in (4.9) are equal[15] and a necessary and sufficient condition for the existence of such probabilities is (as in the linear case)

$$|a_0| + |a_1| < 1. \tag{4.12}$$

Therefore, we can state the following

PROPOSITION 4.1   There exist local 2-SSE of (4.1) if $|a_0| + |a_1| < 1$.

Under the assumptions made and a_0, a_1 being defined as above, notice that this characterization was, in the linear case, not only sufficient but necessary, too. The converse implication cannot be obtained in the general case and examples of systems not satisfying $|a_0| + |a_1| < 1$ but with local 2-SSE can be produced.[16]

The same argument can be extended to characterize the existence of local k-SSE in order to obtain the next proposition.

PROPOSITION 4.2   There exist local k-SSE of (4.1) if $|a_0| + |a_1| < 1$.

The reasoning has to be done in this case in the space of k-tuples of states, i.e., in some piece of R^k, and our former curves become manifolds of dimension $k - 1$ in some neighborhood of $(\overline{x}, \ldots, \overline{x})$. The idea of the proof is essentially the same as before: A sufficient condition for producing an off-diagonal intersection of all the manifolds is the existence of probabilities making all of them tangent at $(\overline{x}, \ldots, \overline{x})$ to a nontrivial affine set.[17] Should there exist such probabilities, the manifolds could be perturbed to intersect at any point in that affine set close enough to $(\bar{x}, \ldots, \bar{x})$.[18] Now a necessary and sufficient condition for the existence of such an affine set is precisely $|a_0| + |a_1| < 1$.[19]

Moreover, as in the linear case, the argument can also be extended to characterize the existence of local k-SSE in systems with arbitrarily long memory

$$x_t = \tilde{f}(x_{t-p}, \ldots, x_{t-1}, \{x_{t+1}^1, \ldots, x_{t+1}^k, m^1, \ldots, m^k\}) \qquad (4.13)$$

and to prove the following proposition.

PROPOSITION 4.3   There exist local k-SSE of (4.13) of if

$$\sum_{i=0}^{p} |a_i| < 1 \qquad (4.14)$$

where $a_0 = \dfrac{1}{\partial_1 f(\bar{x}, \ldots, \bar{x})}$ and $a_i = \dfrac{\partial_{-i} f(\bar{x}, \ldots, \bar{x})}{\partial_1 f(\bar{x}, \ldots, \bar{x})}$,   with   the   usual notation for partial derivatives.

The proof is essentially independent of the length of the memory: it is somewhat irrelevant for the argument that the number of manifolds, whose off-diagonal intersection is considered, varies with the length of the memory.[20]

5   The Connection with Woodford's Conjecture

On the one hand, the systems (4.1) for which the proposition 4.2 guarantees the existence of local k-SSE are actually systems for which the steady state $\bar{x}$ is indeterminate in the perfect foresight dynamics: Any trajectory starting close enough to the steady state converges to the steady state. On the other hand, the so-called Woodford conjecture (Woodford [1984]) links the existence of local sunspot equilibria to indeterminacy of the steady state, a fact that the recent work of Grandmont, Pintus, and de Vilder (1997) illustrate in a more geometric way.

Let us clarify the connections of the above results and of Woodford's conjectures.

Indeed, the dynamics

$$x_t = f(x_{t-1}, x_{t+1}) \tag{5.1}$$

if linearized around the steady state

$$x_t - \bar{x} = \partial_1 f(\bar{x}, \bar{x})(x_{t-1} - \bar{x}) + \partial_2 f(\bar{x}, \bar{x})(x_{t-1} - \bar{x}) \tag{5.2}$$

and written in the form

$$x_{t+1} - \bar{x} = \frac{1}{\partial_2 f(\bar{x}, \bar{x})}(x - \bar{x}) - \frac{\partial_1 f(\bar{x}, \bar{x})}{\partial_2 f(\bar{x}, \bar{x})}(x_{t-1} - \bar{x}) \tag{5.3}$$

can be restated as

$$\begin{pmatrix} x_{t+1} - \bar{x} \\ x_t - \bar{x} \end{pmatrix} = \begin{pmatrix} a_0 & a_1 \\ 1 & 0 \end{pmatrix} \begin{pmatrix} x_t - \bar{x} \\ x_{t-1} - \bar{x} \end{pmatrix} \tag{5.4}$$

where a_0 and a_1 denote $\dfrac{1}{\partial_2 f(\bar{x}, \bar{x})}$ and $-\dfrac{\partial_1 f(\bar{x}, \bar{x})}{\partial_2 f(\bar{x}, \bar{x})}$ respectively.

The point $(\bar{x}, \bar{x})$ is a globally stable fixed point of this dynamics (i.e., $\bar{x}$ is an indeterminate steady state) if no eigenvalue of the matrix of the linearization above is out of the unit circle in the complex plane. These eigenvalues are the solution to

$$\begin{vmatrix} a_0 - \lambda & a_1 \\ 1 & -\lambda \end{vmatrix} = 0 \tag{5.5}$$

i.e., they are the roots of the characteristic equation $\lambda^2 - a_0\lambda - a_1 = 0$, which are $\dfrac{1}{2}(a_0 + \sqrt{a_0^2 + 4a_1})$ and $\dfrac{1}{2}(a_0 - \sqrt{a_0^2 + 4a_1})$.

Simple algebra[21] shows that for the steady state $\bar{x}$ to be indeterminate in the perfect foresight dynamics a_0 and a_1 have to satisfy the inequalities $-1 < a_1$, $a_1 < 1 - a_0$ and $a_1 < 1 + a_0$.

Our condition for the existence of local k-SSE, $|a_0| + |a_1| < 1$, is sufficient for these inequalities to be satisfied, although it is certainly not a necessary one. In other words, the systems for which we have shown the existence of local k-SSE around the steady state constitute a proper subset of those for which this steady state is indeterminate in the corresponding perfect foresight dynamics.

This fact deserves some comments. Woodford (1984) established that the indeterminacy of the steady state is a necessary and sufficient condition for the existence of local sunspot equilibria. Here, we have focused on a special class of sunspot equilibria which have particularly appealing properties: The system oscillates forever between 2 or more states, and displays quasi-cycles; but the sufficient conditions that have been exhibited by Dávila and that have been reproduced here are more restrictive than those of Woodford and are not moreover necessary.[22]

However, and interestingly enough, our characterization, which is only sufficient in general, becomes necessary and sufficient indeed for the linear case, i.e. for dynamics of the form

$$x_{t+1} = a_0 x_t + a_1 x_{t-1}. \tag{5.6}$$

This implies that there are dynamics of this kind with the steady state indeterminate, and thus with local sunspot equilibria according to Woodford, but without local k-SSE. Therefore, the local sunspot equilibria detected by Woodford have to be for these linear dynamics either of non finite support or not markovian (at least with a memory whose length is of the order of magnitude of the cardinality of the support). This underlines the fact that the existence of local sunspot equilibria à la Woodford and that of k-SSE are clearly distinct questions in general: The results emphasized here, as they concern specially simple and appealing types of sunspot equilibria, are less powerful but may have a particular significance for the theory of endogenous fluctuations.

6   Sunspot Equilibria in Multidimensional Systems with Memory

Let us now reconsider the linear case when the dynamics take place in R^n. The dynamics (2.7) becomes thus

$$x_{t+1} = A_0 x_t + A_1 x_{t-1} \tag{6.1}$$

where A_0 and A_1 are $n \times n$ matrices. Assuming A_0 to be regular, these dynamics can be read as

$$x_t = A_0^{-1} x_{t+1} - A_0^{-1} A_1 x_{t-1}. \tag{6.2}$$

i.e., as the state in each period being determined by that of the previous one and the perfectly foreseen next state. Should the next period state be foreseen with uncertainty as a lottery $\{x_{t+1}^1, \ldots, x_{t+1}^k, m^1 \ldots, m^k\}$, and deterministic values replaced by expected values, the equation (6.2) could be rewritten as

$$x_t = A_0^{-1} \sum_{h=1}^{k} m^h x_{t+1}^h - A_0^{-1} A_1 x_{t-1}. \tag{6.3}$$

A k-SSE associated with the dynamics (6.1) will consist of a k-tuple of distinct states $x^1, \ldots, x^k$ and k^2 vectors of probabilities $(m^{ij1}, \ldots, m^{ijk})$, for $i, j = 1, \ldots, k$, such that

$$x^j = A_0^{-1} \sum_{h=1}^{k} m^{ijh} x^h - A_0^{-1} A_1 x^i \tag{6.4}$$

or equivalently,

$$A_1 x^i + A_0 x^j = \sum_{h=1}^{k} m^{ijh} x^h \tag{6.5}$$

for all $i, j = 1, \ldots, k$. Thus $x^1, \ldots, x^k$ and $\{m^{ij}\}$ will be a k-SSE if, and only if, all the vectors $A_1 x^i + A_0 x^j$ are in the convex hull of the states. Obviously, for any $x^1, \ldots, x^k$ such that *the full interior of their convex hull* contains the null vector, if A_1 and A_0 are regular are matrices close enough to the null matrix, then the conditions will be satisfied and $x^1, \ldots, x^k$ will certainly be the states of a k-SSE.

Therefore, A_1 and A_0 being strong enough contractions is sufficient to guarantee the existence of k-SSE of (6.1) of a high enough order ($k \geq n$).

More specifically, it suffices that the norms of A_1 and A_0 add up to less than 1, i.e.,

$$\|A_1\| + \|A_0\| < 1 \tag{6.6}$$

since in that case for any x^i, x^j such that $\|x^i\| = 1$ and $\|x^j\| = 1$ $\|A_1 x^i\| \leq \|A_1\|$ and $\|A_0 x^j\| \leq \|A_0\|$, and since $\|A_1 x^i + A_0 x^j\| \leq \|A_1 x^i\| + \|A_0 x^j\|$, then necessarily

$$\|A_1 x^i + A_0 x^j\| \leq \|A_1\| + \|A_0\| < 1, \tag{6.7}$$

that is to say, for any pair of points x^i, x^j on the unit sphere, $\|A_1 x^i + A_0 x^j\|$ is contained in a sphere strictly contained in the unit sphere. Thus there exist a high enough number[23] of points $x^1, \ldots,$ x^k on the unit sphere such that the sphere of radius $\|A_1\| + \|A_0\|$ is contained in its convex hull and therefore necessarily every $A_1 x^i + A_0 x^j$ too. This means that the equations (6.5) are fulfilled for some probabilities. Hence we have, on the one hand, the next sufficient condition for the existence of k-SSE of (6.1).

PROPOSITION 6.1   There exist k-SSE of (6.1) for k high enough (specifically, if $n = 2$, for any $k > \pi/\arccos(\|A_1\| + \|A_0\|)$) if

$$\|A_1\| + \|A_0\| < 1 \tag{6.8}$$

On the other hand, a necessary condition for the existence of k-SSE of any order k of (6.1) is provided by the following reasoning, for which, and for all what follows, it will be assumed, without loss of generality, that $A_1 + A_0$ has no eigenvalue with modulus 0 or 1.

Conditions (6.5) require the existence of a non-trivial intersection of the null spaces of the matrices

$$\left(m^{ij} \otimes I_n - \left(e^i \otimes A_1 + e^j \otimes A_0\right)\right) \tag{6.9}$$

$i, j = 1, \ldots, k$, and in particular of those where $i = j$. Therefore, should there exist a k-SSE of any order k, then the matrix

$$\begin{pmatrix} m^{11} \otimes I_n - e^1 \otimes (A_1 + A_0) \\ m^{22} \otimes I_n - e^2 \otimes (A_1 + A_0) \\ \vdots \\ m^{kk} \otimes I_n - e^k \otimes (A_1 + A_0) \end{pmatrix} = M \otimes I_n - I_k \otimes (A_1 + A_0) \tag{6.10}$$

(where M is the Markov matrix whose i-th row is m^{ii}) would have to be singular. In other words, $M \otimes (A_1 + A_0)^{-1} - I_{nk}$ would have to be singular (since $A_1 + A_0$ is regular because 0 is not in its spectrum), i.e., 0 would have to be one of its eigenvalues. But the eigenvalues of $M \otimes (A_1 + A_0)^{-1} - I_{nk}$ are of the form[24] $mb - 1$, m being any eigenvalue of the Markov matrix M and b any of $(A_1 + A_0)^{-1}$, hence $mb = 1$ would have to hold for some m and b. Now, since all the eigenvalues of a Markov matrix are within the unit circle, necessarily there ought to be an eigenvalue of $(A_1 + A_0)^{-1}$ within the unit circle, i.e., an eigenvalue of $A_1 + A_0$ outside the unit circle (off the circle since $A_1 + A_0$ has no eigenvalue on it). Thus we have the following:

PROPOSITION 6.2   If (6.1) has a k-SSE, then $A_1 + A_0$ has an eigenvalue within the unit circle.

Let us consider now the general nonlinear case

$$x_t = \tilde{f}(x_{t-1}, \{x_{t+1}^1, \ldots, x_{t+1}^k, m^1, \ldots, m^k\}) \tag{6.11}$$

with the state in R^n. We can now give a necessary condition for the existence of local k-SSE fluctuating around a steady state. Consider the function defined as

$$\tilde{F}(x^1,\ldots,x^k,\{\ldots,m^{ij},\ldots\}) = \begin{pmatrix} x^1 - \tilde{f}(x^1,\{x^1,\ldots,x^k,m^{111},\ldots,m^{11k}\}) \\ \vdots \\ x^k - \tilde{f}(x^1,\{x^1,\ldots,x^k,m^{1k1},\ldots,m^{1kk}\}) \\ \vdots \\ x^1 - \tilde{f}(x^k,\{x^1,\ldots,x^k,m^{k11},\ldots,m^{k1k}\}) \\ \vdots \\ x^k - \tilde{f}(x^k,\{x^1,\ldots,x^k,m^{kk1},\ldots,m^{kkk}\}) \end{pmatrix}.$$

$$(6.12)$$

The zeros of this function are either steady states or k-SSE.[25] Now, for any given probabilities $(m^{ij1},\ldots,m^{ijk})$, $i,j = 1,\ldots,k$, should $D_{(\bar{x},\ldots,\bar{x})}\tilde{F}(\bar{x},\ldots,\bar{x},\{m^{ij}\})$ be full rank (kn), then in some neighborhood of $(\bar{x},\ldots,\bar{x},\{m^{ij}\})$ the set of zeros of $\tilde{F}$ would be a function giving $(x^1,\ldots,x^k)$ in terms of the probabilities. Since for any other probabilities $\tilde{m}^{ijh}$ close enough to m^{ijh} the point $(\bar{x},\ldots,\bar{x},\{\tilde{m}^{ij}\})$ is in that graph, no other point in that neighborhood with at least two states distinct can be a zero of $\tilde{F}$, otherwise the implicit function theorem would be contradicted. Therefore, there cannot be local k-SSE around $(\bar{x},\ldots,\bar{x},\{m^{ij}\})$. Thus if this is the case for all probabilities m^{ijh}, i.e., $D_{(\bar{x},\ldots,\bar{x})}\tilde{F}(\bar{x},\ldots,\bar{x},\{m^{ij}\})$ is full rank whichever the probabilities are, the system does not have local k-SSE. Hence a necessary condition for the existence of local k-SSE around $\bar{x}$ is that for some probabilities $D_{(\bar{x},\ldots,\bar{x})}\tilde{F}(\bar{x},\ldots,\bar{x},\{m^{ij}\})$ is not full rank.

Now, this jacobian can be written as

$$\begin{pmatrix} \vdots \\ -e^i \otimes D_{-1}f(\bar{x},\bar{x}) + e^j \otimes I_n - m^{ij} \otimes D_1 f(\bar{x},\bar{x}) \\ \vdots \end{pmatrix}.$$

$$(6.13)$$

where $D_h f$ denotes the partial derivatives of f with respect to x_{t+h}, $h = -1, 1$. Thus the lack of full rank of the jacobian asks for the non-trivial intersection of the null spaces of the matrices

$$\left(-e^i \otimes D_{-1}f(\bar{x},\bar{x}) + e^j \otimes I_n - m^{ij} \otimes D_1 f(\bar{x},\bar{x})\right)$$

$$(6.14)$$

or equivalently of those (since they are the same subspaces) of these matrices premultiplied by $-D_1 f(\overline{x}, \overline{x})^{-1}$ (assuming $D_1 f(\overline{x}, \overline{x})$ regular)

$$\left(m^{ij} \otimes I_n - \left(e^i \otimes A_1 + e^j \otimes A_0\right)\right) \tag{6.15}$$

for all $i, j = 1, \ldots, k$, where A_1 is $-D_1 f(\overline{x}, \overline{x})^{-1} D_{-1} f(\overline{x}, \overline{x})$ and A_0 is $D_1 f(\overline{x}, \overline{x})^{-1}$. But we have seen in the linear case that a necessary condition for having a non-trivial intersection of the null spaces of these matrices for any probabilities is that $A_1 + A_0$ has an eigenvalue within the unit disk. Hence we have the following:

PROPOSITION 6.3   If (6.1) has local k-SSE of any order k, then $A_1 + A_0$ has an eigenvalue within the unit circle, where A_1 is $-D_1 f(\overline{x}, \overline{x})^{-1} D_{-1} f(\overline{x}, \overline{x})$ and A_0 is $D_1 f(\overline{x}, \overline{x})^{-1}$.

7 Conclusion

We hope that this chapter has provided insights on sunspot equilibria in models with memory that both allow to emphasize, on the one hand, the robustness of the initial message of the sunspot literature (starting from Azariadis [1981b]) on the existence of kind of equilibrium stochastic quasi cycles, on the other hand the specificity of the mechanisms at work and then of the technical apparatus that is required for the analysis of the models under scrutiny here.

One may, from this brief overview, get the impression that we are not yet close to having a general enough understanding of the problem that was here under scrutiny. Naturally, one may expect no basic difficulty in extending the analysis of sunspot equilibria to linear systems that are much more complex than those considered here: multidimensional with long memory several steps forward looking. But the existence of corresponding local sunspot equilibria in nonlinear systems raises a priori difficult technical questions.[26] Such a difficulty is a reflection of a more general fact:

our understanding of rational expectations equilibria (of sunspot or nonsunspot type) of nonlinear dynamical systems, outside the class of one-step forward-looking models, is still rather limited.

Notes

1. Trivially assume $a \neq 0$.

2. The equilibrium future exchange value of the money balances obtained today in exchange for labor depends on future production, i.e., on the amount of labor supplied tomorrow.

3. Actually it is not needed, for the argument to to through, that generation t believes indeed that generation $t + 1$ believes indeed that generation $t + 1$ will make its decision following the rule "x^1 if I see 1, x^2 if I see 2". It suffices that t: i) believes that $t + 1$ believes that $t + 2$ will behave like this and ii) assumes rational behavior at $t + 1$. Of course, following the same line of argument, it is not needed that any generation believes that any other generation will behave according to such a rule, but just that every generation believes that some subsequent generation believes that some other subsequent generation further in the future will behave like this, and moreover assumes all generations in between to be rational. Although no generation has, a priori, any reason for sticking to the sunspot behavior, given these beliefs about the beliefs of others concerning the behavior of others, everybody ends up adopting such a behavior.

4. More could be said, from the present inspection on the structure of SSE for example on the dimensionality of the set of sunspot Markov matrices, (dimension 1), but this is not our present purpose.

5. We assume both $a_0 \neq 0$ and $a_1 \neq 0$.

6. With supports of higher cardinality, if the dimension if 1 there is always as many equations, k^2, as unknowns k states and $k^2 - k$ probabilities. In the linear case necessarily any solution has its support on the diagonal. In the nonlinear one, a common tangent space (which will be sufficient to produce k-SSE as it will be seen in section 4) can be obtained only if the partial derivative of f with respect to the past is null at the steady state! If the dimension n is 2 or more then the nonlinear system has more equations, $k^2 n$, than unknowns, $kn + k^2 - k$.

7. Since all of them are in an affine set not containing a null vector.

8. See lemma 3 in Dávila (1997).

9. Assumptions implicitly used are $a_0 \neq 0$, which amounts to ask for a well-defined link between expectations and the current state, and $a_0 + a_1 \neq 1$, which is the equivalent to ask for the regularity of the steady state of the perfect foresight dynamics.

10. See Prop 4.6 in Dávila (1994).

11. More precisely, such conditions will be sufficient to guarantee the existence of so-called local k-SEE, i.e. uncountably many k-SEE arbitrarily close to a steady state of the system.

12. Trivially these lotteries represent x_{t+1} with certainty whichever the probabilities α^1 and α^2 are.

13. This is the consistency of derivatives condition of Guesnerie (1986) or Chiappori and Guesnerie (1989), who argue that he property should hold in a setting with Bayesian agents.
   The property is in particular satisfied by the dynamics with memory of the Woodford (86) and Reichlin (86) economies and the simple overlapping gnerations economies dynamics without memory, for instance.

14. For a proof of this fact see lemma 1 in Dávila (1997). Essentially, such a perturbation can be done because the gradients in (4.9) depend injectively upon their respective probabilities.

15. Since all of them are in an affine set not containing the null vector.

16. See a counterexample in Dávila (1997), section 3.

17. Proposition 3 in Dávila (1997).

18. See lemmas 1 and 2 in Dávila (1997).

19. Proposition 5 in Dávila (1997).

20. For details see chapter 4, section 5 in Dávila (1997).

21. These roots can be either both real or both complex.

   If both of them are complex, i.e., $a_0^2 + 4a_1 < 0$, then they are $\frac{1}{2}(a_0 + \sqrt{-(a_0^2 + 4a_1)}i)$ and $\frac{1}{2}(a_0 - \sqrt{-(a_0^2 + 4a_1)}i)$, and their modulus $\frac{1}{4}(a_0^2 - (a_0^2 + 4a_1)) = -a_1$. Thus indeterminacy in this case is characterized by the condition $-1 < a_1 < 1$. Actually we just need to check the inequality of $-1 < a_1$ since, from $a_0^2 + 4a_1 < 0$, necessarily $a_1 < 0$ and hence $a_1 < 1$ too. In the case where both eigenvalues are real, i.e., $a_0^2 + 4a_1 \geq 0$, then we need that both $-1 < \frac{1}{2}(a_0 + \sqrt{a_0^2 + 4a_1}) < 1$ and $-1 < \frac{1}{2}(a_0 - \sqrt{a_0^2 + 4a_1}) < 1$ be satisfied or, equivalently, $-2 - a_0 < \sqrt{a_0^2 + 4a_1} < 2 - a_0$ and $-2 + a_0 < \sqrt{a_0^2 + 4a_1} < 2 + a_0$. Note that since the square roots are positive, the second inequalities in these conditions require that both $2 - a_0$ and $2 + a_0$ be positive, i.e., that $-2 < a_0 < 2$. More over for any a_0 between -2 and 2, the expressions $-2 - a_0$ and $-2 + a_0$ are negative and thus the first inequalities in both conditions are trivially satisfied. Therefore the only additional requirement to be fulfilled is that $\sqrt{a_0^2 + 4a_1} < 2 - a_0$ $\sqrt{a_0^2 + 4a_1}$ and $< 2 + a_0$ or, equivalently, $a_1 < 1 - a_0$ and $a_1 < 1 + a_0$.

22. That is to say, we cannot exclude that we have left some dynamics with local k-SSE out of our characterization.

23. Specifically, $k > \pi/\arccos(\|A_1\| + \|A_0\|)$ when the system is of dimension 2.

24. See lemma 2 in Chiappori, Geoffard, and Guesnerie (1992).

25. Actually, some of them may be k'-SSE with $k' < k$.

26. It might, however, be the case that the combination of the insights provided here and of the technical results of Chiappori, Geoffard, and Guesnerie (1992) provides clues for future progresses.

10

Theoretical Tests of the Rational Expectations Hypothesis in Economic Dynamical Models

Roger Guesnerie

1 Introduction

Let us dream of a Martian economist visiting Earth every thirty years; suppose that his last visit had taken place in the early sixties and that he has come back at the beginning of the nineties. One may imagine what his report on the state of economic science on Earth will be. Presumably, he will report on the rapid progresses of mathematical modelling, which thirty years ago was limited to few fields and now embraces most subjects. Also he will stress that Earthian economists have started giving the subject of expectations the importance that its central role in economics deserves (a role that was emphasized and understood at the brightest period of the development of economics on Mars, thousands of years ago). Building on these two facts, our outside observer will also report, probably with more astonishment,[1] that the rational expectations hypothesis has taken over most fields of theoretical modelling. Thirty years ago, even if within the neo-classical general equilibrium tradition some implicit or explicit references to the prediction requirements of the temporal version of the competitive model could be noted, the problem of expectations—and of their appropriate formal treatment—looked as a peripheral subject.[2] The change of situation in the nineties is most striking: expectations have become a systematic and central concern and receive a fairly uniform formal treatment. Economists on Earth nowadays discuss subjects as different as macro economics, money, growth, international trade, industrial organization from theoretical models that assume that economic agents have rational expectations. (Our clever traveller has also noted that in parallel with this rational expectations revolution, there has been a widespread development of the game-theoretical studies of dynamic Nash equilibria.)

The role of my Martian observer stops here. His alleged surprise at acknowledging the deep impact of the rational expectations hypothesis on modern economic theory is indeed the introductory message of this chapter. The assessment of the hypothesis that is now attempted has, I am afraid, to be based on human wisdom.

According to the rational expectations hypothesis, economic agents are able to predict the future history, or at least the part of the future history that is relevant to them, of the system which they live in. If such a prediction may be incomplete, because conditional on the information available to the agent, it has nevertheless the same methodological status as the players' predictions at a game's Nash equilibrium. As well as in a Nash equilibrium, players foresee all the future actions of their opponents, economic agents of rational expectations models predict the future values of the variables relevant to their decision, that are often economic aggregates of the other agents' actions.

How reasonable is the predictability assumption imbedded in rational expectations models? Intellectual positions on this matter have been conflictual. Opponents—although, as already mentioned, they are almost silent in the circles of formalized economic theory—tend to dismiss the assumption as unrealistic or counterfactual; proponents sometimes rally Muth's original justification according to which the rational expectations hypothesis is "nothing else than the extension of the rationality hypothesis to expectations." None of these theoretical or empirical arguments is quite true.[3] In particular, on theoretical grounds, the hypothesis should neither be dismissed nor taken for granted, but discussed from alternative viewpoints and hopefully from more basic principles. Such is indeed the option of an increasing literature on which I will report now.

The critical assessment of the rational expectations hypothesis that is attempted here takes place within a simple class of infinite-horizon models. In these models, four different stability criteria for rational expectations equilibria are proposed (section 2). The comparison of the stability of a rational expectations steady state, according to the different criteria under consideration, is made in section 3 within the framework of the one-dimensional version of the stylized dynamic model, while the *n*-dimensional case is analyzed in section 4.

2   Stability Tests and Model

2.1   Four Stability Criteria for Rational Expectations Equilibria

The four criteria that will now be introduced reflect different ideas on what makes a rational expectations equilibrium "reasonable." These ideas have *a priori* a very different status: they either reflect the need for avoiding confusion that multiplicity is likely to generate (criteria a and c), or refer to a standard learning stability argument (criterion b), or to abstract game-theoretical considerations (criterion d).

2.1.1   Criterion A: The Equilibrium is Isolated or "Determinate"
In the infinite-horizon model we are considering here, an intertemporal equilibrium consists of an infinite sequence of state variables indexed by time *t*, where *t* runs from 1 to infinity.[4] Deciding whether two equilibria are neighbours amounts to deciding whether the two relevant sequences are themselves neighbours. It is indeed the

purpose of a topology over the space of sequences to define a precise notion of neighbourhood.

Having chosen such a topology, one can check whether a given equilibrium—for example, a steady state or a stationary equilibrium—is or is not "isolated."

Formally, an equilibrium is *isolated*, or as we will say later in order to stick to the dominant terminology in the economic literature "determinate," if *there is no other equilibrium in a small enough neighbourhood of the equilibrium under consideration.*

The terminology of "determinacy" or "indeterminacy," advocated in particular by Woodford (1984), directly appeals to the test that is going to be proposed. A rational expectations equilibrium that is indeterminate coexists with many rational expectations equilibria and is not an unambiguous reference, even within the rational expectations framework. In contrast, a determinate equilibrium provides, at least locally, a unique reference. In that sense, indeterminacy signals coordination problems and intuitively affects what could be called the "predictability" of the system.

Let us summarize: our first stability criterion for rational expectations equilibria is that the equilibrium is isolated or "determinate."

2.1.2   Criterion B: Learning Equilibria from Past Observations

As in physics, an equilibrium in economics can be viewed as a "rest point" of the system. So, a Walrasian equilibrium is a rest point of a static competitive system; in the same way, a rational expectations equilibrium of a system in which the basic data remain stationary can be viewed as the "rest point of the system," i.e., a point in which—as forecasts coincide with realizations—agents cease to revise expectations. Such a remark provides a basis for justification of the rational expectations concept. But here, as in the Walrasian case, the rest point argument is not in itself conclusive: in the Walrasian world, the equilibrium should be the outcome of the tatonnement process; here the rational expectations equilibrium is a rest point of the revision process just alluded to, but in addition it has to be the ultimate outcome of the revision process under consideration or, to put it more precisely, the process should converge to it.

The justification of the rational expectations equilibria that we have sketched can be concisely formulated: A *rational expectations equilibrium* is justified whenever it obtains as the ultimate *outcome of a learning process* along which agents *revise expectations* whenever they are falsified by observations.

A basic ingredient of the suggested analysis is the revision process that is used by the economic agents. It depends on the nature of the observations made by the agents; it has to explain how future values are forecasted from past observations: presumably, the function that maps past observations to future values is the same across time (it is called a fixed learning rule).

Our learning scenario is then quite clear: at time t, agents hold information on previous realizations of the economic state variables; using the learning rule, they form expectations on the future values of these variables, and then take actions that generate the date t equilibrium; and so on. This process generates a sequence of temporary equilibria. Our second stability criterion is then nothing else than the stability of the just described learning process. Do the temporary equilibrium dynamics converge to the rational expectations equilibrium? In fact, our criterion will focus attention on *local asymptotic stability*, i.e., it will require convergence subject to the restriction that the starting point is close to the equilibrium under consideration. This is a less strong requirement than global stability, but as we will see later still a demanding one.

Finally, it should be clear that the key ingredient of the analysis, i.e., the fixed learning rule, imbeds a lot of arbitrariness. For example, it should be reasonable, realistic, . . . , but it is unclear whether and to what extent these intuitive requirements can be connected with considerations involving rationality, or perhaps bounded rationality. . . .

In the following we will refer to this criterion as an "evolutive" learning criterion (the word evolutive will be opposed to the word "eductive" introduced later).

2.1.3   Criterion C: No Sunspot Multiplicity

When considering rational expectations equilibria, one is tempted to restrict attention to exogenous factors that may be thought of as strictly relevant to economic functioning. In particular, one is tempted to assume that agents do not record for forecasting purposes factors that are *a priori* irrelevant, such as the color of the moon at night, sunspots, moonspots, etc. In other words, one might expect, using Cass and Shell's (1984) terminology, that the equilibrium only depends on fundamentals. These fundamentals (i.e., preferences, endowments, technologies) may be uncertain; the corresponding uncertainty is then called "intrinsic." By contrast, the *a priori* irrelevant uncertainty alluded to before is said to be "extrinsic."

However, it has been realized that indeed extrinsic uncertainty may matter. This phenomenon is particularly plausible in infinite-horizon economies of the kind we are going to consider here: the set of rational expectations equilibria can be significantly enlarged when equilibria based on extrinsic uncertainty, for short "sunspot equilibria," are taken into consideration.[5]

When discussing our first criterion, we argued that the existence of many rational expectations equilibria (that were equilibria based on intrinsic uncertainty only) close to a reference rational expectations equilibrium would perturb the coordination of expectations. The existence of sunspot equilibria close to (non-sunspot) rational expectations equilibria is also likely to perturb coordination and may, intuitively, even be more disturbing if the neighbour equilibria share some of the regularity properties of the candidate equilibrium. Indeed, along the lines of our first criterion, when testing the determinacy of a stationary equilibrium (for example a steady state) the possible neighbour equilibria—based on fundamentals—that we are considering can only be (in general) non-stationary. The sunspot test that we are now introducing focuses attention on (possible) neighbour equilibria that are themselves stationary.

Let us summarize: our *third stability criterion is the absence of a (stationary) sunspot equilibrium in the neighbourhood of the (stationary) equilibrium* under test (stability is then associated with the absence of sunspot-like multiplicity or, for short, no sunspot confusion).

Before going to the fourth criterion, one comment is in order. This third criterion interprets the occurrence of a sunspot equilibrium as a threat to the stability of rational expectations equilibria, while in part of the sunspot literature sunspot equilibria are viewed as constructs that can explain positive facts.[6] There is clearly a difference of perspective between this literature and the present paper but, as we will argue later, it may be less basic than it *a priori* looks.

2.1.4   Criterion D: Learning Equilibria from "Introspection" or "Educing" Equilibria

It has often been argued that the rational expectations hypothesis only reflects the fact that agents "understand" the system which they live in. This fourth criterion is indeed about "understanding." However, it does not make understanding a synonym of coordinating on Nash outcomes. It takes a more basic, and as well more realistic, viewpoint from which Nash-like coordination can or cannot be deduced.

This criterion is, as is the second criterion, a learning criterion; but learning is here a mental process, a kind of collective introspection, that may result in expectations coordination. Contrary to the evolutive process associated with the second criterion, that takes place in real time, the "eductive" process considered here is instantaneous (at least in every period) or, if one prefers, takes place in "virtual" time.

As the reader may guess, the application of the fourth criterion requires that some game-theoretical structure has been given to the economic model under consideration. Also, the more basic assumptions—alluded to above—on which the criterion rests are two-fold: first, agents are *Bayesian rational*; second, rationality as well as the system structure are *common knowledge* among the agents. The second assumption is clearly a strong assumption; it has however the merit of having a very clear conceptual status. In a game in which both assumptions are valid, the outcome should be a "rationalizable solution."[7]

For the sake of completeness, the precise definition of a rationalizable solution is recalled below. The fourth criterion can however already be defined: An *equilibrium* is said to be *stable*, according to the *fourth criterion*, if it is the unique—or more precisely in the following, *locally unique*—*rationalizable solution of the associated game*. (In fact, as will be seen later, the definition has to make precise, in a way that cannot be stated now, some initial *common knowledge assumption*.)

In the following we will refer to this criterion as an "eductive" learning criterion (in opposition to the evolutive criteria introduced above). Also, when it will be satisfied we will say that the *equilibrium is (locally) strongly rational*.

The formal definition of a rationalizable solution refers to a game in "normal form." Let me index the players by $f \in F$.

The strategy sets are denoted S_f. Pay-off functions depend on the strategies played by all players.

Let us consider the following process of elimination of nonbest response strategies:

$S(0, f) = S_f,$

$S(1, f) = \{S_f \setminus s_f \in S_f$ s.t. s_f is not a "best response" to some profile
of mixed strategies of players f', $f' \neq f$, the support of
which is in $S_{f'}\}$,

$S(\tau, f) = \{S(\tau - 1, f) \setminus s_f \in S(\tau - 1, f)$ s.t. s_f is not a "best response"
to some mixed strategies of players f', $f' \neq f$, the
support of which is in $S(\tau - 1, f')\}$,

$R = \prod_f \left(\bigcap_\tau S(\tau, f) \right)$ is the set of rationalizable strategies.[8]

In the above formulas, the precise definition of the standard concept of "best response" is left to the reader.

The interpretation of the process is then easy: at virtual time 1, agents delete from their strategy sets those strategies that are "useless" in the sense of not being best response to any set of strategies that can possibly be played by the other players. But this first-step deletion being known and even being common knowledge, a second-step deletion is (possibly) in order, and so on. This infinite process may leave only a subset of each initial strategy set, the product of which defines the set of rationalizable solutions. Our criterion refers to cases in which, under some conditions, the set reduces to a point.

2.2   The Dynamic Model Under Consideration

We will be considering an abstract dynamic model that has the following features:

The state variables are n-dimensional; at time t the state vector is denoted by x_t, a vector of $\mathbb{R}^n_+$.

The system has no predetermined variables (or no memory) and is one-step-forward looking. In other words, the equilibrium value of the state vector x_t today is determined by the agents' expectations on the values of state variables tomorrow (these expectations are assumed at this stage to be homogeneous across agents).

Hence, when expectations are deterministic point expectations, the dynamics of the system is determined by the mapping F:[9]

$$F: (x_{t+1}^e) \rightarrow x_t = F(x_{t+1}^e),$$

where x_t is the vector of state variables at period t and x_{t+1}^e is the vector of point expectations for period $t + 1$.

When expectations are stochastic, the dynamics is then governed by the mapping $\tilde{F}$:

$$\tilde{F}: (\mu_{t+1}) \rightarrow x_t = \tilde{F}(\mu_{t+1}),$$

where x_t has the same meaning as before and μ_{t+1} is a probability measure over state vectors of period $t + 1$.

Naturally, F and $\tilde{F}$ are not independent mappings. They necessarily have connections: $\tilde{F}$ must coincide with F when μ_{t+1} is a Dirac measure; also a "consistency of derivatives" condition holds in most economic models.[10]

In this setting, a *perfect foresight equilibrium* consists of an infinite sequence, $x_1, x_2, \ldots, x_t, \ldots$, that satisfies

$$x_t = F(x_{t+1}).$$

A *steady state* consists of a n-dimensional vector $\bar{x}$ such that

$$\bar{x} = F(\bar{x}).$$

A *stationary sunspot equilibrium* (with finite support) consists of k state vectors, $\bar{x}_1, \bar{x}_2, \ldots, \bar{x}_k$, and a Markov matrix, whose lth row is $m_l = (m_{l1}, m_{l2}, \ldots, m_{lk})$, such that

$$\bar{x}_l = F(\bar{x}_1, \bar{x}_2, \ldots, \bar{x}_k, m_l), \quad \forall l = 1, \ldots, k,$$

where $\bar{x}_1, \bar{x}_2, \ldots, \bar{x}_k, m_l$ designates the probability distribution that gives the probability m_{lj} to state $x_j, j = 1, \ldots, k$.

The sunspot equilibrium is called *"local"* when the support is in a small neighbourhood of the steady state.

The first two definitions do not require comments, the third one is only a formal translation of the informal description of sunspot equilibria that was introduced before: the extrinsic phenomenon is a Markov chain with k states, the equations only say that the prophecy "when the extrinsic phenomenon is in state l, the equilibrium is $\bar{x}_l$" is self-fulfilling.

3   Comparison of the Four Criteria: The One-dimensional Case

3.1   The Equivalence Theorem

When the dimension of the state variable of the above abstract model is one, the comparison of the four rational expectations stability criteria (discussed in section 2.1) becomes strikingly simple when applied to a steady state. The main result is now stated as an equivalence theorem (whose precise status will be discussed later):

EQUIVALENCE THEOREM   Consider a steady state $\bar{x}$ of the one-dimensional version of the model of section 2.2. Then, the four following statements are equivalent:

A. The steady state is determinate.

B. Every "reasonable" adaptive learning process is locally asymptotically stable.

C. There is no local (stationary) sunspot equilibrium in the neighbourhood of the steady state.

D. If it is common knowledge that in the distant future the system will remain in a (small enough) neighbourhood of the steady state, then the steady state is (almost) strongly rational.

The word "theorem" should indeed be used with quotation marks: the definition of a "reasonable" learning process will be given later; and similarly, the statement of point D will only be made fully explicit at the end of the section.

However, before going to a finer understanding of the theorem, we should stress that the four criteria introduced in the previous section reflect stability ideas that were *a priori* of very different origin. The equivalence result is then, whatever its precise form, rather striking.

The next part of this section provides (more or less) unformal proofs of the four parts of the equivalence theorem, while making precise statements B and C. We proceed as follows: first we examine the equivalence of A and C, then we show the connections between A and B, and finally we examine the relationship between A and D.

3.2   Equivalence—Determinacy—No Local Sunspot Equilibria

In conformance with intuition, indeterminacy here is equivalent to the existence of a perfect foresight equilibrium $x_1, x_2, \ldots, x_t, \ldots$, such that x_t converges to $\bar{x}$. Linearizing around the steady state, we note that $x_t - \bar{x} = F'(x_{t+1} - \bar{x})$ so that indeterminacy relates to the fact that $|F'| > 1$.

Suppose now that we have $|F'| > 1$, so that the steady state is indeterminate, and let us explain the principles of the construction of a stationary sunspot equilibrium (from now on S.S.E.) in the neighbourhood of the steady state. The intuition of this construction is well conveyed by Figure 10.1.

Here, $\bar{x}$ is such that $\bar{x} = F(\bar{x})$ and y_1 "rationalizes" x_1 [in the sense that $x_1 = F(y_1)$]: if the agents believe that y_1 will occur tomorrow, then x_1 is the equilibrium state today. Also, y_2 (deterministically) rationalizes x_2 (the diagram corresponds to the case where $F' > 0$, $F' > 1$).

Figure 10.1

Consider now the random expectation: x_1 with probability α, x_2 with probability $1 - \alpha$. If the mapping $\tilde{F}$ is locally linear with respect to probabilities, as it is when agents in the underlying model maximize expected utility, then the random perspective x_1, x_2, with respective probabilities α and $1 - \alpha$, (stochastically) rationalizes x_1 for appropriately chosen α; similarly x_2 can be "stochastically rationalized" by the random perspective x_1, x_2 with well-chosen probabilities β and $1 - \beta$.

It follows that x_1, x_2 is a S.S.E. associated with the Markov matrix $\begin{pmatrix} \alpha & 1-\alpha \\ 1-\beta & \beta \end{pmatrix}$.

The just sketched argument conveys the flavour of the implication: indeterminacy implies the existence of "local" S.S.E. Pursuing along the lines of the same argument, the reader is invited to sketch a proof of the converse implication (for S.S.E. of order 2).

The close relationship between indeterminacy and existence of local S.S.E. was already apparent in the early example and analysis of Azariadis (1981); and the validity of the proposition that indeterminacy implies the existence of local S.S.E. within a prototype two-period-lived agents O.L.G. model with a single steady state follows from the sufficiency results of Azariadis and Guesnerie (1982), reproduced in Azariadis and Guesnerie (1986). In a similar framework where however two steady states coexist, Farmer and Woodford (1984) exhibit S.S.E. in the neighbourhood of an indeterminate "low" steady state. Further, the nature of the connection was better ascertained through the work of Spear (1984), Woodford (1984), and also Grandmont (1986), Chiappori and Guesnerie (1989), etc.

3.3   Equivalence Determinacy—"Evolutive" Learning Stability

Here the detailed analysis is rather intricate and only a crude intuition can be conveyed through the following consideration: take
the "passive" learning rule $x_{t+1}^e = x_{t-1}$, which says that agents expect
that yesterday's state will be tomorrow's state. With such a learning rule, the dynamics of the system is simply $x_t = F(x_{t-1})$, i.e., the
reversed perfect foresight dynamics. Hence, the learning dynamics
converge (resp. diverge) whenever the perfect foresight dynamics
diverge (resp. converge). This establishes our proposition for the
very special learning rule under consideration, but not for the class
of learning rules that are labelled "reasonable" in the statement of
the theorem. The definition of such reasonable learning processes is
now in order. It incorporates two ingredients:

First, the revision of expectations is adaptive: the difference
between the forecast and the (relevant) past realization is a fraction
of the difference between the (relevant) past expectation and the
past realization (such learning rules have been first studied by
Cagan, Nerlove, etc.).

Second, the rule must be able to detect cycles of order two; in
other words, if the system has a cycle of order two, then such a cycle
must be a possible rest point of the learning process. The simplest
adaptive learning rules would not fit this latter requirement; in fact,
the combination of the two conditions leads to considering learning rules of the following form:

$$x_{t+1}^e = \alpha x_{t-1} + (1-\alpha)x_{t-1}^e, \quad \alpha \in (0,1).$$

According to this formula, the revision rule is adaptive but differs
according to whether the time period is odd or even.

It turns out that "reasonable processes," as just defined, *are locally
asymptotically stable if and only if the steady state is "determinate."*

The proof of this statement is rather intricate: it follows from
the analysis of the necessary and sufficient conditions of local

asymptotic stability of a class of adaptive processes that includes the processes under consideration here [Guesnerie and Woodford (1991)]. In fact, Guesnerie and Woodford give a necessary and sufficient condition[11] for local stability of an adaptive learning rule with coefficient α that detects cycles of order k. Viewing the steady state as degenerate two cycles, this necessary and sufficient condition—for a learning rule that does detect cycles of order two—reduces, independently of α, to $(F')^2 < 1$. Hence, the result.

A brief bibliography on learning studies in intertemporal dynamical models includes Fuchs (1976), Grandmont (1985), and Grandmont and Laroque (1986). The two latter contributions stressed the requirement that learning processes should be able to detect cycles of higher order than the one that was "learnt," a fact that is part of our definition of "reasonableness."[12] The motivation for such a requirement is straightforward: the learning rule should leave some room as regards the nature of the stationary state that may be attained; for example, here a steady state is being learnt but a cycle of order two is not *a priori* ruled out—more generally, the order of the cycle should be left (at least partly) open.

The literature has often considered learning rules that do not belong to the class of adaptive rules (and I admit that the association of reasonable and adaptive is not entirely justified) and/or more complex systems. Some of these studies will be considered later in section 4, but one may already mention some recent relevant references for the subject, such as Grandmont and Laroque (1990a,b), Marcet and Sargent (1988, 1989a,b), Evans and Honkapojha (1990, 1994b).

3.4   Equivalence Indeterminacy—"Eductive" Stability

Let us suppose here that the state at period $t + T$ is restricted to belong to some subset R of the state space, i.e., $R \subset X$. This fact can reflect a Government commitment to appropriate intervention in case the state variable would leave R, or any other consideration that justifies a concentration of expectations on R. Assume now that this state space restriction is not only universally known but also common knowledge (abbreviated as C.K.). Then the following sequences of implications is in order:

It is C.K. that $x_{t+T-1} \in F(R)$.

It is C.K. that $x_{t+T-2} \in F(F(R)) = F^2(R)$.

$\vdots$

It is C.K. that $x_t \in F(F(F \ldots (R)) = F^T(R))$.

Noting that determinacy is equivalent to the fact that F is contracting around $\bar{x}$, one checks that if R is a small enough neighbourhood of the steady state and T is large enough, then it is common knowledge that x_t is arbitrarily close to $\bar{x}$.

The argument is rather straightforward, although it should be qualified since it makes an implicit assumption on the homogeneity of the sign of agents' reaction.[13]

4   Comparison of the Stability Tests in the N-Dimensional Case

We are now going to examine the general version of the model introduced in section 2.1. The system is still forward looking, without predetermined variables, but the state space is now n-dimensional. What happens then to the equivalence theorem?

Let us examine successively within this more general setting the connections between indeterminacy and the existence of local sunspot equilibria, the problem of eductive stability, and the problem of convergence of evolutive learning rules.

4.1   Indeterminacy and the Existence of Local Sunspot Equilibria in the N-Dimensional Case

Here the condition of determinacy for the steady state is that the Jacobian matrix $DF(\overline{X})$, at the steady state, has all its eigenvalues inside the unit circle.

Assume now that DF has one eigenvalue outside the unit circle, called b; take then a $(k \times k)$ Markov matrix M with $1/b$ as eigenvalue (such a matrix can indeed be shown to exist, at least for a large enough k); take then an appropriate path of Markov matrices that "crosses" the matrix M; at this crossing point there is a *bifurcation* of the equilibrium equations: before the bifurcation the steady state is the (locally) unique equilibrium, after the bifurcation a stationary sunspot equilibrium appears—with support arbitrarily close to the steady state and for beliefs triggered by matrices close to M. This result is precisely stated and proved in Chiappori, Geoffard, and Guesnerie (1992). The proof rests on standard bifurcation theorems [as in Guesnerie (1986)] when the eigenvalue under consideration is real; it is more delicate when the eigenvalue is complex since the bifurcation becomes then of codimension two.

The just described result shows that indeterminacy implies the existence of local sunspot equilibria, and these equilibria are triggered by Markovian extrinsic phenomena that have finite support. What about the converse? Indeed, combining the previous result together with an earlier result of Woodford (1986)—see below—and a representation theorem for Markov matrices, one can show [cf. Guesnerie and Woodford (1992)] that indeterminacy is equivalent to the existence of local S.S.E. that are triggered by one-period *Markovian* processes with finite support.

The generality of the relationship between indeterminacy and the occurrence of local sunspot equilibria has been conjectured by Woodford (1984) in a survey of the early results of the sunspot literature. The argument of Woodford (1986), who shows that, in a model more complex than the present one (with predetermined variables), there exist local S.S.E. close to an indeterminate steady state, further confirms this conjecture. There is however room for further in-depth exploration work.

4.2   Locally Strongly Rational Expectations Equilibria

The procedure for checking the local strong rationality of the equilibrium (that has been presented in section 3.4) is reminiscent of the procedure for checking expectational stability (from now "E-stability"), a concept introduced by Lucas (1978) and De Canio (1979), and extensively used—particularly in linear rational expectations models—by Evans (1983, 1985). In fact E-stability focuses attention on some x_{t+1} in a neighbourhood of the steady state $\bar{x}$ and considers $x_t = F(x_{t+1})$, $F(x_t) = F^2(x_{t+1}), \ldots, F^n(x_{t+1}), \ldots$ Here the sequence is viewed as an alternate sequence of expectations (x_{t+1}) realisations $[F(x_{t+1})]$; the realisation becomes the basis for new expectations that generate new realisations, etc. E-stability is, by definition, associated with the convergence of this process.

Also, the transposition in the n-dimensional model of the argument in section 3.4 concluding to locally strong rationality is immediate: it leads to considering a neighbourhood R (where it would be common knowledge that the steady state lies) and to examining $F(R), F^2(R), \ldots, F^k(R)$. The test is formally analogous to the E-stability test just described. In both cases, convergence requires that the mapping F is contracting—a property that again obtains whenever the steady state is determinate.

Should we conclude that the application of the game-theoretical ideas developed in section 3.4 leads to the same stability test as E-stability, providing, at least in the present context, a more basic justification to a concept of somewhat atheoretic inspiration?

For $n = 1$ (i.e., the case of section 3.4), local strong rationality and E-stability indeed coincide, but this property ceases to hold true for $n \neq 1$, except in the special case where the economic agents of the model under consideration are all similar. In other words, the implications of a common knowledge assumption on the situation of the initial state, as derived some lines above, implicitly assume that all agents are homogeneous. Beyond the domain of validity of this restrictive assumption, strong local rationality is a more demanding criterion than E-stability.

In order to elaborate on this point, let us assume that the more precise law of motion of the system under consideration here is: $x_t = \int F(x_{t+1}^{e,w}, w)dw$, where $x_{t+1}^{e,w}$ is the (point) expectation of agent w who is itself an infinitisimally small agent within a (large) set of agents associated with the Lebesgue measure on $[0-1]$; for short, $F(x_{t+1}^{e,w}, w)$ represents some kind of contribution of agent w, when its expectation of tomorrow is $x_{t+1}^{e,w}$, to the aggregate today state. Without discussing the generality of the proposed setting, we should note the following sufficient condition for strong local rationality derived in Evans and Guesnerie (1992):[14]

Note that with our previous notation $F(x) = \int F(x, w)dw$; call $DF(\overline{x})$ the Jacobian matrix of F in $\overline{x}$ and denote $\|A\|$ the norm of a matrix A.

Take β as the basis in R^n in which $\|DF(\overline{x})\| = \max |\rho|$, where $|\rho|$ is the modulus of an eigenvalue of the matrix DF;[15] call $\rho(w)$ the norm of $DF(\overline{x}, w)$ measured in the basis β.

Then, $\int_{[0,1]} \rho(w)dw < 1$ implies local strong rationality.

In the case where agents are homogeneous, the integral equals the modulus of the eigenvalue of highest modulus and the statement reduces to: determinacy implies local strong rationality (and the converse also holds true). As determinacy itself is equivalent to E-stability, then, as announced, E-stability and local strong rationality are identical criteria in the homogeneous case.[16] They, however, differ in the general case where E-stability ceases to imply local strong rationality. (E-stability remains a necessary condition for local strong rationality in the heterogeneous case.)

4.3   "Evolutive" Stability and Reasonable Learning Rules

The study of evolutive learning rules in n-dimensional dynamic models (either in the present setting or in more complex setting involving predetermined variables) has generated a number of contributions. A survey of this literature goes beyond the scope of the present paper, and I will limit myself to some remarks that only concern convergence towards steady states (a lot of the literature considers periodic equilibria) and that stress key points already evoked.

(1) The fact that determinacy is likely to be a necessary condition for local stability of learning rules is confirmed in models of increasing generality by the studies of Grandmont and Laroque (1986, 1990a) who consider "general" learning rules with finite memory.

(2) Determinacy is however not a sufficient condition, at least when accepting rather broad notions of "reasonable" rules. In order to illustrate this idea, let us consider a determinate steady state and an eigenvector of DF associated with a real eigenvalue (smaller than one), say c; and let us consider the sequence $c^{n+1}, c^n, \ldots, c^2, c, 1, 1/c, 1/c^2, \ldots, 1/c^n$. Assume that at time $t - 1$ the history of the system consists of $\ldots c^n, \ldots, c^2, c$. If the system "extrapolates growth rates" in the sense of Grandmont and Laroque (1990b), then the expectation of x at time $t + 1$ will be $1/c$; hence the realisation will be one (naturally this is strictly true only for the linearized version of the model). But the constant growth rate hypothesis will be maintained so that the after-tomorrow forecast will be $1/c^2$, validating a tomorrow price of $1/c$; and so on, Also assume that the agents believe that

the system follows a stationary random walk, the support of which is the set of points along the eitenvector under consideration and the law of which is to switch from state n to state $n + 2$ with probability α and to state $n - 2$ with probability $1 - \alpha$. Taking $\alpha = (1 - c^2)/(1 - c^4)$, one checks that at time t the agents' expectations consist of the random variable c^2 with probability α, $1/c^2$ with probability $1 - \alpha$, with mean one. This validates (locally and approximately) the random walk theory and defines in the terminology of Chiappori and Guesnerie (1988) a *"germ"* of *an heteroclinic equilibrium.*

(3) The just sketched analysis suggests that the extension of the above equivalence result is unlikely to obtain without a very restrictive definition of "reasonable". Indeed, reasonable may have to mean that it is known that the process does not leave some compact neighbourhood of the steady state [as illustrated in the recent work of Marcet and Sargent (1988, 1989a,b)]. Naturally this fact is reminiscent of the C.K. neighbourhood hypothesis used in the analysis of strong rationality.

(4) There may be significant differences between learning in non-noisy systems—such as those considered here—and learning in noisy systems: an approach to the second problem can be found in the just quoted contribution of Marcet and Sargent as well as in Evans and Honkappojha (1994a,b)

5   Conclusion

The chapter has presented and discussed alternative criteria for testing the validity of the rational expectations hypothesis. When one (or all) of these criteria is met, then there is a presumption that the agents can "predict" (in the sense of having rational expectations) the system which they belong to. The (obviously provisional) conclusion stresses three different facts:

(1) The whole analysis has remained *local*: all the stability criteria discussed here refer to a small area of the state space in which the rational expectations equilibria lies. Indeterminacy is a local property; we have focused attention on local sunspot equilibria, local stability of learning processes; and the eductive criterion under consideration explicitly refers to some local (common) knowledge. The nature of the relationship between global criteria— no sunspot equilibria, global stability of learning processes, global strong rationality—is an open question.[17]

(2) Attention has been limited here to a simple class of economic dynamic models. Although understanding this class is likely to be a key step in the process of understanding more complex models, the generality of the connections emphasised here is far from being fully elucidated. As argued above, the equivalence between indeterminacy and the existence of local sunspot equilibria is likely to be a very robust phenomenon, but in the present state of the theory, we understand it only in a limited class of models [including the models with predetermined variables of Woodford (1986)]. We know that the close relationship between the existence of sunspot equilibria and the strong rationality of equilibria does not extend to finite-horizon models, where the existence of sunspot equilibria is a more exceptional phenomenon although the failure of eductive stability is a rather frequent one [see Guesnerie (1992), Guesnerie and Rochet (1992)]. Also, even if as suggested by Milgrom and Roberts (1990), there should be a general relationship between evolutive stability and eductive stability, the form it takes within our framework remains unclear.

(3) Finally, in testing the validity of the rational expectations hypothesis, the present paper focuses attention only on steady states. Using the same tests in order to evaluate the stability of other stationary equilibria (periodic equilibria, even sunspot equilibria,

. . .) provides a natural direction of extension of the studies surveyed here.

Notes

1. Although this would remind him of some forgotten footnotes of the famous volumes on Mars' history of economic analysis.

2. But for some exceptions, and in particularly one that our penetrating observer carefully noticed in his thirty-years-old report [Muth (1961)].

3. For a discussion of Muth's argument see the introduction of Guesnerie (1992). Also, empirical tests of the rational hypothesis suggest mixed conclusions.

4. As it will become clear later, this first criterion only considers equilibria that are based on "fundamentals" or that are intrinsic in the terminology introduced later.

5. The first systematic analyses of the effect of extrinsic uncertainty in infinite-horizon models are reported in Azariadis (1981b) and Azariadis and Guesnerie (1982a). Note however that Shell's paper (1977) refers to an O.L.G. framework. For additional bibliography on the sunspot literature, see section 2.

6. This viewpoint is particularly taken by Woodford in several articles [see Guesnerie and Woodford (1992) for a review of these articles and of the sunspot literature].

7. For a proof that Bayesian rationality plus common knowledge of rationality "justify" the rationalizability concept, see Tan and Werlang (1985).

8. This standard definition assumes—conformably with the Bayesian axiom—that players assign (subjective) probability to the strategies played by others. One question that does not matter for the purpose of this chapter, and that our somewhat vague definition leaves open, is whether these (mixed) strategies should be correlated. Indeed, according to the answer to the question, two different concepts of rationalizability can be defined.

9. Here, we "solve" the equilibrium equation in x_t. This is not too restrictive for the local analysis we are undertaking although, in general, it would eliminate interesting phenomena.

10. See Guesnerie (1986), Chiappori and Guesnerie (1991a,b).

11. Theorem 1 in Guesnerie and Woodford (1991, p. 120).

12. Note that the combination of a sufficiency result of Grandmont (1985) and a necessity result of Grandmont and Laroque (1986) suggests another definition of "reasonable," for which the statement would remain true.

13. Also, in spite of some oral record of a (possibly) similar argument, I have not seen it in print as such. However, there are early discussions of the O.L.G. model that convey arguments with similar flavour.

14. Evans and Guesnerie (1992) analyze the static model $x_t = \int F(x_{t+1}^{e,w}, w)dw$, but their result carries over to the dynamic model considered here, following the lines of the argument in section 3.4 above.

15. Such a basis exists almost everywhere, and we restrict attention on the generic case.

16. We leave it to the reader to check equivalence in the one-dimensional case.

17. For example, the only necessary and sufficient conditions known for the existence of sunspot equilibria have been derived within the simple framework of a two-period-lived O.L.G. model with a unique steady state. In this framework, Azariadis and Guesnerie (1986) indeed showed that S.S.E. of order two existed if and only if there were cycles of order two. The further results of Grandmont (1986) and Woodford (1988) have shown that "S.S.E. of order two" can be replaced by "S.S.E." in the previous proposition.

References

Allais, M. (1947). Economie et Intérêt, Paris, Imprimerie Nationale.

Arrow, K. J. (1953). "Le rôle des valeurs boursières pour la répartition la meilleure des risques." {Econométrie}, Paris, CNRS, pp. 41–48 (1953). English translations as "The role of Securities in the Optimal Allocation of Risk-Bearing," *Review of Economic Studies* 31 (1964):91–96.

Azariadis, C. (1981a). "A reexamination of natural rate theory." *American Economic Review* 71:944–960.

Azariadis, C. (1981b). "Self-Fulfilling Prophecies." *Journal of Economic Theory* 25:380–396.

Azariadis, C. (1993). "Intertemporal macroeconomics." Cambridge, Mass.: Blackwell.

Azariadis, C., and R. Guesnerie (1982a). "Propheties Créatrices et Persistance des Théories." *Revue Economique* 33:787–806. English translation: "Creative Prophecies and Persistence of Theories," chapter 1, this volume.

Azariadis, C., and R. Guesnerie (1982b). "The persistence of self-fulfilling Theories." Mineo, unpublished.

Azariadis, C., and R. Guesnerie (1986). "Sunspots and Cycles." *Review of Economic Studies* 53:725–736, chapter 2, this volume.

Balasko, Y., and K. Shell (1981). "The overlapping-generations model, I, II." *Journal of Economic Theory* 24.

Balasko, Y., D. Cass, and K. Shell (1980). "Existence of competitive equilibrium in a general overlapping generations model." *Journal of Economic Theory* 23:307–322.

Balasko, Y., D. Cass, and K. Shell (1988). "Market Participation and Sunspot Equilibria." CAE w. p., Cornell University.

Benhabib, J., and R. Farmer (1999). "Indeterminacy and Sunspots in Macroeconomics." Mimeo.

Benassy, J. P. (1991). "Incomplete markets and the suboptimality of rational expectations." *Economics Letters* 36:343–346.

Bernheim, B. D. (1984). "Rationalizable Strategic Behavior." *Econometrica* 52:1007–1028.

Bewley, T. (1980). "The Optimum Quantity of Money." In *Models of Monetary Economies*, ed. J. H. Kareken and N. Wallace. Minneapolis: Federal Reserve Bank of Minneapolis.

Blanchard, O., and F. Fisher (1989). *Macroeconomic Theory*. Cambridge, Mass.: MIT Press.

Boudon, R. (1979). *"La logique du social."* Paris: Hachette.

Bray, M. (1982). "Learning, Estimation and the Stability of Rational Expectations Equilibria." *Journal of Economic Theory* 36:318–339.

Brock, W. A. (1974). "Money and Growth: The Case of Long-Run Perfect Foresight." *International Economic Review* 15:750–777.

Broze, L., C. Gourieroux, and A. Szafars (1985). "Solution of linear rational expectations models." *Econometric Theory* 1:341–368.

Broze, L., and A. Szafars (1985). "On an Econometric Model with Rational Expectations." Centre d'Economie Mathématique et d'Econométrie, Université Libre de Bruxelles, Working Paper.

Calvo, G. A. (1983). "Comments on Rational Expectations in Macroeconomic Models." In *Individual Forecasting and Aggregate Outcomes*, ed. R. Frydman and E. Phelps. Cambridge: Cambridge University Press.

Cass, D., M. Okuno, and L. Zilcha (1979). "The Role, of Money in supporting the Pareto Optimality of Competitive Equilibrium." *Journal of Economic Theory* 20:40–81.

Cass, D., and K. Shell (1980). "In defense of a basic approach." In *Models of monetary economics*, Federal Reserve Bank of Minneapolis, 251–260.

Cass, D., and K. Shell (1983). "Do sunspots matter?" *Journal of Political Economy* 91:193–227.

Caspi, Y. (1974). "Optimum Allocation of Risk in a Market with Many Traders." In *Uncertainty Equilibrium, Optimality*, ed. J. Dreze. London: MacMillan.

Chiappori, P.-A., and R. Guesnerie (1985). "Indeterminacy, Expectations, and The Non-neutrality of Money." Mimeo, CEQC, Paris.

Chiappori, P.-A., and R. Guesnerie (1988). "Self-fulfilling theories: The sunspot connection." Mimeo, Delta.

Chiappori, P.-A., and R. Guesnerie (1989). "On Stationary Sunspots of Order k." In W. Barnett, J. Geweke, and K. Shell, eds., *Economic Complexity: Chaos, Sunspots, Bubbles and Nonlinearities* (Cambridge: Cambridge University Press), chapter 3, this volume.

Chiappori, P.-A., and R. Guesnerie (1990). "Anticipations, indetermination et non neutralité de la monnaie." *Annales d'Économie et statistiques* 19:1–25.

Chiappori, P.-A., and R. Guesnerie (1991a). "Lucas Equation, Indeterminacy, and Non-Neutrality." In *Economic Analysis of Markets and Games*, ed. P. Dasgupta, D. Gale, O. Hart, and E. Maskin. Cambridge, Mass.: MIT Press, 445–465, chapter 4 this volume.

Chiappori, P.-A., and R. Guesnerie (1991b). "Sunspot Equilibria in Sequential Markets Models." In *Handbook of Mathematical Economics*, ed. W. Hildenbrand and H. Sonnenschein. Amsterdam: North Holland, 1684–1760.

Chiappori, P.-A., and R. Guesnerie (1993). "Rational Random Walks." *Review of Economic Studies* 60:837–864, chapter 5, this volume.

Chiappori, P.-A., P. Y. Geoffard, and R. Guesnerie (1992). "Sunspot fluctuations around a steady state: The case of multidimensional one-step forward looking economic models. *Econometrica* 60:1097–1126, chapter 7, this volume.

Chow, S. N., and J. K. Hale (1982). "Methods of Bifurcation Theory." New York: Springer-Verlag.

Dávila, J. (1994). "Indétermination de l'équilibre à anticipations rationnelles: équilibres à taches solaires et systèmes dynamiques." Ph.D. dissertation, Ecole des Hautes Etudes en Sciences Sociales, Paris.

Dávila, J. (1997). "Sunspot Equilibria in Dynamics with Predetermined Variables." *Economic Theory* 10:483–495.

Day, R. (1980). "Irregular growth cycles." Ph.D. dissertation, University of Southern California.

De Canio, S. J. (1979). "Rational Expectations and Learning from Experience." *Quarterly Journal of Economics* 93:47–58.

Desgranges, G., and R. Guesnerie (1996). "Common Knowledge and the information revealed through prices: Some conjectures" to appear F. Gardes and G. Prat, ed. "Prices on good and financial markets: new results in theory and empirical research." Elgar, forthcoming.

Dupuy, J.-P. (1982). "Mimesis et Morphogénèse." In *Ordres et désordres*, ed. J. P. Dupuy and L. Dumonchel. Paris: Le Seuil.

Evans, G. W. (1983). "The stability of rational expectations in macroeconomic models." In *Individual forecasting and aggregate outcomes*, ed. R. Frydman and E. S. Phelps. Cambridge: Cambridge University Press.

Evans, G. W. (1985). "Expectational stability and the multiple equilibria problem in rational expectations models." *Quarterly Journal of Economics* 100:1217–1233.

Evans, G., and R. Guesnerie (1993). "Rationalizability, Strong Rationality and Expectational Stability." *Games and Economic Behaviour* 5:632–646.

Evans, G., and R. Guesnerie (1999). "Coordination on saddle path solutions: The "eductive" viewpoint 1-linear univariate models." Delta DP 99-15.

Evans, G. W., and S. Honkapohja (1990). "Learning, Convergence and Stability with Multiple Rational Expectations Equilibria." STICERD Disc. Paper no. TE-90-212, London School of Economics, June.

Evans, G., and S. Honkhappojha (1994a). "On the Local Stability of Sunspot Equilibria under adaptive learning rules." *Journal of Economic Theory* 64:142–161.

Evans, G., and S. Honkappojha (1994b). "Economic dynamics with learning: new stability results." Mimeo, June.

Evans, G., and S. Honkhappojha (1997). "Learning Dynamics." Mimeo, forthcoming in *The Handbook in Macroeconomics*.

Farmer, R., and Woodford, M. (1984). "Self-fulfilling Prophecies and the Business Cycle." CARESS, Working Paper 84-12, University of Pennsylvania.

Farmer, R., and M. Woodford (1989). "Self-fulfilling Prophecies and the Business Cycle." CARESS W. P. 84. 12, University of Pennsylvania, published in Spanish in *Cuadernos Economicos* 35:1–37.

Fourgeaud, C. Gourieroux, and J. Pradel (1986). "Learning Procedures and Convergence to Rationality." *Econometrica* 54:845–868.

Frankel, D., and A. Pauzner (1997). "History not expectations." Mimeo, Tel Aviv.

Fuchs, G. (1976). "Asymptotic stability of stationary temporary equilibria and changes in expectations." *Journal of Economics* 13:201–216.

Gale, D. (1973). "Pure Exchange Equilibrium in Dynamic Economic Models." *Journal of Economic Theory* 6:12–36.

Geanakoplos, J., and H. Polemarchakis (1991). "Overlapping Generations." In *Handbook of Mathematical Economics*, vol. 4, ed. W. Hildenbrand and H. Sonnenschein. Amsterdam: Elsevier Science Publishers, 1899–1960.

Gourieroux, C., J.-J. Laffont, and A. Monfort (1982). "Rational Expectations in Dynamical Linear Models: Analysis of the Solutions." *Econometrica* 50:409–426.

Grandmont, J.-M. (1985). "On Endogenous Competitive Business Cycles." *Econometrica* 33:995–1045.

Grandmont, J. M. (1986). "Stabilizing Competitive Business Cycles." *Journal of Economic Theory* 40:57–76.

Grandmont, J.-M. (1989). "Local bifurcations and stationary sunspots." In *Economic Complexity: Chaos Sunspots, Bubbles and Non Linearity* ed. W. Barnett, J. Geweke, and K. Shell. Cambridge: Cambridge University Press, 45–60.

Grandmont, J.-M. (1992). "Expectations drivers non linear business cycles." Mimeo, CEPREMAP.

Grandmont, J. M., and G. Laroque (1986). "Stability of Cycles and Expectations." *Journal of Economic Theory* 40:138–151.

Grandmont, J.-M., and G. Laroque (1990a). "Stability, Expectations and Predetermined Variables." In *Essays in Honor of Edmond Malinvaud*, vol. 1., ed. P. Champsaur et al. Cambridge, Mass.: MIT Press.

Grandmont, J. M., and G. Laroque (1990b). "Economic Dynamics with Learning: Some Instability Examples." CEPREMAP W. P. 90-07, Paris.

Grandmont, J.-M., P. Pintus, and R. de Vilder (1997). "Capital labour substitution and competitive nonlinear endogenous business cycles." *Journal of Economic Theory*.

Grossmann, S. (1976). "On the Efficiency of Competitive Stock markets where Traders have Diverse Information." *Journal of Finance* 31:573–585.

Grossmann, S., and J. Stiglitz (1976). "Information and Competitive Price Systems." *American Economic Review* 66:246–253.

Guesnerie, R. (1986). "Stationary sunspot equilibria in an n-commodity World." *Journal of Economic Theory* 40, no. 1:103–128, chapter 6, this volume.

Guesnerie, R. (1989). "A propos de la rationalité des anticipations Rationnelles." In *Théorie Economique et Crise des Marchés Financiers*, 31–43.

Guesnerie, R. (1992). "An Exploration of the Eductive Justifications of the Rational Expectations Hypothesis." *American Economic Review* 82, no. 5:1254–1278.

Guesnerie, R. (1993). "Theoretical tests of the rational expectations hypothesis in economic dynamical models." *Journal of Economics Dynamic and Control* 17:847–864, chapter 10, this volume.

Guesnerie, R., and J. Y. Jaffray (1974). "Optimality of Equilibria of Plans, Prices and Price Expectations." In *Uncertainty, Equilibrium, Optimality*, ed. J. Dreze. London: MacMillan, 71–86.

Guesnerie, R., and J.-J. Laffont (1988). "Notes on Sunspot Equilibria in Finite Economies." In *Volume en l'honneur d'Edmond Malinvaud*, Economica, EHESS, 118-143. English translation in *Essays in Honor of Edmond Malinvaud*, Cambridge, Mass.: MIT Press, 1990.

Guesnerie, R., and Woodford, M. (1991). "Stability of cycles with adaptive learning rules." In Equilibrium Theory and Applications, *Proceedings of the Sixth International Symposium in Economic Theory and Econometrics*. Cambridge: Cambridge University Press, 110–133, chapter 8, this volume.

Guesnerie, R., and J.-C. Rochet (1993) "(De) Stabilizing Speculation: an Alternative Viewpoint." *European Economic Review* 37:1043–1063.

Hahn, F. (1982). *Money and Inflation*. Oxford: Blackwell.

Hirsch, M. W. (1976). *Differential Topology*. New York: Springer-Verlag.

Heinemann, F. (1995). "Rationalizable Expectations and Sunspot Equilibria in an Overlapping Generations Economy." Mimeo, Mannheim University.

Irwin, M. C. (1980). *Smooth Dynamical Systems*, Orlando, Fla.: Academic Press.

Kehoe, T. J., and D. K. Levine (1984). "Intertemporal separability in overlapping generations models." *Journal of Economic Theory* 34:216–226.

Kehoe, T. J., and D. K. Levine (1985). "Comparative statics and perfect foresight in infinite horizon economies." *Econometrica* 53:433–454.

Laitner, J. (1985). "Sunspot Equilibrium and Stability." *Journal of Economic Theory* 47:39–50.

Lucas, R. (1972). "Expectations and the Neutrality of Money." *Journal of Economic Theory* 4:101–124.

Lucas, R. E., Jr. (1978). "Asset Prices in an Exchange Economy." *Econometrica* 46:1429–1445.

Lucas, R. E. (1983). "Expectations and the neutrality of money: A corrigendum." *Journal of Economic Theory* 31:197–199.

Lucas, R. E., Jr., and N. L. Stokey (1987). "Money and Interest in a Cash—in Advance Economy." *Econometrica* 55:491–514.

Mcleod, J. B., and D. H. Sattinger (1973). "Loss of Stability and Bifurcation at a Double Eigenvalue." *Journal of Functional Analysis*, 62–84.

Malinvaud, E. (1969). "First Order Certainty Equivalence." *Econometrica* 37:706–718.

Malinvaud, E. (1977). "The Theory of Unemployment Reconsidered." Oxford: Basil Blackwell.

Marcet, A., and T. J. Sargent (1988). "The Fate of Systems with 'Adaptive' Expectations." *American Economic Review*, Papers and Proceedings, 78 (May):168–172.

Marcet, A., and Sargent, J. (1989a). "Convergence of Least Squares Learning Mechanisms in Self Referential Linear Stochastic Models." *Journal of Economic Theory* 48:337–368.

Marcet, A., and Sargent, J. (1989b). "Convergence of Least Squares Learning in Environments with Hidden State Variables and Private Information." *Journal of Political Economy* 97:1306–1322.

Maskin, E., and Tirole, J. (1987). "Correlated Equilibria and Sunspots." *Journal of Economic Theory* 43:364–373.

Milgrom, P., and J. Roberts (1990). "Rationalizability, Learning and Equilibrium in Games with Strategic Complementarities." *Econometrica* 47:1337–1351.

Milnor, J. (1965). *Topology from the Differentiable Viewpoint*. Charlottesville: University Press of Virginia.

Moulin, H. (1979). "Dominance Solvable Voting Schemes." *Econometrica* 47:1337–1351.

Muth, J. (1961). "Rational Expectations and the Theory of Price Movements." *Econometrica* 29:315–335.

Peck, J. (1988). "On the Existence of Sunspot Equilibria in an Overlapping Generation Model." *Journal of Economic Theory* 44:19–42.

Phelps, E. (1961). "The Golden Rule of Accumulation: A Fable for Growthmen." *American Economic Review* 51:638–643.

Poincaré, H. (1980). "Sur les équations de le dynamique et le problème des trois corps." *Acta Mathematica* 13:1–270.

Popper, K. (1959). *The Logic of Scientific Discovery*, London: Hutchinson and Co, London. English translation of *Logik der Forschung* 40:128–137.

Radner, R. (1972). "Equilibrium of plans, prices and price expectations." *Econometrica* 40:289–303.

Radner, R. (1979). "Rational expectations Equilibrium: Existence and the Information Revealed by Prices." *Econometrica* 47:655–678.

Reichlin, P. (1986). "Equilibrium cycles in an overlapping generations economy with production." *Journal of Economic Theory* 40:89–102.

Samuelson, P. A. (1958). "An exact consumption-loan model of interest with or without the social contrivence of money." *Journal of Political Economy* 66:467–482.

Sargent, T. J. (1984). "Consumption, loans, and currency: II." Unpublished lecture notes.

Shell, K. (1977). "Monnaie et allocation intertemporelle." Mémoire CEPREMAP.

Shiller, R. (1978). "Rational Expectations and the Dynamical Structures of Macroeconomic Models." *Econometrica* 46:467–482.

Shefrin, S. (1983). *Rational Expectations*. Cambridge University Press.

Spear, S. (1984). "Sufficient Conditions for the Existence of Sunspot Equilibria." *Journal of Economic Theory* 35:360–370.

Spear, S., S. Srivastava, and M. Woodford (1990). "Indeterminacy of Stationary Equilibrium in Overlapping Generations Models." *Journal of Economic Theory* 50:265–284.

Taylor, I. (1977). "Conditions for Unique Solutions in Stochastic Macroeconomic Models for Rational Expectations." *Econometrica* 45:1372–1385.

Tan, T., and S. R. Costa da Werlang (1988). "On Aumann's Notion of Common Knowledge, an Alternative Approach." *Journal of Economic theory* 45:370–391.

Tobin, D. (1979). "Price Flexibility and Output Stability: An Old Keynesian View." *Journal of Economic Perspectives* 7:45–65.

Topkis, D. (1979). "Equilibrium points in nonzero-sum-n-Person Submodular Games." *Siam Journal of Control and Optimization* 17, no. 6:773–787.

Townsend, R. M. (1978). "Market Anticipations, Rational Expectations and Bayesian Analysis." *International Economic Review* 19:481–494.

Vives, X. (1990). "Nash Equilibria with Strategic Complementarities." *Journal of Mathematical Economics* 19, no. 3:305–321.

Woodford, M. (1984). "Indeterminacy of equilibrium in the overlapping generations model: a survey." Mimeo, Columbia University, May.

Woodford, M. (1986). "Stationary sunspot equilibria: the case of small fluctuations around a deterministic steady state." Mimeo, University of Chicago, September.

Woodford, M. (1988a). "Expectations, finance, and aggregate instability." In *Finance Constraints, Expectations and Macroeconomics*, ed. M. Kohn and S. C. Tsiang. Oxford: Oxford University Press.

Woodford, M. (1988b). "Monetary policy and price level indeterminacy in a cash in advance economy." Mimeo, University of Chicago.

Woodford, M. (1990a). "Learning to believe in sunspots." *Econometrica* 58:277–307.

Woodford, M. (1990b). "Equilibrium models of endogenous fluctuations: an introduction." NBER Working Paper no. 3360, May.

Sources

1. "Prophéties créatrices et Persistance des Théories," with C. Azariadis, *Revue Economique* 33 (1982): 787–806, translated by Susan Clay as "Creative Prophecies and Persistence of Theories," reprinted with the permission of Presses de la Fondation Nationale des Sciences Politiques.

2. "Sunspots and Cycles," with C. Azariadis, *Review of Economic Studies* 53 (1986): 725–836, reprinted with the permission of The Review of Economic Studies Ltd.

3. "On Stationary Sunspot Equilibria of Order k," with P.A. Chiappori, in *Economic Complexity: Chaos, Sunspots, Bubbles and Nonlinearities*, ed. W. Barnett, J. Geweke, and K. Shell (Cambridge: Cambridge University Press, 1989), 21–44. Reprinted with the permission of Cambridge University Press.

4. "Lucas Equation, Indeterminacy and non-Neutrality: An example," with P.A. Chiappori, in *Economic Analysis of Markets and Games*, ed. P. Dasgupta, D. Gale, O. Hart, and E. Maskin (Cambridge, Mass.: MIT Press, (1991), 445–465. Reprinted with the permission of MIT Press.

5. "Rational Random Walks," with P.A. Chiappori, *The Review of Economic Studies* 60 (1993): 837–864, reprinted with the permission of The Review of Economic Studies Ltd.

6. "Stationary Sunspot Equilibria in an N-commodity World," *Journal of Economic Theory* 40 (1986): 103–128, reprinted with the permission of Academic Press.

7. "Sunspot Fluctuations around a Steady State: The Case of Multidimensional, One-Step Forward Looking Economic Models," with P.A. Chiappori and P.-Y. Geoffard, *Econometrica* 60 (1992): 1097–1126. Reprinted with the permission of The Econometric Society.

8. "Stability of Cycles with Adaptive Learning Rules," with M. Woodford, in *Equilibrium Theory and Applications, Proceedings of the Sixth International Symposium*

in Economic Theory and Econometrics (Cambridge University Press, 1991), 110–133, Reprinted with the permission of Cambridge University Press.

9. "Sunspot Equilibria in Systems with Memory: An Introductory Presentation," with J. Dávila. Delta DP 9905.

10. "Theoretical Tests of the Rational Expectations Hypothesis in Economic Dynamic Models," *Journal of Economic Dynamics and Control* 17 (1993): 847–864. Reprinted with the permission of Elsevier Science.

Index